SAT Wars

The Case for Test-Optional Admissions

SAT Wars

The Case for
Test-Optional Admissions

Edited by

JOSEPH A. SOARES

Foreword by

DAVID HAWKINS

Teachers College, Columbia University
New York and London

Published by Teachers College Press, 1234 Amsterdam Avenue, New York, NY 10027

Library of Congress Cataloging-in-Publication Data

SAT wars : the case for test-optional college admissions / edited by Joseph A. Soares ; foreword by David Hawkins.
   p. cm.
Includes bibliographical references and index.
ISBN 978-0-8077-5262-3 (pbk. : alk. paper)
ISBN 978-0-8077-5263-0 (hardcover : alk. paper)
   1. Universities and colleges—United States—Entrance examinations.
2. Education—Standards—United States. 3. Educational evaluation—United States. 4. SAT (Educational test). I. Soares, Joseph A.

LB2353.2.S22 2011
378.1'6620973—dc23   2011017002

ISBN 978-0-8077-5262-3 (paper)
ISBN 978-0-8077-5263-0 (hardcover)

Printed on acid-free paper
Manufactured in the United States of America

19 18 17 16 15 14 13 12   8 7 6 5 4 3 2 1

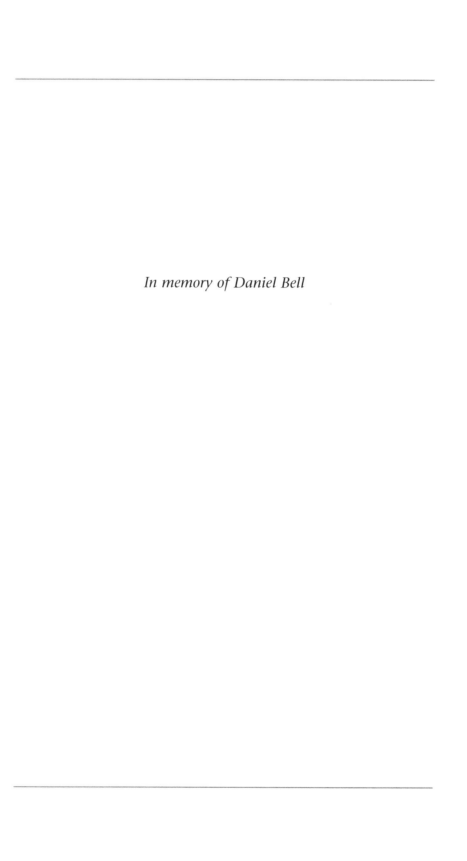

In memory of Daniel Bell

Contents

PART III
Evaluations of Test-Optional Policies

Foreword

There are thousands of admissions professionals working across the United States in high schools, in colleges, and independently to advise, assist, and evaluate college-bound youths. The National Association for College Admission Counseling (NACAC), with more than 11,000 members, provides a democratic forum for those in the field to explore "best admissions practices." One long-term concern of NACAC is the impact of standardized tests on equity and excellence in college admissions.

In 2008, NACAC issued the *Report of the Commission on the Use of Standardized Tests in Undergraduate Admission* (2008), which included, among others, the following recommendations for colleges and universities:

1. Regularly question and reassess the foundations and implications of standardized test requirements.
2. Draw attention to possible misuses of admissions test scores.
3. Understand differences in test scores among different groups of people, and continually assess the use of standardized test scores relative to the broader social goals of higher education.
4. Contemplate a future direction for admissions testing, which includes ideas about alternative tests, the consideration of subject tests, and the consideration of options not yet developed.

At the association's annual conference in 2008, a group that included NACAC staff, college admissions officers, and high school counselors was discussing the report with a reporter from the *New York Times*. In response to a question about the effect of the report, one experienced and highly respected high school counselor said, "Nothing is going to change." The counselor meant no disrespect to the Commission or to NACAC but was simply making the point that the inertia behind the use of standardized tests in college admissions was too great for a single report to alter.

Of course, the intent of the Commission was not to end the use of all standardized tests at colleges and universities, whether in the short term or in the long term. The discussions around the table were too varied to settle on such a definitive course of action. However, the unanimous consensus reached by the committee was that the discussion about standardized testing had to be reignited—that colleges and universities had a responsibility to "take back the conversation" about standardized testing from the array of organizations and individuals that have misappropriated the discussion over the years.

As the recommendations suggest, any change resulting from the Commission's work would be carefully conceived and well researched by individual colleges and universities—by definition limiting change (if it is to happen) to an incremental process. The Commission's first recommendation—to *regularly question and reassess the foundations and implications of standardized test requirements*—was its most profound. For decades, Commission members believe, colleges and universities have adopted standardized admissions tests for reasons that are not always well researched or evaluated. As a result, admissions tests have become a sort of "received wisdom," not just in the eyes of prospective students and their families but also by the colleges themselves. Given that admissions test use has raised the stakes for students, families, and colleges in many ways—the report notes the misuse of tests in rankings, bond ratings, and scholarship programs, as well as the growth of the billion-dollar test preparation industry—institutional decisions about the use of tests have implications far beyond their originally intended boundaries. As such, institutions of higher education have an obligation to their students and other stakeholders to understand whether such tests serve as appropriate measures of student eligibility for admission to their institutions.

This book is an important contribution to the reassessment of the use of standardized tests in college admissions. Although colleges and universities will have various reactions to its content, they will all be better served by a conversation about testing—and about all of the factors in the admissions process—that includes research and perspectives that challenge the "received wisdom." Colleges that are well prepared for a discussion about standardized admissions tests will understand how their research aligns with the information provided in this publication and will be able to communicate clearly to students, colleagues, university administrators, and policymakers how their admissions requirements do or do not serve the institution's interests.

The work of the NACAC Commission on the Use of Standardized Tests in Undergraduate Admission was a turning point in colleges' decades-long journey with standardized admissions tests. It signified a recognition that to some degree, colleges and universities have created a phenomenon that is now operating beyond their ability to control it. Colleges can effect change if they deem it desirable or needed, but their ability to act unilaterally is limited by the number and prominence of stakeholders, both inside and outside institutions, who believe they have a role in interpreting or otherwise taking ownership of admissions tests. The Commission did not espouse or encourage a wholesale movement away from admissions tests— its recommendations were far less radical but may be no less far-reaching. If more researchers and institutions take the time to fully evaluate test-use policies and practices, changes will almost inevitably result.

—David Hawkins
National Association for College Admission Counseling

Reference

National Association for College Admission Counseling (NACAC). (2008). *Report of the Commission on the Use of Standardized Tests in Undergraduate Admission.* Arlington, VA: Author.

Acknowledgments

I am grateful for support, both material and emotional, received during the production of this book from Wake Forest University, especially from its Provost, Jill Tiefenthaler; its "Rethinking Admissions" conference administrator, Debra Alty; my departmental colleagues, in particular Catherine Harris, Ian Taplin, and Robin Simon; and our administrative assistant, Joan Habib. I also greatly appreciate the hard work of many with Teachers College Press in seeing this project through: Brian Ellerbeck, my senior editor; Lynne Frost, for copy editing and page layout; and Karl Nyberg, for overseeing production. My overall happiness was sustained by my spouse, Dr. Felicitas Opwis, as my spirits were modulated by our children, Axel and Isabella; may they never feel compelled to take a high-stakes college-entrance exam.

Introduction

JOSEPH A. SOARES

This book presents a call to rethink, and a toolkit for redoing, college admissions. Admissions are the lifeblood of higher education. Through admissions, universities and colleges entrust their mission to a new generation. But which social and institutional goals should be addressed by admissions policies? How well are schools and society served by the decisions of admissions officers? Are colleges successfully selecting students who will creatively contribute the most to the campus today and to humanity tomorrow? What can an admissions officer safely predict about the future of a 17-year-old?

Admissions professionals are the gatekeepers who make decisions on membership in an association that extends from alumni, dead and living, to next year's class; their policies and practices change the lives of youths and families, who, in turn, shape the learning experience and cultural climate of a campus. Admissions are the nexus where the promise of opportunity and excellence meets the realities of limited resources and conflicts over the criteria used in evaluating a candidate's virtues.

Admissions associates, from deans down to campus tour guides, live with these issues daily, yet everyone has a stake in the discussion. The issues raised in this volume transcend the campus—they go to the heart of how we, as a society, think about talent, creativity, knowledge, and wisdom. Are the best and the brightest the ones who can check off the most correct boxes on a standardized multiple-choice exam? Or do we need other ways of measuring ability and promise?

This book strives to inspire a general rethinking of college admissions. The particular impetus for this work, however, comes from a sense that our society allows too much weight to be placed on standardized, fill-in-the-blank college admissions tests. (For now, consideration of K–12 testing is left to others.)

High-stakes standardized college admissions tests have a gigantic and mostly negative impact on American life. Currently, approximately 3 million youths graduate each year from high school, 2 million attend college, more than 1.5 million take the SAT, and (with much overlap) more than 1.5 million take the ACT. The testing industry rakes in more than $4 billion annually. Inappropriate uses of test scores are legion. Even the backers of the SAT warn, to little effect, against misusing test scores as proxies for the quality of a high school (Deike, 2010). Nonetheless, realty agencies, newspapers, and school-board members report high school SAT averages as reflections on the education a youth receives in a particular school. SAT tests are not based on the curriculum taught in high schools; they tell us more about the socioeconomic status of the families sending youths to that school than they say about the school itself. The same is true of colleges. Aggregate student body test scores do not define the quality of a college; they tell us little about its capacity to educate or nurture creative leading talents. The magazine industry's ranking of colleges by test scores is not an accurate or healthy way for a youth to think about his or her choices. Misuses and misunderstandings do not end there. Bond rating agencies believe average SAT/ACT scores at a college are a meaningful reflection of a college's finances; National Merit Scholarships require a cutoff PSAT score for eligibility; and, perhaps worst of all, many individuals believe their test scores are a truthful reflection of their intelligence, encouraging snobbery or shame.

All of this is done for tests (SAT and ACT) that are less valuable than the high school transcript for an admissions officer's ability to estimate how well a youth will do in college. Rather than leveling the playing field, these tests reinforce social disparities: women score lower than men, but earn higher college grades; there is a linear relation between family income and test score that does not exist for high school grades; and the racial disparities in test scores are a constant source of controversy.

In May 2008, Wake Forest University announced a new admissions policy, no longer requiring SAT/ACT scores as part of the application process. With this change in policy, Wake Forest joined approximately 750 other four-year-degree-granting institutions that were test-optional. And those ranks have grown: as this book nears publication, approximately 850 institutions have gone test-optional. Wake Forest was singled out as the first highly ranked national university to go test-optional. News outlets ranging from the *Charlotte Observer* to the *New York Times* covered the change, including several positive editorials.

In the buzz over Wake Forest's decision, the connection between testing and racial disparities in America was highlighted. According to *The Journal of Blacks in Higher Education*, "Wake Forest presents the most serious threat so far to the future of the SAT. . . . University admissions officials say that one reason for dropping the SAT is to encourage more black and minority applicants. Blacks now make up 6 percent of the undergraduate student body" ("Wake Forest Presents," 2008, p. 9). The year after the new policy was announced, Wake Forest's minority applications went up by 70%, and the first test-optional class (which enrolled in the fall of 2009) was 23% black and Hispanic, a big leap forward. For Wake Forest, as for many other colleges, there is an inverse relationship between the weight placed on high-stakes test scores and the diversity of an applicant pool and matriculating class.

Wake Forest was getting racial and social class diversity from its new policy, but was it also getting more engaged and academically stronger students than before? It would take the passage of time, at least the few years that have so far elapsed, before those questions could be answered. The balance sheet in the concluding chapter of this book provides that answer, with an update on the current social composition and academic performance of Wake Forest's test-optional classes.

Wake Forest's announcement in May 2008 was fortuitously followed by the National Association for College Admission Counseling's (NACAC) release in September 2008 of its *Report of the Commission on the Use of Standardized Tests in Undergraduate Admission.* The NACAC Commission urged educators to "take back the conversation" on testing from the hands of the testing industry. It began by noting the "growing number of postsecondary institutions [that] have adopted 'test-optional' admissions policies" and then proceeded to suggest that many more could fruitfully follow the same route. The Commission wrote that while "many colleges find benefit in using admission tests in admission decisions, *it is the view of the Commission that there may be more colleges and universities that could make appropriate admissions decisions without requiring standardized tests* such as the ACT and SAT. *The Commission encourages institutions to consider dropping the admission test requirements if it is determined that the predictive utility of the test or the admission policies of the institution . . . support that decision*" (NACAC, 2008, p. 7, emphasis added).

All but three of the chapters in this book originated as presentations at national conferences. Some papers were presented at a 3-day event organized by Wake Forest University in April 2009; others were given at meetings of NACAC in September 2009 or 2010; one was presented at the American Educational Research Association's meeting in April 2009. The contributors to this volume include three university presidents or provosts, three admissions directors or deans, two admissions office statisticians, four economists, three sociologists, two leaders in the field of test preparation and test critique (from FairTest and the Princeton Foundation), one historian, one American Enterprise Institute Fellow, and one journalist.

Everyone who contributed to this book is deeply engaged with admissions practices and problems.

This book examines admissions questions in chapters organized into three topical sections. Part I, "Overview and History of Admissions and Testing," offers broad arguments about the history of selective college admissions in America. Part II, "New Techniques, Removing Test Bias, and Institutional Case Studies," addresses the limitations of the SAT and ACT: these tests do not address qualities, such as creativity and problem solving, that are crucial to success in college; the SAT in particular may continue to be contaminated by racial and gender biases; and institutional case studies demonstrate that SAT scores add little or nothing that is superior to the high school record. Part III, "Evaluations of Test-Optional Policies," reviews practical experiences with, and statistical models of, test-optional admissions and the challenges of crafting an undergraduate class to meet academic and societal goals without relying on SAT/ACT scores.

Part I presents historical overviews and analytical arguments urging us to go beyond conventional practices. In Chapter 1, Daniel Golden, who won a Pulitzer Prize for his reporting on admissions in the *Wall Street Journal*, provides examples of the many systematic ways selective colleges opt for the offspring of the rich and well connected over students with special talents and academic merit.

Chapter 2 is an extensive essay on a century of experience with standardized tests in admissions by Richard Atkinson, former President of the University of California, and Saul Geiser, who is affiliated with the Center for Studies in Higher Education, University of California, Berkeley. Atkinson and Geiser's critique of the SAT in 2001 was a turning point in the national discussion of testing. California made the SAT a successful nationwide test in the late 1960s when it decided to require it, and in 2001 California threatened to pull the pillars out of the very testing edifice it helped to create by abandoning the SAT. California found high school grades and subject tests to best predict college performance, and to do so without as many disparities between social groups as are found with the SAT. In reaction, the Educational Testing Service (ETS) offered to create a new test that would address California's concerns about fairness and predictive power, if only California would give it another chance. California accepted ETS's proposal, which, like the second-marriage cliché on the triumph of hope over experience, brought sad results. The New SAT, which was released in 2005, has been widely judged a failure. Relative to the older SAT, it is longer and more expensive, it has no more predictive power, and it has *higher* test-score disparities between racial groups.

Chapter 3, by John Aubrey Douglass, rounds out the California story with a historical review of the politics of standardized tests at the University of California. Douglass is the author of the definitive history of admissions at the University of California (2007).

Chapter 4 is by Charles Murray, who is famous for his controversial work on intelligence and social inequalities (Herrnstein & Murray, 1994). Murray is unusual in that he both endorses the technical validity of the test and yet urges us to drop it. In his contribution to this discussion, he writes:

> The evidence has become overwhelming. . . . [S]o I find myself arguing that the SAT should be abolished. Not just deemphasized, but no longer administered. . . . [T]he SAT score, intended as a signal flare for those on the bottom, has become a badge flaunted by those on top. (this volume, pp. 69, 80)

It says something very profound about the role of the SAT today if Charles Murray has abandoned it.

Part II begins by rejecting the notion that underpins the SAT (explicitly in the past, implicitly at present): that there is only one type of intelligence. Theories of multiple intelligences, famously associated with the names of Howard Gardner and Robert J. Sternberg, argue in favor of colleges selecting for a diversity of intelligences beyond the analytic ability tapped by tests like the SAT.

When DePaul University went test-optional in 2011, becoming then the largest private university in the United States to do so, it knew that high school grades best predicted college grades, and that SAT/ACT scores transmitted social disparities, but it was also impressed by the multiple-intelligence alternative of "noncognitive assessment." As the *Chronicle of Higher Education* reported, "DePaul officials began investigating noncognitive assessments several years ago. In 2008 the university added four short essay questions to its freshman application. Those questions were based on the research of William E. Sedlacek, a professor emeritus of education at the University of Maryland at College Park and author of *Beyond the Big Test: Noncognitive Assessment in Higher Education* [2004]" (Hoover, 2011). Admissions practices, such as DePaul used, that are sensitive to multiple intelligences are urged by authors in this book.

In Chapter 5, Robert J. Sternberg describes his four types of intelligence (analytical, creative, practical, and wisdom) and how new tests can measure those four and do so with greater predictive power than, and without any of the social biases of, the SAT. Sternberg's admissions experiment, as Dean of the School of Arts and Sciences at Tufts University, pointed to a new direction, moving beyond the scientific pitfalls and social disparities of the past. Impressed with Sternberg's results, Oklahoma State University persuaded him to leave Tufts to become OSU's Provost. In an interview with *Inside Higher Ed*, Sternberg explained the move as an opportunity to implement a new admissions system. He said, "our society has a real problem . . . its obsessive preoccupation with test scores. . . . We need to be concentrating on developing wise and ethical leaders—instead we are developing people who are consummate multiple-choice test-takers" ("Following His Values," 2010).

The limitations of the SAT beyond its one-dimensional view of intelligence may also include racial, ethnic, and gender biases that are due to the mechanics of test design. Chapter 6, by Jay Rosner, Executive Director of the Princeton Review Foundation, explains how the test question selection process may penalize women, ethnic minorities, and racial minorities.

The statistical case against the SAT (which also applies to the ACT) is that it does not significantly enhance the ability of admissions staff to predict the academic potential of applicants. Insofar as the SAT is a measure of analytic ability, it contributes little beyond what we already know from high school about cognitive performance. Lest there be any confusion about this, one should keep in mind that high school grade-point average (HSGPA) has always been the best single academic variable predicting college grades—that point has been repeatedly admitted even by the SAT's sponsor, the College Board (Kobrin, Patterson, Shaw, Mattern, & Barbuti, 2008).

New in-depth studies described in Chapters 7–9 by authors from Wake Forest University, the University of Georgia, and Johns Hopkins University explore the relative merits of the academic and demographic data available in an applicant's file as predictors of college grades. We accept limited terms of debate about the SAT—the metric of first-year college grades—because this is the measure used by the ETS and the College Board to justify their test (Kobrin et al., 2008). The independent case studies presented here—from three types of selective institutions (liberal arts college, flagship public university, private research university)—offer similar findings that are dramatically different from the claims made by the testing industry. These studies show that the New SAT adds 1–4 percentage points to a regression model's ability to predict grades—and that is not a very impressive justification for the troubles and expenses endured by millions of America's test-taking families. Furthermore, there are important variations in the effectiveness of the test among types of institutions and types of students, but *not* in the effectiveness of high school grades. Test scores, for example, tell us less about how well a black youth will do at a public university than they do about how the same individual will perform at a private liberal arts college; but high school grades work equally well at both. These three case studies show that test scores are unreliable and inconstant predictors, whereas high school grades are dependable and uniform—and that is a complete reversal of the conventional wisdom offered by the testing industry.

If regression models predicting college performance typically explain 20–30% of what matters to one's grade-point average, then clearly admissions remain more art than science. Our best models fail to capture 70–80% of what predicts grades, and that leaves a lot of room for the discerning judgment of admissions staff. There is nothing that can replace human judgment based on a conscientious examination of each applicant's file and, whenever possible, face-to-face interviews.

More disturbing than the SAT's small statistical contribution is its significant social cost. If we employ SAT scores to set the limits of our qualified applicant pool, rather than rely on HSGPA, we end up selecting from candidates who are overwhelmingly white and affluent. The social case against the SAT is that racial and socioeconomic status disparities are transmitted by the test. As the NACAC report on admissions states, "test scores appear to calcify differences based on class, race/ethnicity, and parental educational attainment" (NACAC, 2008, p. 11). Many researchers attribute the test's fossilizing effects to its correlation with family socioeconomic status. The SAT appears to be a more reliable proxy for privilege than for college performance. As noted in a 2007 report from Berkeley's Center for Studies in Higher Education (CSHE),

> SAT I Verbal and Math scores exhibit a strong, positive relationship with measures of socioeconomic status (SES) such as family income, parents' education and the academic ranking of a student's high school, whereas HSGPA is only weakly associated with such measures. As a result, standardized admissions tests tend to have greater adverse impact than HSGPA on underrepresented minority students, who come disproportionately from disadvantaged backgrounds. (Geiser & Santelices 2007, p. 2)

SAT-sensitive admissions reduce all types of social diversity.

Part III of this book presents the experience of schools going test-optional and offers research and advice on how to manage test-optional admissions. In practice, there are three ways to move past test-restricted admissions: by going test-optional, as done by Wake Forest University; by refusing to look at any test scores whatever, as done by Sarah Lawrence; and by not requiring test scores from certain categories of applicants. The most researched example of the third option, the exemption policy, is in place at the University of Texas. Their 10% solution, in which admission is guaranteed to all high school seniors who graduate in the top 10% of their local high school—regardless of test scores—has been in place since 1997.

The University of California in 2009 adopted a similar policy (to go into effect for the entering class in 2012), guaranteeing admission to all in the top 9% of their local California school.

In Chapter 10, Robert Schaeffer of FairTest reports on the record of colleges going test-optional, and in Chapter 11, Martha Allman, Dean of Admissions at Wake Forest, describes its test-optional experience. Chapter 12 is a study by a Princeton sociologist and a demographer, Thomas Espenshade and Chang Young Chung, who use a unique national database to explore the impact of different test-optional strategies on the social diversity and academic preparation of one's incoming class. Espenshade and Chung clarify the social and academic costs and benefits of going test-optional.

The authors in this collection do not all agree on exactly how to proceed, but there is a consensus that admissions must change. Views on what should be done with existing standardized tests range from supplementing them with noncognitive assessment, to replacing the norm-scored SAT/ACT tests with criterion-scored subject tests, to rejecting high-stakes tests entirely in favor of relying on high school records. The critique of high-stakes tests stands on three arguments. First, and most fundamentally, those tests assume a one-dimensional theory of intelligence that is both antiquated and dysfunctional. Second, those tests are weak predictors of college grades and degree attainment. And third, use of those tests transmits social biases—it is a type of social Darwinism. A strong case is made in the pages of this volume that public universities should ignore the SAT/ACT and partner with their states' high schools. The case is compelling for private liberal arts colleges and research universities to be test-optional, and to consider adapting Sternberg's methods for identifying creative, ethical problem-solvers. The need to move beyond the wasteful big-test industry is critical—for the sake of our youth, our educational system, and our social health.

References

Deike, R. (2010, May). Standardized test scores—How should they be used? *Admissions Insights.* New York: College Board.

Douglass, J. A. (2007). *The conditions for admission: Access, equity, and the social contract of public universities.* Stanford, CA: Stanford University Press.

Following his values from Tufts to Oklahoma State. (2010, April 23). Quick takes. *Inside Higher Ed.* Retrieved from http://www.insidehighered.com/news/2010/04/23/qt

Geiser, S., & Santelices, M. V. (2007). Validity of high-school grades in predicting student success beyond the freshman year: High-school record vs. standardized tests as indicators of four-year college outcomes. *Research and Occasional Papers Series: CSHE.9.07*. Berkeley: Center for Studies in Higher Education, University of California. Retrieved from http://cshe.berkeley.edu/publications/publications.php?id=265

Herrnstein, R., & Murray, C. (1994). *The bell curve: Intelligence and class structure in American life*. New York: Free Press.

Hoover, E. (2011, February 17). DePaul becomes biggest private university to go "test optional." *Chronicle of Higher Education*. Retrieved from http://chronicle.com/article/DePaul-U-Will-Make-SAT-and/126396/

Kobrin, J. L., Patterson, B. F., Shaw, E. J., Mattern, K. D., & Barbuti, S. M. (2008). *Validity of the SAT for predicting first-year college grade point average*. (College Board Research Report No. 2008-5.) New York: College Board.

National Association for College Admission Counseling (NACAC). (2008). *Report of the Commission on the Use of Standardized Tests in Undergraduate Admission*. Arlington, VA: Author.

Sedlacek, W. E. (2004). *Beyond the big test: Noncognitive assessment in higher education*. San Francisco: Jossey-Bass.

Wake Forest presents the most serious threat so far to the future of the SAT. (2008, Summer). *Journal of Blacks in Higher Education*, (60), 9.

PART I

Overview and History of Admissions and Testing

1

The Preferences of Privilege

DANIEL GOLDEN

Equal opportunity for all, regardless of income and family background, is widely regarded as a cornerstone of American democracy. Yet, unlike their counterparts in the rest of the world, selective colleges in the United States tilt their admissions policies to favor children of the rich and powerful. While professing to foster upward mobility, they often base acceptance and rejection less on the applicant's merit than on the propensity of his or her family to donate to their endowments. In this chapter, I will analyze admissions preferences for privileged groups, such as alumni children and athletes who play predominantly upper-class sports.

I was reminded of the inequities in college admissions when I saw the 2008 film *Slumdog Millionaire,* which won eight Academy Awards in 2009, including Best Picture. It concerns Jamal, a homeless, motherless, destitute youth from a Bombay ghetto, who overcomes numerous hurdles to become the unlikeliest winner of India's version of the game show *Who Wants to Be a Millionaire?*

The obstacles have a certain familiar ring. Hardly anyone from Jamal's social class even competes as a contestant on the show. The program's host pretends to be his friend but actually doesn't want him to win. The questions—such as, "Who's on the face of the U.S. $100 bill"—have a built-in moneyed, upper-class bias. And when Jamal, baffled by one question, opts to "phone a friend," he lacks the usual array of knowledgeable mentors; instead he has to turn to an uneducated—though gorgeous—ex-girlfriend.

As I watched, a sequel began running through my head. Call it *Slumdog Ivy Leaguer.* In this imaginary tale, a low-income student in the United States—let's make it a young woman this time, Jamie—from an inner-city public high school wants to attend a top private university. Bright and hard-working, she yearns to soak up knowledge from academia's best minds and fulfill her intellectual potential. But her dream seems almost as far-fetched as Jamal's game-show fantasy, and it is blocked by similar barriers. Few of her classmates have such lofty aspirations; few high-ranking universities recruit at her low-performing high school; and her overburdened guidance counselor scoffs at her hopes and tries to steer her to a community college.

Just as the host of *Who Wants to Be a Millionaire* feigns friendship with Jamal, so admissions officials at the top colleges encourage Jamie. But they don't tell her that they want to boost application numbers to make their schools look even more selective—or that many of the slots in the freshman class are already spoken for, reserved for the children of alumni and donors, and for athletes who play upper-crust sports never offered at her humble high school. Like Jamal, Jamie is barraged with questions—on standardized tests, in alumni interviews—that presuppose a cultural and family background far more privileged than her own. And, again like Jamal, she can't "phone a friend" for serious help—the analogy, in her case, being to hire a tutor, a test-prep service, or a private college counselor.

I'll concede that my movie premise is susceptible to some of the same criticisms that reviewers leveled at *Slumdog Millionaire*. It's exaggerated, a bit of a caricature, and a tad old-fashioned. Elite colleges actually are making some progress toward economic diversity. They're trying harder to find promising low-income students. They're dropping early-decision programs that deny applicants the ability to shop around for the best financial aid deal. Or, like Wake Forest, they offer applicants the option to not take the SAT, on which scores correlate closely with income.

Still, it is indisputable that students from rich families and private schools are overrepresented at America's top universities. Low-income students remain almost as scarce on these campuses as college presidents who earn less than half a million dollars a year or professors who give grades of D and F. In fact, *The Chronicle of Higher Education* reported in 2008 that the percentage of students at elite colleges receiving Pell Grants—the financial aid program for the neediest students—was actually declining (Fischer, 2008).

The recent reforms do not disturb the fundamental building blocks of an inequitable system—the whole array of admissions preferences that favor the rich, powerful, and famous. Although colleges enjoy nonprofit, tax-free status because they are presumed to serve a social purpose—namely, educating the best students of all backgrounds—these "preferences of privilege" serve a different master: fund-raising. As documented in my book, *The Price of Admission* (Golden, 2006), more applicants receive special consideration under the preferences of privilege than under affirmative action, and in some cases the admissions break is as big or bigger than the advantage affirmative action confers. At schools that admit only 1 in 10 or 1 in 8 of their applicants, and are the gateway to power and influence in our society, affluent but second-rate students regularly get in ahead of candidates with greater intellectual ability or artistic aptitude. These colleges, most of which have not increased their student body size significantly in years, seek donations by reserving slots for children of privilege while turning away outstanding middle-class and working-class applicants. As Notre Dame's admissions dean told me, "The poor schmuck who has to get in on his own has to walk on water."

The Preference for Legacy

The best-known and most widespread of the preferences of privilege is the boost for alumni children. Except for a few private universities in Japan, the United States is the only country where colleges formally favor alumni offspring. Here, legacy preference is almost universal among private colleges, and it is widespread even at flagship public universities. At most top colleges, 10–25% of students are legacies, and they are admitted at two to four times the rate of nonlegacies. Brown University, for instance, admitted 33.5% of legacy applicants for the class of 2010, almost three times its overall acceptance rate of 13.8% (Golden, 2010, pp. 73–76).

A recent study of legacies at one elite university found that as a group they are more likely than their classmates to be white, to be Protestant, and to have attended prep schools. They are also wealthier, with an average family income of $240,000 a year. Yet, despite their affluent backgrounds, alumni children frequently enjoy tuition discounts. At the University of Arkansas in 2008–2009, 185 children of out-of-state alumni received legacy scholarships reducing their tuition to the in-state rate, a reduction of about $9000 a year. That translates into a loss of $1.7 million in university revenue that could have funded scholarships for low-income students (Golden, 2010, p. 77).

College officials often defend legacy preference on the grounds that it is valuable to maintaining tradition. That is at most a half-truth, concealing the profit motive. In the early 1990s, one study of Harvard admissions showed that if an alumni child who applied needed financial aid, the legacy boost disappeared almost entirely (Golden, 2010, p. 79). The implication was that if an alumnus could not earn enough to pay his child's tuition, Harvard was not going to make the same mistake twice.

As admissions rates at top colleges have declined for all students, including alumni children, the economic motive behind legacy preference has become increasingly transparent. Legacies have, in effect, been divided into two groups. The children of graduates who are also big donors or celebrities or politicians enjoy as much of an edge as ever. And then there is everybody else. One high-ranking development official at a top university told me recently that, because the cost of educating a student is one and a half times tuition, alumni who do not donate should not expect admissions preference for their children. "Just because you drank at a trough that others filled does not entitle your child to drink at the same trough," this official told me recently. "There are trough-fillers and there are just drinkers. Those two people are treated differently" (Golden, 2010, p. 80).

Even as colleges rely on legacy preference as a fund-raising tool, the idea that this preference is indispensable to alumni giving is becoming increasingly dubious. Several fine schools, such as Caltech, admit students purely on merit, and do not favor alumni children, and yet they still raise plenty of money, partly through creative approaches to fund-raising. For instance, Gordon Moore, the cofounder of Intel Corp., who earned his Ph.D. at Caltech, gave $600 million to the institute, in tribute to what he calls its "fantastic intellectual climate." Dr. Moore's two sons did not go there, but he received a different kind of reward: Caltech named an asteroid after him (Golden, 2010, p. 97).

Harrison Frist was not in the top 20% of his class at his prep school. When he applied to Princeton, the admissions office gave him the lowest ranking on its academic scale. Nevertheless, Princeton's president considered him a top priority, and he was admitted. Why? Harrison's father, Bill Frist, was a U.S. Senator at the time, and was about to become majority leader. He was also an alumnus and a former Princeton trustee. And the Frist family had given Princeton $25 million to build the Frist Campus Center. Once enrolled, Harrison joined Princeton's rowdiest student club and was arrested for drunk driving. Undeterred, Princeton admitted his younger brother, who was then photographed wearing a Confederate uniform.

Several selective public universities that have dropped legacy preference in recent years have seen no adverse effect on fund-raising. Since Texas A&M eliminated legacy preference in 2004 under pressure from civil rights groups, it has successfully completed a $1.5 billion campaign, and gifts to its foundation almost doubled, from $62 million in 2004 to $114 million in 2007 (Golden, 2010, p. 93).

One secret to Texas A&M's fund-raising success was the ability of its administrators to explain to worried alumni why they had jettisoned legacy preference. Robert Gates, then President of Texas A&M and most recently U.S. Secretary of Defense, told one alumni audience about his own family and about how hard he and his forebears in Kansas had worked for their own college educations. "Texas A&M was built by men who had rough hands," Gates said. One person who attended the speech told me there were tears in the audience, and the alumni gave him a standing ovation. They understood and appreciated Gates's message—that Texas A&M aspired to be elite, but not elitist (Golden, 2010, p. 94).

The Preference for Development

The second preference of privilege does not even have the excuse of tradition. It is known as development preference—for students recommended by the development, or fund-raising office, because their nonalumni parents or relatives are considered to be in a position to help the institution with money or visibility. These parents may be corporate tycoons, Hollywood celebrities, or politicians in a position to provide earmarked funding. This preference can be equivalent to hundreds of SAT points or a full point on the four-point grading scale, depending on the importance of the family.

The family of Texas oil billionaire Robert Bass is a classic example of development preference. Of his four children, two went to Stanford, one to Harvard, and one to Duke, while these same institutions rejected academically stronger classmates. Mr. Bass, a Stanford trustee, has given each of those universities at least $10 million—in Stanford's case, $50 million (Golden, 2006, pp. 61–65).

Incidentally, the Nixon administration, notorious for ethical transgressions, was not above muscling universities for development admits. Nixon's chief counsel, Charles W. Colson, who later served time for obstruction of justice, called Princeton directly from the White House to advocate for his son, Wendell. After Wendell enrolled, Chuck Colson drove to Princeton in September 1972, to visit the freshman on his first weekend there. He reported back to President Nixon, in a conversation preserved on the Watergate tapes, that, "I just had to make sure my son wasn't in the hands of radicals, and he isn't."

The President replied, "Not yet."

The Preference for Athletes

The third preference of privilege is for athletes. Fans watch racially and economically integrated college basketball and football teams on television and think that college sports are diverse. They do not realize that colleges also give admissions breaks to athletes in many prep-school sports that ordinary American kids never have a chance to play: crew, horseback riding, sailing, squash, even polo. College athletics are weighted toward these rich people's sports to attract wealthy donors who rowed crew or played squash themselves, want their alma mater to have a winning team, and are eager to pay for the boathouse or the polo ponies.

Title IX, the law requiring gender diversity in colleges, has worsened this socioeconomic inequity, because it has prompted colleges to start women's teams in blueblood sports such as crew and equestrian events—

for which they can easily find donors—while eliminating men's teams in working-class sports such as wrestling and track and field.

Once enrolled at a top college, children of the rich and famous have a leg up in making varsity rosters. The last player on the bench on many college teams tends to be a legacy or a development admit. From 2003 to 2007, for instance, Joe Pagliuca, a basketball player of modest talents, enjoyed a coveted spot on Duke University's men's team, one of the nation's top programs. Joe did not score a single point in his entire college career. But his presence on the team fulfilled the dream of his father, Boston Celtics co-owner Steve Pagliuca, a Duke graduate and former junior varsity basketball player, who has given more than $1 million to his alma mater (Golden, 2006, pp. 168–169).

The Preference for Faculty and Administrators

The fourth preference of privilege is the edge for children of faculty and administrators. I include this preference because college faculty and administrators, while mostly not millionaires—except for some college presidents—are highly educated. Because the level of parental education is one of the biggest predictors of student accomplishment, the children of these Ph.D.s and M.B.A.s should not need a boost, but they get it anyway. The admissions break is a side effect of the tuition subsidy most colleges give to children of employees. Admissions deans are afraid to reject the child of a prominent professor or administrator because it means the parent will not only be embarrassed but will also have to pay full tuition someplace else (Golden, 2006, pp. 179–194).

The Preference for the Wealthy

As social injustices go, these preferences for the privileged may not seem too hurtful. The worst outcome is that somebody with the ability to excel at a top-tier school goes to a second-tier school instead.

Still, there is something about these admissions benefits for the rich that violates our basic notions of what America stands for—fairness, equal opportunity, and upward mobility—particularly in an era of growing social and economic inequality. The unfairness breeds cynicism among teenagers, who represent America's future and learn even before they are old enough to vote that money talks louder than merit. It is also the bane of high school guidance counselors, who must console their spurned valedictorians, and of the admissions staff at the colleges themselves, who consider themselves professionals and generally want to pick the best candidates. Often, the beneficiaries of preference are imposed on them over their objections.

Many colleges have developed special back-channel routes to admissions for the rich. In September 2006, Harvard eliminated early decision, which, the university contended "advantages those that are already advantaged" and hurts low-income applicants. But, while professing to discard early admissions in the interest of fairness, Harvard preserved what might be called "late admissions"—its Z-list. Students on the Z-list tend to be children of well-connected alumni and big donors with less than peak credentials. Although they often are told in advance that they will be admitted, they are officially wait-listed until the school year ends. Then, after their rejected classmates have gone home and are in no position to complain, Z-listers are admitted not for the following September but for the year after (Golden, 2006, pp. 37–39, 223).

These preferences of privilege come on top of numerous other advantages for the wealthy in the educational process. These individuals generally go to excellent high schools that offer a much wider range of courses, foreign languages, sports, and clubs than inner-city schools do. Their parents introduce them to the world of books and travel. They can afford tutors, SAT prep, independent college counselors, and expensive extracurricular activities. Moreover, many colleges are not what is known in admissions jargon as need-blind—in other words, they have a limited pool of financial aid and consequently give preference to students who can pay their own way. So the rich should not even need legacy, development, and athletic preference—those advantages are just the cherry on the sundae.

Bias Against Asian American Students

The preferences of privilege squeeze out one ethnic group in particular: Asian American students. Data for Harvard, Yale, and other schools show that Asian American applicants need higher SAT scores for admission than any other group, including whites. While Asian American students make up about 30% of winners and finalists for the most prestigious high school awards—AP National Scholar, Presidential Scholar, Intel Science Talent Search, and the like—they make up only about 15% of Ivy League students (Golden, 2006, pp. 197–224).

A few years ago, I visited Hunter College High School in New York City. It is an exam school, very difficult to get into, and one of the best high schools in the country. I interviewed a group of top Asian American students there, including Elizabeth Wai. She told me that she had a 3.7 GPA and a 1530 SAT score (out of 1600; this was before the writing test). When I congratulated her, she said, "No, you don't understand. We call that an 'Asian fail.'"

Or consider Navonil Ghosh, who comes from a middle-class South Asian family and graduated in 2008 from a public magnet school in Austin, Texas. He received perfect scores on the SAT and ACT, one of only a handful of students in the country to accomplish that feat, and he was fourth in his high school class. Yet he was rejected by Harvard, Yale, Stanford, Princeton, Penn, and MIT. These universities love to boast about how many valedictorians and students with perfect SAT scores they turn down, giving the impression that the Navonil Ghoshes of the world do not measure up—when the reality is that they could make room for Navonil by turning down weaker candidates whose parents happen to be alumni or donors.

When the rejection letter from Harvard arrived, "my son was devastated," said Nirmalendu Ghosh. "He told me he could not study anymore and went to bed." Navonil enrolled at Rice University in Houston—and has learned, I hope, that this country has many fine educational institutions outside the Ivy League.

Much of Navonil's case for admission rested on his SATs—a test that has become increasingly beleaguered. Some, including colleges such as Wake Forest that have made it optional, argue that using the SAT in admissions amounts to a preference for privilege, because of the sizable scoring gap between whites and minorities, and between high- and low-income students.

The SAT as a Counterweight to Privilege

While I have relied heavily on SAT scores in my research to document preferences for children of alumni and donors, I have very ambivalent feelings about the test. I agree with the SAT's critics that disparities in scoring by race and social class, exacerbated by test prep and other coaching options available to affluent students, are profoundly disturbing. At the same time, though, I am a product of the SAT generation. I was one of the thousands of bright, middle-class, public high school students who were able to attend an elite college at least partly because the test helped extend the vision and reach of the Ivy Leagues beyond a cluster of old-boy prep schools. Ironically, a test that broadened opportunity for so many young people now stands accused of denying that same opportunity to others.

Opponents of the SAT often talk as if it is the only instrument of privilege in college admissions—ignoring the preferences for children of legacies and donors. Unlike those preferences, the SAT at least tries to gauge the candidate's individual merit. And, even granting a bias toward the white and the wealthy, the SAT may remain useful in comparing two candidates within the same racial and economic groups—or when a score goes against type. For instance, if a minority applicant from a low-performing high school does well on the SAT, that score could be a noteworthy indication of academic potential.

But if—as in so many of the examples I cited in my book (Golden, 2006)—a legacy or a development applicant, with all of the advantages of wealth and parental education, does poorly on the SAT, that can be a strong signal that he or she may not be serious about learning—and that the admissions staff should resist lobbying on the applicant's behalf by the development or alumni office. Indeed, without SAT scores to act as a check on these preferences, it is likely that the number of legacies and development admits at elite universities would be even greater than it already is.

What Is the Future of College Admissions?

Today, curbing the clout of alumni and donors in college admissions is more important—and perhaps more difficult—than ever before. With endowments having plummeted in the deepest economic downturn since the Great Depression, admissions officials face intense pressure to accept candidates whose parents could replenish the college coffers and to reject more applicants who need financial aid. As Northwestern University President Morton Schapiro observed in 2009, "You've always been in an advantaged position to be rich and smart. Now you're at an even greater advantage" (Fitzpatrick, 2009).

Conditions are also ripe for the preferences of privilege to spread to universities in European and Asian countries also affected by the economic downturn. As the public funding on which they are accustomed to relying dries up, such universities are increasingly seeking alumni donations. Can legacy preference be far behind?

At the same time, a movement to stop the preferences of privilege is gaining momentum. The latest strategy is to attack legacy preference in the courts. Legacy preference had been considered untouchable legally under civil rights laws because it does not overtly discriminate on the basis of race. But now there are efforts to challenge legacy preference under other, older laws that prohibit rights and titles based on heredity or nobility.

In a 2006 interview in the *Wall Street Journal*, Princeton President Shirley Tilghman was asked to justify legacy preference. She responded with admirable candor that alumni are "extremely important to the financial well-being of this university." The reporter, John Hechinger, followed up, "And wouldn't they continue to be even if you didn't give their children the preference?" President Tilghman responded, "We've never done the experiment" (Golden, 2010, pp. 78–79).

Let us assume that, perhaps voluntarily, perhaps under a court order, a college does try this experiment—eliminating preferences for children of the wealthy, famous, and powerful. What would that mean? It would open more slots for students of demonstrated intellectual brilliance or creative talent, as well as more spaces for children of poverty with tremendous academic potential that has been suppressed because they went to bad high schools or bounced around from one school to another.

It would lead to more demanding courses and more stimulating class discussions, both because the intellectual quality of the student body would rise and because the students would represent a wider spectrum of society. For children of the rich and famous, it would mean an end to guilt and self-doubt and wondering—as many do—whether they got in on their own merits or their parents' wallets. And, most importantly, eliminating the preferences of privilege would be an important step toward reducing the gap between rich and poor and making this a great country not just for some people but for all Americans.

Note

This chapter is based on the keynote lecture delivered by Daniel Golden at the "Rethinking Admissions" conference held April 15–16, 2009, at Wake Forest University.

References

Fischer, K. (2008). Top colleges admit fewer low-income students. *Chronicle of Higher Education, 54*(34), A1, A19+.

Fitzpatrick, L. (2009, March 26). Colleges face a financial-aid crunch. *Time.*

Golden, D. (2006). *The price of admission: How America's ruling class buys its way into elite colleges—and who gets left outside the gates.* New York: Crown.

Golden, D. (2010). An analytic survey of legacy preference. In R. D. Kahlenberg (Ed.), *Affirmative action for the rich: Legacy preferences in college admissions* (pp. 33–69). New York: Century Foundation Book.

2

Reflections on a Century of College Admissions Tests

RICHARD C. ATKINSON and SAUL GEISER

Standardized testing for college admissions has seen extraordinary growth over the past century and appears to be on the cusp of still more far-reaching changes. Fewer than 1000 examinees sat for the first College Boards in 1901. Today more than 1.5 million students take the SAT, 1.4 million sit for the ACT, and many students take both. This does not count many more who take preliminary versions of college entrance tests earlier in school, nor does it include those who take the SAT Subject Tests and Advanced Placement (AP) exams. Admissions testing continues to be a growth industry, and further innovations such as computer-based assessments with instant scoring, adaptive testing, and "noncognitive" assessment are poised to make their appearance.

Despite this growth and apparent success, the feeling persists that all is not well in the world of admissions testing. College entrance tests and related test preparation activities have contributed mightily to what has been called the "educational arms race"—the ferocious competition for admission to highly selective institutions (Atkinson, 2001). Many deserving low-income and minority students are squeezed out in this competition, and questions about fairness and equity are raised with increasing urgency. The role of the testing agencies themselves has also come into question, and some ask whether the testing industry holds too much sway over the colleges and universities it purports to serve. Underlying all of these questions is a deeper concern that the current regime of admissions testing may impede rather than advance our educational purposes.

This chapter reflects on the first century of admissions testing with a view to drawing lessons that may be useful as we now contemplate the second century. Our aim is not to extrapolate from the past or to predict the specific forms and directions that admissions tests may take in the future. Rather, our intent is to identify general principles that may help guide test development going forward.

Putting Tests in Perspective:
Primacy of the High School Record

A first order of business is to put admissions tests in proper perspective. High school grades are the best indicator of student readiness for college, and standardized tests are useful primarily as a supplement to the high school record.

High school grades are sometimes viewed as a less reliable indicator than standardized tests because grading standards differ across schools. Yet although grading standards do vary by school, grades still outperform standardized tests in predicting college outcomes: irrespective of the quality or type of school attended, cumulative grade point average (GPA) in academic subjects in high school has proved to be the best overall predictor of student performance in college. This finding has been confirmed in the great majority of "predictive-validity" studies conducted over the years, including studies conducted by the testing agencies themselves (see Burton & Ramist, 2001, and Morgan, 1989, for useful summaries of studies conducted since 1976).[1]

In fact, traditional validity studies tend to understate the true value of the high school record, in part because of the methods employed and in part because of the outcomes studied. Such studies usually rely on simple correlation methods. For example, they examine the correlation between SAT scores and college grades, and the size of the correlation is taken to represent the predictive power of the SAT. At most, these studies report multiple correlations involving only two or three variables, as, for example, when they examine the joint effect of SAT scores and high school grades in predicting first-year college grades (see, e.g., Kobrin, Patterson, Shaw, Mattern, & Barbuti, 2008).

However, correlations of this kind can be misleading because they mask the contribution of socioeconomic and other factors to the prediction. Family income and parents' education, for example, are correlated with SAT scores and also with college outcomes, so much of the apparent predictive power of the SAT actually reflects the proxy effects of socioeconomic status. Berkeley economist Jesse Rothstein (2004) conservatively estimates that traditional validity studies that omit socioeconomic variables overstate the predictive power of the SAT by 150%.[2] High school grades, on the other hand, are less closely associated with students' socioeconomic background and thus retain their predictive power even when controls for socioeconomic status are introduced, as shown in validity studies that employ more fully specified multivariate regression models. Such models generate standardized regression coefficients that allow one to compare the predictive weight of different admissions factors when all other factors are held constant. Using this analytical approach, the predictive advantage of high school grades over standardized tests is more evident (Geiser, 2002; Geiser & Santelices, 2007).[3]

The predictive superiority of high school grades has also been obscured by the outcome measures typically employed in validity studies. Most studies have looked only at freshman grades in college; relatively few have examined longer term outcomes such as 4-year graduation rate or cumulative GPA in college. A large-scale study at the University of California (UC) that did track long-term outcomes found that high school grades were decisively superior to standardized tests in predicting 4-year graduation rate and cumulative college GPA (Geiser & Santelices, 2007). The California findings have been confirmed in a recent national study of college completion by William Bowen and his colleagues, *Crossing the Finish Line,* based on a sample of students from a broad range of public colleges and universities: "High school grades are a far better predictor of both four-year and six-year graduation rates than are SAT/ACT test scores—a central finding that holds within each of the six sets of public universities that we study" (Bowen, Chingos, & McPherson, 2009, pp. 113–114).

Why high school grades have a predictive advantage over standardized tests is not fully understood. It is undeniable that grading standards differ across high schools, yet standardized test scores are based on a single sitting of 3 or 4 hours, whereas high school GPA is based on repeated sampling of student performance over a period of years. In addition, college preparatory classes present many of the same academic challenges that students will face in college—term papers, labs, final exams—so it should not be surprising that prior performance in such activities would be predictive of later performance.

Whatever the precise reasons, it is useful to begin any discussion of standardized admissions tests with acknowledgment that a student's record in college preparatory courses in high school remains the best indicator of how the student is likely to perform in college. Standardized tests do add value, however. In our studies at the University of California, for example, we have found that admissions tests add an increment of about 6 percentage points to the explained variance in cumulative college GPA, over and above about 20% of the variance that is accounted for by high school GPA and other academic and socioeconomic factors known at the point of admission (Geiser & Santelices, 2007). And tests can add value in other important ways, beyond prediction, that we shall consider later in this chapter.

Testing for Ability: The Saga of the SAT

The SAT, or Scholastic Aptitude Test, first made its appearance in 1926 as an alternative to the earlier College Boards. Whereas the older tests were written, curriculum-based examinations designed to assess student learning in college preparatory subjects, the SAT promised something entirely new: an easily scored, multiple-choice instrument for measuring students' general ability or aptitude for learning (Lemann, 1999).

The similarity between the early SAT and IQ testing was not coincidental, and the two shared a number of assumptions that most now regard as problematic. The SAT grew out of the experience with IQ tests during World War I, when 2 million men in military service were tested and assigned an IQ based on the results. The framers of those tests assumed that intelligence was a unitary, inherited attribute; it was not subject to change over a lifetime and could be measured in a single number. Although the SAT was more sophisticated from a psychometric standpoint, it evolved from the same questionable assumptions about human talent and potential.

Despite the test's questionable underpinnings, especially in the years after World War II, the idea of the SAT resonated strongly with the meritocratic ethos of American college admissions. The SAT was standardized in a way that high school grades were not, and it could be administered relatively inexpensively to large numbers of students. If aptitude for learning could be reliably measured, the SAT could help identify students from disadvantaged circumstances who were deserving of admission—thus improving access and equity in college admissions. Above all, the SAT offered a tool for prediction, providing admissions officers a means to distinguish between applicants who were likely to perform well or poorly in college. It is easy to understand why the test gained widespread acceptance in the postwar years.

The SAT has evolved considerably since that time, and both the name of the test and the terminology describing what it is intended to measure have changed. In an effort to alter the perception of the test's link to the older IQ tradition, in 1990 the College Board changed the name to the Scholastic Assessment Test and then in 1996 dropped the name altogether, so that the initials no longer stand for anything. Official descriptions of what the test is supposed to measure have also changed over the years from "aptitude" to "generalized reasoning ability" and now "critical thinking," and the test items and format have been more or less continuously revised (Lawrence, Rigol, Van Essen, & Jackson, 2003). Throughout these changes, the one constant has been the SAT's claim to gauge students' general analytic ability, as distinct from their mastery of specific subject matter, and thereby to predict performance in college.

Questioning the SAT

By the end of the 20th century, however, the SAT had become the object of increasing scrutiny, partly as a result of developments at our own institution, the University of California. After Californians voted to end affirmative action in 1996, the UC system undertook a sweeping review of its admissions policies in an effort to reverse plummeting Latino and African American enrollments. What we found challenged many established beliefs about the SAT.

Far from promoting equity and access in college admissions, we found that—compared with traditional indicators of academic achievement—the SAT had a more adverse impact on low-income and minority applicants.[4] The SAT was more closely correlated than other indicators with socioeconomic status and so tended to diminish the chances of admission for underrepresented minority applicants, who come disproportionately from lower socioeconomic backgrounds. For example, when UC applicants were rank ordered by SAT scores, roughly half as many Latino, African American, and American Indian students appeared in the top of the applicant pool as when the same students were ranked by high school grades (Geiser & Santelices, 2007).

Another surprise was the relatively poor predictive power of the SAT (then also known as the SAT I) as compared not only with high school grades but also with curriculum-based achievement tests, such as the SAT II subject tests and AP exams, which measure students' mastery of specific subjects. The SAT I's claim to assess general analytic ability, independent of curriculum content, was long thought to give it an advantage over achievement tests in predicting how students will perform in college.

The University of California had required applicants to take both the SAT I and a battery of achievement tests since 1968, and thus had an extensive database to evaluate that claim. Our data showed that the SAT I reasoning test was consistently *inferior* to the SAT II subject tests in predicting student performance, although the difference was small and there was substantial overlap between the tests. It was not the size of the difference but the consistency of the pattern that was most striking. The subject tests—particularly the writing exam—held a predictive advantage over the SAT I reasoning test at all UC campuses and within every academic discipline (Geiser, 2002).[5] And in later studies we found that the AP exams, which require the greatest depth of subject knowledge, exhibited an even greater predictive advantage (Geiser & Santelices, 2006). Mastery of curriculum content, it turns out, is important after all.

Another concern with the SAT I was its lack of fit with the needs of K–12 schools. After affirmative action was dismantled, UC massively expanded its outreach to low-performing schools throughout California in an effort to restore minority admissions over the long term. At their height, before later state budget cuts, UC outreach programs were serving 300,000 students and 70,000 teachers, and UC campuses had formed school–university partnerships with 300 of the lowest performing schools in the state. College admissions criteria can have a profound influence, for good or ill, on such schools—what Michael Kirst has called a "signaling effect" (Kirst & Venezia, 2004)—and it was evident that the SAT was sending the wrong signals.

The SAT I sent a confusing message to students, teachers, and schools. It featured esoteric items, such as verbal analogies and quantitative comparisons, rarely encountered in the classroom. Its implicit message was that students would be tested on materials that they had not studied in school and that the grades they achieved could be devalued by a test that was unrelated to their coursework. Especially troubling was the perception of the SAT I as a test of basic intellectual ability, which had a perverse effect on many students from low-performing schools, tending to diminish academic aspiration and self-esteem. Low scores on the SAT I were too often interpreted as meaning that a student lacked the ability to attend the University of California, notwithstanding his or her record in high school.[6]

These concerns prompted the coauthor of this chapter and then President of the University of California, Richard Atkinson, to propose dropping the SAT I in favor of curriculum-based achievement tests in UC admissions (Atkinson, 2001).[7] The University of California accounts for a substantial share of the national market for admissions tests, and the College Board responded to our concerns with a revised SAT in 2005.

The New SAT

The New SAT (now also known as the SAT-R, for "Reasoning") is clearly an improvement over the previous version of the test. The SAT II writing exam has been incorporated into the test, and verbal analogies have been dropped. Instead of deconstructing esoteric analogies, students must now perform a task they will actually face in college—writing an essay under a deadline. The old SAT featured math items, such as quantitative comparisons, that were known for their trickery but required only an introductory knowledge of algebra; the New SAT math section is more straightforward and covers some higher level topics in algebra. Reports indicate that the changes have galvanized a renewed focus on math and especially writing in many of the nation's schools (Noeth & Kobrin, 2007).

Nevertheless, as an admissions test, the New SAT still falls short in important respects. The New SAT has three sections: Writing, Mathematics, and a third called Critical Reading. Not surprisingly, given the University of California's earlier findings, research by the College Board shows that writing is the most predictive of the three sections. Yet College Board researchers also find that, overall, the New SAT is not statistically superior to the old test in predicting success in college: "The results show that the changes made to the SAT did not substantially change how well the test predicts first-year college performance" (Kobrin et al., 2008, p. 1). This result was unexpected, given the strong contribution of the writing test and the fact that the New SAT is almost an hour longer than the old test.[8]

A possible explanation is provided by a study by economists at the University of Georgia (Cornwell, Mustard, & Van Parys, 2008). That study found that adding the writing section to the New SAT has rendered the critical reading section almost entirely redundant, so that it does not add significantly to the prediction. The critical reading section is essentially the same as the verbal reasoning section of the old SAT I. It appears that the College Board was trying to have the best of both worlds. The College Board could and did tell admissions officers that the critical reading and math sections of the New SAT were comparable to the verbal and mathematical reasoning sections of the old SAT I. If admissions officers disliked the New SAT, they could ignore the writing exam and then for all practical purposes the old and New SATs would be equivalent.[9]

A more fundamental question is what, exactly, the new test is intended to measure. The SAT's underlying test construct has long been ambiguous, and the recent changes have only added to the confusion. Although inclusion of the writing test and some higher level math items is evidently intended to position the New SAT as more of an achievement test, its provenance as a test of general analytic ability remains evident as well. The verbal and math sections continue to feature items that are remote from what students encounter in the classroom, and the College Board has emphasized the psychometric continuity between the old and new versions of the test (Camara & Schmidt, 2006). In a phrase, the New SAT appears to be "a test at war with itself" (Geiser, 2009), and it will be interesting to see which impulse prevails in future iterations of the test.

Although a significant improvement over the old test, the New SAT remains fundamentally at odds with educational priorities along the pathway from high school to college. The New SAT's lack of alignment with high school curricula has become especially conspicuous now that more and more states have moved toward standards-based assessments at the K–12 level. Standards-based tests seek to align teaching, learning, and assessment. They give feedback to students and schools about specific areas of the curriculum where they are strongest and weakest, providing a basis for educational improvement and reform (Darling-Hammond, 2003). Aligning admissions tests with the needs of our schools—especially schools serving populations that have been traditionally underserved by higher education—must be a priority as we look to the next generation of standardized admissions tests.

Testing for Achievement: Enter the ACT

The ACT was introduced in 1959 as a competitor to the SAT. From its inception, the ACT has reflected an alternative philosophy of college admissions testing espoused by its founder, E. F. Lindquist (1958):

> If the examination is to have the maximum motivating value for the high school student, it must impress upon him the fact that his chances of being admitted to college . . . depend not only on his "brightness" or "intelligence" or other innate qualities or factors for which he is not personally responsible, but even more upon how hard he has worked at the task of getting ready for college. . . . The examination must make him feel that he has *earned* the right to go to college by his own efforts, not that he is entitled to college because of his innate abilities or aptitudes, regardless of what he has done in high school. In other words, the examination must be regarded by him as an *achievement* test. (pp. 108–109)

From our vantage point half a century later, Lindquist's vision of admissions testing seems remarkably fresh and prescient. His understanding of the signaling effect of college admissions criteria for K–12 students and schools reflects a modern sensibility, as does his admonition that educators must not allow their standards to be set, by default, by the tests they use. Assessment should flow from standards, not the other way round. Lindquist's concept of achievement testing was also quite sophisticated: as against those who would caricature such tests as measuring only rote recall of facts, he insisted that achievement tests can and should measure students' reasoning skills, albeit those developed within the context of the curriculum.

Reflecting Lindquist's philosophy, the ACT from the beginning has been tied more closely than the SAT to high school curricula. The earliest forms of the test grew out of the Iowa Tests of Educational Development and included four sections—English, mathematics, social studies reading, and natural sciences reading—reflecting Iowa's high school curriculum. As the ACT grew into a national test, its content came to be based on national curriculum surveys as well as analysis of state standards for K–12 instruction. In 1989 the test underwent a major revision and the current four subject areas were introduced (English, mathematics, reading, and science), and in 2005 the ACT added an optional writing exam in response, in part, to a request from the University of California.

The ACT exhibits many of the characteristics that one would expect of an achievement test. It is developed from curriculum surveys. It appears less coachable than the SAT, and the consensus among the test prep services is that the ACT places less of a premium on test-taking skills and more on content mastery. The ACT also has a useful diagnostic component to assist students as early as the eighth grade to get on and stay on track for college—another function that Lindquist believed an admissions test should perform (ACT, 2009b).

Yet the ACT still falls short of being a true achievement test in several ways. Like the SAT, the ACT remains a norm-referenced test and is used by colleges and universities primarily to compare students against one another rather than to assess curriculum mastery. The ACT is scored in a manner that produces almost the same bell curve distribution as the SAT. It is true that the ACT also provides standards-based interpretations indicating the knowledge and skills that students at different score levels generally can be expected to have learned (ACT, 2009a). But those interpretations are only approximations and do not necessarily identify what an examinee actually knows. It is difficult to reconcile the ACT's norm-referenced scoring with the idea of a criterion-referenced assessment or to understand how one test could serve both functions equally.

The ACT lacks the depth of subject matter coverage that one finds in other achievement tests such as the SAT Subject Tests or AP exams. The ACT science section, for example, is intended to cover high school biology, chemistry, physics, and earth/space science. But the actual test requires little knowledge in any of these disciplines, and a student who is adept at reading charts and tables quickly to identify patterns and trends can do well on this section—unlike the SAT Subject Tests or AP exams in the sciences, which require intensive subject matter knowledge.

In a curious twist, the ACT and SAT appear to have converged over time. Whereas the SAT has shed many of its trickier and more esoteric item types, such as verbal analogies and quantitative comparisons, the ACT has become more SAT-like in some ways, such as the premium it places on students' time management skills. It is not surprising that almost all U.S. colleges and universities now accept both tests and treat ACT and SAT scores interchangeably.

Finally, another fundamental problem for the ACT—or for any test that aspires to serve as the nation's achievement test—is the absence of national curriculum standards in the United States. The ACT has tried to overcome this problem through its curriculum surveys, but the "average" curriculum does not necessarily reflect what students are expected to learn in any given state, district, or school. The lack of direct alignment between curriculum and assessment has led the National Association for College Admissions

Counseling (NACAC, 2008) to criticize the practice followed by some states, such as Colorado, Illinois, and Michigan, of requiring all K–12 students to take the ACT, whether or not they plan on attending college, and using the results as a measure of student achievement in the schools. This practice runs counter to the American Educational Research Association's guidelines on testing: "Admission tests, whether they are intended to measure achievement or ability, are not directly linked to a particular instructional curriculum and, therefore, are not appropriate for detecting changes in middle school or high school performance" (American Educational Research Association, American Psychological Association, & National Council on Measurement in Education, 1999, p. 143).

Of course, using the ACT to assess achievement in high school is not the same as using it to assess readiness for college. But the same underlying problem—the loose alignment between curriculum and assessment—is evident in both contexts. It may be that no one test, however well designed, can ever be entirely satisfactory in a country with a strong tradition of federalism and local control over the schools. Developing an effective and robust single national achievement test may be impossible in the absence of a national curriculum.

Assessing Achievement in Specific Subjects: SAT Subject Tests and AP Exams

In place of a single test, another approach taken at some colleges and universities is to require several achievement tests in different subjects. The assessments most often used are the SAT II subject tests and AP exams.

During the 1930s, the College Board developed a series of multiple-choice tests in various subject areas to replace its older written exams. These later became known as the SAT IIs. and they are now officially called the SAT Subject Tests. In 1955 the College Board introduced the Advanced Placement program and, with it, the AP exams. As their name indicates, the AP exams were originally intended for use in college placement. Colleges and universities used AP exam scores mainly to award course credits, allowing high-achieving students to place out of introductory courses and move directly into more advanced college work. Over time, however, AP has come to play an increasingly important role in admissions at selective institutions, and its role in admissions is now arguably more important than its placement function.[10]

Of all nationally administered tests used in college admissions, the SAT Subject Tests and AP exams are the best examples of achievement tests currently available. The SAT Subject Tests are offered in about 20 subject areas and the AP exams in more than 30. The SAT Subject Tests are hour-long, multiple-choice assessments, whereas the AP exams take 2–3 hours and include a combination of multiple-choice, free-answer, and essay questions. Students frequently sit for the tests after completing high school coursework in a given subject, so the tests often serve, in effect, as end-of-course exams. Test prep services such as the Princeton Review advise students that the most effective way to prepare for subject exams is through coursework, and in a telling departure from its usual services, the Review offers content-intensive coursework in mathematics, biology, chemistry, physics, and U.S. history to help students prepare for these tests (Princeton Review, 2009).

Until the SAT II Writing exam was discontinued and became part of the New SAT in 2005, the University of California had for many years required three subject tests for admission to the UC system: SAT Writing, SAT II Mathematics, and a third SAT II subject test of the student's choosing.[11] The elective test requirement was established to give students an opportunity to demonstrate particular subjects in which they excel and to assist them in gaining admission to particular majors. Students can also elect to submit AP exam scores, which, though not required, are considered in admission to individual UC campuses.[12]

The idea that students should be able to choose the tests they take for admission may seem anomalous to those accustomed to viewing the SAT or ACT as national "yardsticks" for measuring readiness for college. But the real anomaly may be the idea that all students should take one test or that one test is suitable for all students. Our research showed that a selection of three SAT II subject tests—including one selected by students—predicted college performance better than either of the generic national assessments, although scores on all of the tests tended to be correlated and the predictive differences were relatively small. Of the individual SAT II exams, the elective SAT II subject test proved a relatively strong predictor, ranking just behind the SAT II Writing test (Geiser, 2002; Geiser & Santelices, 2007). The AP exams proved even better predictors. Although mere participation in AP classes bore no relation to performance in college, students who took and scored well on the AP exams tended to be very successful: AP exam scores were second only to high school grades in predicting student performance at the University of California (Geiser & Santelices, 2006).

Our findings in California on the superiority of achievement tests, and especially the AP exams, have been confirmed by Bowen et al.'s (2009) recent national study of college completion. Based on a large sample of students at public colleges and universities, Bowen and his colleagues found that AP exam scores were a far better incremental predictor of graduation rates than were scores on the regular SAT/ACT and, as in the case of the SAT IIs, including this achievement test variable in the regression equation entirely removed any positive relationship between the SAT/ACT scores and graduation rates. It is also important to emphasize that achievement tests are better predictors than SAT scores for all students, including minority students and students from lower socioeconomic backgrounds (pp. 130–131). In the national admissions community there is growing awareness of the value of subject tests. NACAC (2008) has recently called on colleges and universities to reexamine their emphasis on the SAT and ACT and to expand use of subject tests in admissions.

NACAC's commission on testing, which wrote the 2008 report, included many high-profile admissions officials and was chaired by William Fitzsimmons, Dean of Admissions at Harvard. The report is unusually thoughtful and is worth quoting at some length:

> There are tests that, at many institutions, are both predictive of first-year and overall grades in college and more closely linked to the high school curriculum, including the College Board's AP exams and Subject Tests as well as the International Baccalaureate examinations.
>
> What these tests have in common is that they are—to a much greater extent than the SAT and ACT—achievement tests, which measure content covered in high school courses; that there is currently very little expensive private test preparation associated with them, partly because high school class curricula are meant to prepare students for them; and that they are much less widely required by colleges than are the SAT and ACT. . . . By using the SAT and ACT as one of the most important admission tools, many institutions are gaining what may be a marginal ability to identify academic talent beyond that indicated by transcripts, recommendations, and achievement test scores. In contrast, the use of . . . College Board Subject Tests and AP tests, or International Baccalaureate exams, would create a powerful incentive for American high schools to improve their curricula and their teaching. Colleges would lose little or none of the information they need to make good choices about entering classes, while benefiting millions of American students who do not enroll in highly selective colleges and positively affecting teaching and learning in America's schools. (NACAC, 2008, p. 44)

The main counterargument to expanding use of such tests in college admissions is the fear that they might harm minority, low-income, or other students from schools with less rigorous curricula. Currently the SAT Subject Tests and AP exams are considered in admissions only at a few highly selective colleges and universities, and the population of test takers is smaller, higher achieving, and less diverse than the general population that takes the SAT or ACT. The fear is that if subject tests were used more widely, students from disadvantaged schools might perform more poorly on them than on tests less closely tied to the curriculum.

Experience at the University of California suggests that this fear is unfounded. After introducing its Top 4 Percent Plan in 2001, which extended eligibility for admission to top students in low-performing high schools, the university saw a significant jump in the number of students in these schools who took the three SAT II subject tests that the university required. Low-income and minority students performed at least as well on these tests, and in some cases better, than they did on the SAT I reasoning test or the ACT. Scores on the SAT II subject tests were in most cases *less* closely correlated than SAT I or ACT scores with students' socioeconomic status.[13] Interestingly, the elective SAT II subject test had the lowest correlation of any exam with students' socioeconomic status, while remaining a relatively strong indicator of their performance at the University of California (Geiser, 2002).

Nevertheless, as achievement tests, the SAT Subject Tests and AP exams do have limitations. Scoring on both tests is norm referenced, despite the fact that colleges often treat them as proficiency tests (especially the AP exams, which are used for college placement as well as admissions). Oddly, for tests designed to assess curricular achievement, scores are not criterion referenced even though they are often interpreted as such.

Another issue is how well the tests actually align with high school curricula. The SAT Subject Tests and AP exams differ in this regard. The latter exams are intended primarily for students who have completed AP courses in high school. This arrangement has both advantages and disadvantages. The advantage is that the exams are tied to the AP curriculum, but it also means that the tests are not necessarily appropriate for students who have not taken AP courses, thus limiting the usefulness of the exams in college admissions. Also, the AP program has come under fire from some educators, who charge that, by "teaching to the test," AP classes too often restrict the high school curriculum and prevent students from exploring the material in depth; a number of leading college preparatory academies have dropped AP courses for that reason (Hammond, 2008).

The SAT Subject Tests, on the other hand, are not tied as directly to particular instructional approaches or curricula but are designed to assess a core of knowledge common to all curricula in a given subject area: "Each Subject Test is broad enough in scope to be accessible to students from a variety of academic backgrounds, but specific enough to be useful to colleges as a measure of a student's expertise in that subject" (College Board, 2009b). This enhances their accessibility for use in admissions, but at a cost. The SAT Subject Tests are less curriculum intensive than the AP exams, and perhaps for that reason, they are also somewhat less effective in predicting student success in college (Geiser & Santelices, 2006). Without question, the SAT Subject Tests and AP exams have the strongest curricular foundations of any college entrance tests now available, and more colleges and universities should find them attractive for that reason. But both fall short of being fully realized achievement tests.

Adapting K–12 Standards-Based Tests for Use in College Admissions

The best examples of pure achievement tests now available are employed not in U.S. higher education but in our K–12 schools: standards-based assessments developed by the various states as part of the movement to articulate clearer standards for what students are expected to learn, teach to the standards, and assess student achievement against those standards.[14] The schools are well ahead of colleges and universities in this regard. In its recent report, NACAC's commission on testing raised the possibility of adapting K–12 standards-based assessments for use in college admissions:

> These tests vary in quality; the better ones, such as those in New York, include end-of-course tests that students take upon completion of specific courses. Not all state high school exams are sufficient to measure the prospect of success in postsecondary education. However, if such tests can be developed so they successfully predict college grades as well as or better than the SAT, ACT, AP, International Baccalaureate exams, and Subject Tests do, and align with content necessary for college coursework, the Commission would urge colleges to consider them in the admission evaluation process. (NACAC, 2008, p. 44)

The idea of adapting K–12 standards-based assessments for use in college admissions has obvious attractions. In the ideal case, students' performance on end-of-course tests or exit exams could serve the dual function of certifying both their achievement in high school and their readiness for college. The burden on students and the amount of testing they must endure could be greatly reduced. College entrance criteria would be aligned directly with high school curricula, and the message to students would be clear and unequivocal: working hard and performing well in one's high school coursework is the surest route to college.

This is surely a compelling and worthwhile vision. At the same time, however, there are significant obstacles to its realization. Our experience in California is not necessarily representative of other states but may help illustrate some of the difficulties involved.

University of California's Experience with K-12 Assessments

In 2000 the University of California began to explore possible alternative assessments to the SAT and ACT that were more closely aligned with California's K–12 curriculum yet suitable for use in UC admissions. Some UC faculty were skeptical of this effort in view of the volatile political environment surrounding the state's K–12 assessment system, where new testing regimes came and went with alarming frequency. In 1997, however, the State Board of Education launched a major effort to articulate clear curriculum standards for the schools and to align all state tests with those standards, which seemed to promise greater stability and continuity going forward.

It soon became evident, however, that most statewide tests were inadequate for use in UC admissions. Designed to measure achievement across the entire range of the K–12 student population, the California Standards Test lacked sufficient differentiation and reliability at the high end of the achievement distribution, from which the University of California draws its students. A similar problem existed with the California High School Exit Exam, then in its planning stages. An exam designed to determine whether students meet the minimum standards required for high school graduation is unlikely to be useful in a highly selective admissions environment.

But one test did hold promise: the Golden State Examinations (GSEs), which had been established in 1983 to assess achievement in specific academic subjects. The California Department of Education, the state's K–12 administrative arm, had long championed the GSEs as part of a broader program to improve student achievement, similar to the national AP program. The exams were voluntary and were geared as honors-level assessments. Matching the state's test records to our own student database, we found that GSE scores predicted first-year performance at the University of California almost as well as the SAT I reasoning test, although not nearly as well as the SAT II subject tests. Although the GSEs lacked some of the technical sophistication of the national tests, we were hopeful that those issues could be resolved; the state had contracted with ACT, Inc., to help improve the tests' psychometric quality.[15]

Those hopes were dashed when funding for the GSE program was eliminated from the state's 2003 budget. The test had fallen victim to political infighting between the California Department of Education, which was promoting the test, and the State Board of Education, which viewed the GSEs as a departure from its new curriculum standards. Some state education officials also viewed the University of California's efforts to adapt the

GSEs for use in admissions as an incursion on the Board of Education's authority over K–12 curriculum standards.

California's experience illustrates a more general problem likely to confront efforts to develop standards-based assessments that bridge the institutional divide between state university and K–12 school systems. Standards for what is expected of entering freshmen at selective colleges and universities are different and usually much more rigorous than K–12 curriculum standards. They overlap, to be sure, but they are not the same, and institutional conflicts over standards and testing are probably inevitable for this reason. College and university faculty are right to be skeptical about using K–12 tests in admissions if it means relinquishing control over entrance standards. And it is understandable that secondary school educators are concerned that, in seeking to adapt and modify K–12 tests for use in admissions, colleges and universities may exert undue influence over curriculum standards for the schools.

A first step toward getting past this problem is for colleges and universities to band together in articulating their own standards for what is expected of entering freshmen, as distinct from high school graduates. This has occurred in California. The academic senates of the three main segments of the state's higher education system—the University of California, the California State University, and the California Community Colleges—have collaborated on a joint statement of specific "competencies" in both English and mathematics expected of all students entering California higher education (Intersegmental Committee of the Academic Senates, 1997, 1998). The statements are intended to inform students about the preparation they will need for college beyond the minimum requirements for high school graduation, so that students will not graduate only to find themselves unready for college-level work. Although it is a useful first step, the standards have yet to result in any changes in admissions tests.

Nationally, the most ambitious effort to develop standards of college readiness is Standards for Success, a project sponsored by the American Association of Universities (AAU) and the Pew Charitable Trusts. Led by David Conley at the Center for Education Policy Research at the University of Oregon, the project convened representatives from AAU institutions to identify content standards for what students need to know to succeed in entry-level courses at those institutions. The standards covered English, mathematics, natural sciences, social sciences, second languages, and the arts. Then, in the most interesting phase of the project, researchers used the standards as a reference point to evaluate alignment of K–12 standards-based tests. The project evaluated 66 exams from 20 states, finding that although a few were closely aligned with the standards, most bore only an inconsistent relationship to the knowledge and skills needed for college (Brown & Conley, 2007).

Whether K–12 standards-based assessments can be successfully adapted for use in college admissions may depend in part on the response of the testing agencies. The Standards for Success project ended in 2003, and the standards were subsequently licensed to the College Board. The College Board has announced that the standards are now being used in reviewing test specifications for the SAT, the Preliminary SAT/National Merit Scholarship Qualifying Test, and AP exams. Like ACT, the College Board has sought to have its tests adopted by the states for assessing K–12 student achievement (Hupp & Morgan, 2008), but there is as yet no indication that the standards will be used to adapt state-level exams for admissions purposes (College Board, 2009a).

In its call for American colleges and universities to "take back the conversation" on standardized admissions testing, NACAC's (2008) blue-ribbon commission on testing had this to say about the role of the testing agencies:

> Institutions must exercise independence in evaluating and articulating their use of standardized test scores. There is also a need for an independent forum for inter-institutional evaluation and discussion of standardized test use in admission that can provide support for colleges with limited resources to devote to institutional research and evaluation. While support for validity research is available from the testing agencies, the Commission does not believe that colleges and universities should rely solely on the testing agencies for it. . . . Rather, this Commission suggests that colleges and universities create a new forum for validity research under the auspices of NACAC. Such an independent discussion might begin to address questions the Commission and other stakeholders have posed about the tests. (pp. 21, 23)

NACAC's call for independent research on admissions tests is a useful reminder that until now most research on the SAT and ACT has been conducted by the testing agencies themselves. Much of this work is published outside the academic journals, without benefit of normal peer review, and the findings are invariably supportive of the agencies' test products. Whether or not there is an actual conflict of interest, the appearance of a conflict is inevitable, and the parallel with some recent issues in medical research is troubling.

These considerations underscore the need for colleges and universities collectively to reclaim their authority over admissions testing—and, most vitally, over the standards on which admissions tests are built. Only college and university faculty are in a position to set academic standards for what is expected of matriculants, and this critical task can be neither delegated to the schools nor outsourced to the testing agencies.

Shifting the Paradigm:
From Prediction to Achievement

Looking back at the arc of admissions testing over the 20th century, the signs of a paradigm shift are increasingly apparent. Ever since the 1930s, when Henry Chauncey suggested that Carl Brigham's new Scholastic Aptitude Test could predict student success at Harvard, the idea of prediction has captivated American college admissions. The preoccupation continues to this day and still drives much research on admissions testing. Yet the preoccupation with prediction has gradually given way to another idea. Lindquist's philosophical opposition to the SAT and his introduction of the ACT, the renewed interest in subject tests at some colleges and universities, the explosion of standards-based tests in K–12 schools, and the as-yet unsuccessful efforts to adapt them for use in college admissions—all point the way to assessment of achievement and curriculum mastery as an alternative paradigm for admissions testing.

Our ability to predict student performance in college on the basis of factors known at the point of admission remains relatively limited. After decades of predictive-validity studies, our best prediction models (using not only test scores but high school grades and other academic and socioeconomic factors) still account for only about 25–30% of the variance in outcome measures such as college GPA. This means that some 70–75% of the variance is unexplained. That should not be surprising in view of the many other factors that affect student performance after admission, such as social support, financial aid, and academic engagement in college. But it also means that the error bands around our predictions are quite broad. Using test scores as a tiebreaker to choose between applicants who are otherwise equally qualified, as is sometimes done, is not necessarily a reliable guide, especially where score differences are small.

Moreover, there is little difference among the major national tests in their ability to predict student performance in college. Although the New SAT, ACT, SAT Subject Tests, and AP exams differ in design, content, and other respects, they tend to be highly correlated and thus largely interchangeable with respect to prediction. It is true that subject-specific tests (in particular the AP exams) do have a statistically significant predictive advantage (Bowen et al., 2009; Geiser & Santelices, 2006), but the statistical difference by itself is too small to be of practical significance or to dictate adoption of one test over another. The argument for achievement tests is not so much that they are better predictors than other kinds of tests but that they are no worse: "The benefits of achievement tests for college admissions—greater clarity in admissions standards, closer linkage to the high-school curriculum—can be realized without any sacrifice in the capacity to predict success in college" (Geiser, 2002, p. 25).

For these reasons, we believe that prediction will recede in importance, and other test characteristics will become more critical in designing standardized admissions tests in the future. We will still need to "validate" our tests by demonstrating that they are reasonably correlated with student performance in college; validation remains especially important where tests have adverse impacts on low-income and minority applicants. But beyond some acceptable threshold of predictive validity, decisions about what kinds of assessments to use in college admissions will be driven less by small statistical differences and more by educational policy considerations.

In contrast to prediction, the idea of achievement offers a richer paradigm for admissions testing and calls attention to a broader array of characteristics that we should demand of our tests:

1. Admissions tests should be *criterion referenced* rather than norm referenced: Our primary consideration should not be how an applicant compares with others but whether he or she demonstrates sufficient mastery of college preparatory subjects to benefit from and succeed in college.
2. Admissions tests should have *diagnostic utility*: Rather than a number or a percentile rank, tests should provide students with curriculum-related information about areas of strength and areas where they need to devote more study.
3. Admissions tests should exhibit not only predictive validity but *face validity*: The relationship between the knowledge and skills being tested and those needed for college should be transparent.
4. Admissions tests should be *aligned with college preparatory coursework*: Assessments should be linked as closely as possible to materials that students encounter in the classroom and should reinforce teaching and learning of a rigorous academic curriculum in our high schools.
5. Admissions tests should *minimize the need for test preparation*: Although test prep services will probably never disappear entirely, admissions tests should be designed to reward mastery of curriculum content over test-taking skills, so that the best test prep is regular classroom instruction.

6. Finally, admissions tests should *send a signal to students*: Our tests should send the message that working hard and mastering academic subjects in high school is the most direct route to college.

The core feature of achievement testing is criterion-referenced or standards-based assessment. This approach to assessment is now widely established in the nation's K–12 schools but has yet to take hold in college admissions, where norm-referenced assessments still prevail. Norm-referenced tests like the SAT or ACT are often justified as necessary to help admissions officers sort large numbers of applicants and evaluate their relative potential for success in college.

Once started, however, norm-referenced assessment knows no stopping point. The competition for scarce places at top institutions drives test scores ever higher, and average scores for this year's entering class are almost always higher than last year's scores. Tests are used to make increasingly fine distinctions within applicant pools where almost all students have relatively high scores. Small differences in test scores often tip the scales against admission of lower scoring applicants, when in fact such differences have marginal validity in predicting college performance. The ever-upward spiral of test scores is especially harmful to low-income and minority applicants. Even where these students achieve real gains in academic preparation, as measured on criterion-referenced assessments, they lag further behind other applicants on norm-referenced tests.[16] The emphasis on "picking winners" makes it difficult for colleges and universities to extend opportunities to those who would benefit most from higher education. And the preoccupation with test scores at elite institutions spreads outward, sending mixed messages to other colleges and universities and to the K–12 schools.

Criterion-referenced tests, on the other hand, presuppose a very different philosophy and approach to college admissions. Their purpose is to certify students' knowledge of college preparatory subjects, and they help to establish a baseline or floor for judging applicants' readiness for college. Along with high school grades, achievement test scores tell us whether applicants have mastered the foundational knowledge and skills required for college-level work.

When we judge students against this standard, two truths become evident. First is that the pool of qualified candidates who could benefit from and succeed in college is larger than can be accommodated at selective institutions. Second is that admissions criteria other than test scores—special talents and skills, leadership and community service, opportunity to learn, and social and cultural diversity—are more important in selecting whom to admit from among this larger pool. Admissions officers often describe their work as "crafting a class," a phrase that nicely captures this meaning.

Achievement testing reflects a philosophy of admissions that is at once more modest and more expansive than predicting success in college. It is more modest in that it asks less of admissions tests and is more realistic about what they can do. Our ability to predict success in college is relatively limited, and the most we should ask of admissions tests is to certify students' mastery of foundational knowledge and skills. It is more expansive in holding that beyond some reasonable standard of college readiness, other admissions criteria must take precedence over test scores if we are to craft an entering class that reflects our broader institutional values. And beyond the relatively narrow world of selective college admissions, testing for achievement and curriculum mastery can have a broader and more beneficial "signaling effect" throughout all of education.

It is not our intention to try to anticipate the specific forms or directions that admissions testing may take in the 21st century. Yet we believe that the general principles just outlined—and the paradigmatic idea of achievement testing that unites them—will be useful and relevant as a guide for evaluating new kinds of assessments that may emerge in the future. For example, these principles lead us to be initially skeptical about efforts to develop "noncognitive" assessments for use in college admissions insofar as those efforts sometimes blur the crucial distinction between achievement and personality traits over which the student has little control. On the other hand, notwithstanding the many difficulties involved in adapting K–12 standards-based tests for use in admissions, we conclude that this is unquestionably a worthwhile goal if it can be realized.

It should be evident that no existing admissions tests satisfy all of the principles we have outlined. Our purpose is not to endorse any particular test or set of tests but to contribute to the national dialogue about admissions testing and what we expect it to accomplish. Two decades ago in their classic brief *The Case Against the SAT,* James Crouse and Dale Trusheim (1988) argued persuasively for a new generation of achievement tests that would certify students' mastery of college preparatory subjects, provide incentives for educational improvement, and encourage greater diversity in admissions tests. What is new is that today, more than at any time in recent memory, American colleges and universities seem open to the possibility of a fresh start in standardized admissions testing.

Notes

1. The superiority of high school grade point average (GPA) over standardized test scores in predicting college outcomes is sometimes obscured in descriptions of validity studies. For example, in a recent survey of predictive-validity studies conducted over the past several decades, College Board researchers described their findings this way:

"The SAT has proven to be an important predictor of success in college. Its validity as a predictor of success has been demonstrated through hundreds of validity studies. These validity studies consistently find that high school grades and SAT scores together are substantial and significant predictors of achievement in college. In these studies, *although high school grades typically are slightly better predictors of achievement* [italics added], SAT scores add significantly to the prediction" (Camara & Echternacht, 2000).

2. In a recent study sponsored by the College Board, Paul Sackett and his colleagues defend the SAT, asserting that its predictive power is not substantially diminished when controls for socioeconomic status (SES) are introduced (Sackett, Kuncel, Arneson, Cooper, & Waters, 2009). Sackett's study, however, examined the extent to which SES affected the overall, bivariate correlation between SAT scores and college outcomes (first-year college grades) but failed to consider the independent contribution of high school grades (HSGPA) and other indicators in predicting college outcomes. In real-world admissions, the key question is what SAT scores uniquely add to the prediction of college outcomes, beyond what is already provided by a student's HSGPA and other indicators. Looking at the unique portion of the variance in SAT scores—the portion *not* shared with HSGPA or other indicators—studies using more fully specified regression models have found that the predictive power of the SAT is significantly reduced when controls for SES are introduced (Geiser, 2002; Rothstein, 2004). Thus, there is no actual conflict between Sackett's study and others that show that the value added by the SAT is heavily conditioned by SES, as Sackett acknowledges (personal communication, January 14, 2009).

3. An example of how simple correlations can be misleading is a study cited on the College Board's website in introducing the New SAT: "In the California study, SAT scores were slightly more predictive than high school grade point average (HSGPA)" (College Board, 2009c). The study referred to was conducted at the University of California (UC). The claim that the New SAT is more predictive than HSGPA was based on the UC study's initial finding that the univariate correlation between New SAT scores and first-year college GPA (FYGPA) was slightly greater than that between HSGPA and FYGPA (Agronow & Studley, 2007, Figure 1, Models 1 and 4). The same study, however, also presented more fully specified, multivariate regression models that allowed direct comparison of the predictive weights of HSGPA and SAT scores when both were included side by side in the same model along with other academic and socioeconomic factors. In the more fully specified models, HSGPA had by far the greatest predictive weight (Agronow & Studley, 2007, Table 1, Model 22).

4. It is important to be clear about what is meant by the term *adverse impact*. Both the College Board and ACT go to great lengths to eliminate test bias, and we do not question those efforts. Notwithstanding those efforts, however, it remains the case that, compared with other admissions indicators such as high school grades and the SAT II subject tests, SAT scores are more closely correlated with measures of socioeconomic status such as family income and parental education. As a result, the latter test has a greater adverse statistical impact on underrepresented minority applicants, who come disproportionately from lower socioeconomic backgrounds.

5. Given the highly selective nature of UC admissions, some have questioned whether range restriction might account for the diminished predictive value of the SAT I as compared with high school GPA and SAT II subject tests in the UC sample. The UC data were examined carefully for range restriction effects, however, and there was no evidence that this was the case. Comparing the variances in HSGPA, SAT I, and SAT II scores in the UC applicant pool versus the pool of admitted students, we found that

HSGPA—the primary selection criterion used in UC admissions—was the most range restricted of all admissions criteria even though it retained the greatest predictive weight. Restriction on both SAT I and SAT II scores was less pronounced and quite similar. Range restriction, in short, does not appear to account for the relative predictive weights of HSGPA, SAT I, and SAT II scores found in the UC sample (Geiser, 2002, note 4; Geiser & Santelices, 2007, note xix).

In an independent reanalysis of the UC data, Zwick and her colleagues found the same small but consistent predictive advantage for the SAT II subject tests (Zwick, Brown, & Sklar, 2004). The same finding was also confirmed in a 2001 College Board study of a larger sample of institutions that required both the SAT I and SAT II, including Barnard, Bowdoin, Colby, Harvard, Northwestern, and Vanderbilt, as well as four UC campuses (Bridgeman, Burton, & Cline, 2001).

6. These and other conclusions about the problematic effects of the SAT for California's K–12 schools were summarized in a policy paper, "The Use of Admissions Tests by the University of California," adopted by the UC faculty in 2001 after intensive debate and study. The paper was one of the first comprehensive policy statements on standardized admissions tests to be adopted by a major U.S. university and strongly endorsed "curriculum-based achievement tests" over "aptitude-type" tests (University of California, 2002).

7. For an account of events immediately leading up to and following Atkinson's 2001 address to the American Council on Education, proposing elimination of the SAT at the University of California, see "College Admissions and the SAT: A Personal Perspective" (Atkinson, 2004).

8. College Board researchers had expected inclusion of the writing exam in the New SAT "to add modestly to the prediction of college performance when critical reading and mathematics scores are considered" (Kobrin & Kimmel, 2006, p. 7).

9. In a recent article reviewing the New SAT, the authors suggested significantly reducing or even eliminating the critical-reading section, which would not only shorten the test but also possibly improve its predictive validity. Along with this shortened SAT, students might be required to take two subject tests in areas of their choosing (Atkinson & Geiser, 2008).

10. About 70% of all U.S. high schools now award "bonus points" for Advanced Placement (AP) classes, according to a survey by the National Association for College Admissions Counseling (2004). This boosts students' GPAs and improves admissions profiles, and a growing number of students now enroll in AP for this reason.

11. The University of California currently requires two SAT Subject Tests, both of which are now elective. These must be in two different areas, chosen from the following: English, history and social studies, mathematics (Level 2 only), science, or language other than English.

12. The UC regents have recently approved a policy change that would appear to reverse that institution's long-standing reliance on achievement tests in admissions. As part of a broader set of changes in UC admissions policies, in February 2009 the regents approved a proposal to eliminate the SAT Subject Tests and require only the New SAT (or ACT with writing) for admission to the UC system beginning in 2012. Understandably, some have viewed the regents' action as an endorsement of the New SAT and a rejection of previous UC policy favoring achievement tests. But, according to UC President Mark Yudof, this is not the case: "It is important to note that although the subject examinations will no longer be *required*, students for whom these tests represent an opportunity to demonstrate achievement in a particular area are still *encouraged* to take

the tests. . . . Eliminating the subject exam requirement in no way validates or confirms the use of other tests like the SAT reasoning exam" (letter to Asian Pacific Islander Legislative Caucus, February 24, 2009).

13. Regarding our contention that, compared with the SAT I, curriculum-based achievement measures such as the SAT II subject tests are less affected by students' socioeconomic status (SES), one reviewer of this article objected that achievement tests are also correlated with SES. Our point, however, is not that achievement test scores are *un*related to SES—virtually all academic indicators are correlated with SES to one degree or another—but that achievement indicators are *less* correlated with SES compared with the SAT. The UC studies showed that high school GPA had by far the lowest correlation with measures of SES such as family income, parental education, and high school quality; the SAT I had the strongest correlation; and the SAT II subject tests fell generally in between (Geiser, 2002; Geiser & Santelices, 2007). College Board researchers have also noted the stronger association between SAT I scores and SES than between SAT II scores and SES (see Kobrin, Camara, & Milewski, 2002, Figure 1A).

14. There are substantial differences among the states in the quality of their assessments and the extent to which their curriculum standards are integrated with comprehensive school reform efforts. As Linda Darling-Hammond (2003) has noted, "In a number of states, the notions of standards and 'accountability' have become synonymous with mandates for student testing that are detached from policies that might address the quality of teaching, the allocation of resources, or the nature of schooling. . . . States and districts that have relied primarily on test-based accountability emphasizing sanctions for students and teachers have often produced greater failure, rather than greater success, for their most educationally vulnerable students. More successful reforms have emphasized the use of standards for teaching and learning to guide investments in better prepared teachers, higher quality teaching, more performance-oriented curriculum and assessment, better designed schools, more equitable and effective resource allocations, and more diagnostic supports for student learning" (para. 3, 6).

15. For an overview of the assessments used in California secondary and postsecondary education, and the alignment (or lack thereof) between them, see Venezia (2000).

16. As Darling-Hammond (2003) notes, "Use of norm-referenced tests . . . makes it impossible to gauge progress accurately, as items are removed from the test as greater numbers of students can answer them, thus guaranteeing continuing high rates of failure, especially for certain subpopulations of students" (para. 9). One of the main problems with No Child Left Behind, she argues, is that its testing requirements "push states back to the lowest common denominator, undoing progress that has been made to improve the quality of assessments and delaying the move from antiquated norm-referenced tests to criterion-referenced systems" (para. 11).

References

ACT. (2009a). *College readiness standards for the ACT.* Iowa City, IA: Author. Retrieved July 26, 2009, from http://www.act.org/standard/guides/act/index.html

ACT. (2009b). *Educational planning and assessment.* Iowa City, IA: Author. Retrieved July 26, 2009, from http://www.act.org/epas/index.html

Agronow, S., & Studley, R. (2007). *Prediction of college GPA from new SAT test scores—A first look.* Paper presented at annual meeting of the California Association for Institutional Research, Monterey, CA.

American Educational Research Association, American Psychological Association, & National Council on Measurement in Education. (1999). *Standards for educational and psychological testing.* Washington, DC: American Educational Research Association.

Atkinson, R. C. (2001). *Standardized tests and access to American universities.* The 2001 Robert H. Atwell Distinguished Lecture, 83rd Annual Meeting of the American Council on Education, Washington, DC. Retrieved November 18, 2009, from http://www.rca.ucsd.edu/comments/satspch.html

Atkinson, R. C. (2004). *College admissions and the SAT: A personal perspective.* Invited address at the annual meeting of the American Educational Research Association, San Diego, CA. (Republished in *Observer: Journal of the Association for Psychological Science, 18,* 15–22, 2005.)

Atkinson, R. C., & Geiser, S. (2008). The new SAT: A work in progress. *Observer: Journal of the Association for Psychological Science, 21*(10), 23–24.

Bowen, W., Chingos, M., & McPherson, M. (2009). *Crossing the finish line: Completing college at America's public universities.* Princeton, NJ: Princeton University Press.

Bridgeman, B., Burton, N., & Cline, F. (2001). *Substituting SAT II: Subject tests for SAT I: Reasoning tests: Impact on admitted class composition and quality.* (College Board Research Report No. 2001-3.) New York: College Board.

Brown, R., & Conley, D. (2007). Comparing state high school assessments and standards for success in entry-level university courses. *Educational Assessment, 12,* 137–160.

Burton, N., & Ramist, L. (2001). *Predicting success in college: SAT studies of classes graduating since 1980.* (College Board Research Report No. 2001-2.) New York: College Board.

Camara, W., & Echternacht, G. (2000). *The SAT I and high school grades: Utility in predicting success in college.* (College Board Report No. RN-10.) New York: College Board.

Camara, W., & Schmidt, A. (2006). *The new SAT facts* [PowerPoint presentation]. New York: College Board. Retrieved March 7, 2009, from http://www.collegeboard.com/prod_downloads/forum/forum06/the-new-sat_a-comprehensive-report-on-the-first-scores.PPT

College Board. (2009a). *College Board standards for college success.* New York: College Board. Retrieved March 10, 2009, from http://professionals.collegeboard.com/k-12/standards

College Board. (2009b). *Frequently asked questions about SAT subject tests.* New York: College Board. Retrieved March 6, 2009, from http://www.compassprep.com/subject_faq.shtml#faq2

College Board. (2009c). *SAT validity studies.* New York: College Board. Retrieved July 22, 2009, from http://professionals.collegeboard.com/data-reports-research/sat/validity-studies

Cornwell, C. M., Mustard, D. B., & Van Parys, J. (2008, June 25). *How does the New SAT predict academic achievement in college?* (Working Paper). Athens: University of Georgia. Retrieved November 18, 2009, from http://www.terry.uga.edu/~mustard/New%20SAT.pdf

Crouse, J., & Trusheim, D. (1988). *The case against the SAT.* Chicago: University of Chicago Press.

Darling-Hammond, L. (2003). Standards and assessments: Where we are now and what we need. *Teachers College Record* (ID No. 11109). Retrieved November 18, 2009, from http://www.tcrecord.org

Geiser, S. (with Studley, R.). (2002). UC and the SAT: Predictive validity and differential impact of the SAT I and SAT II at the University of California. *Educational Assessment, 8,* 1–26.

Geiser, S. (2009). Back to the basics: In defense of achievement (and achievement tests) in college admissions. *Change, 41*(1), 16–23.

Geiser, S., & Santelices, M. V. (2006). The role of advanced placement and honors courses in college admissions. In P. Gandara, G. Orfield, & C. Horn (Eds.), *Expanding opportunity in higher education: Leveraging promise* (pp. 75–114). Albany: State University of New York Press.

Geiser, S., & Santelices, M. V. (2007). Validity of high-school grades in predicting student success beyond the freshman year: High-school record vs. standardized tests as indicators of four-year college outcomes. *Research and Occasional Papers Series: CSHE.9.07.* Berkeley: Center for Studies in Higher Education, University of California. Retrieved November 18, 2009, from http://cshe.berkeley.edu/publications/ publications.php?id=265

Hammond, G. (2008). Advancing beyond AP courses. *Chronicle of Higher Education, 54*(34), B17.

Hupp, D., & Morgan, D. (2008). *The SAT as a state's NCLB assessment: Rationale and issues confronted.* Paper presented at the National Conference on Student Assessment, Orlando, FL. Retrieved July 29, 2009, from the College Board website: http:// professionals.collegeboard.com/data-reports-research/cb/other-conf/nclb-state -assmt

Intersegmental Committee of the Academic Senates. (1997). *Statement of competencies in mathematics expected of entering college students.* Sacramento: California Education Round Table. Retrieved from http://www.certicc.org

Intersegmental Committee of the Academic Senates. (1998). *Statement of competencies in English expected of entering college students.* Sacramento: California Education Round Table. Retrieved from http://www.certicc.org

Kirst, M., & Venezia, A. (Eds.). (2004). *From high school to college: Improving opportunities for success in postsecondary education.* San Francisco: Jossey-Bass.

Kobrin, J. L., Camara, W. J., & Milewski, G. B. (2002). *The utility of the SAT I and SAT II for admissions decisions in California and the nation.* (College Board Research Report No. 2002-6.) New York: College Board.

Kobrin, J., & Kimmel, E. (2006). *Test development and technical information on the writing section of the SAT reasoning test.* (College Board Research Report No. RN-25.) New York: College Board.

Kobrin, J. L., Patterson, B. F., Shaw, E. J., Mattern, K. D., & Barbuti, S. M. (2008). *Validity of the SAT for predicting first-year college grade point average.* (College Board Research Report No. 2008-5.) New York: College Board.

Lawrence, I., Rigol, G., Van Essen, T., & Jackson, C. (2003). *A historical perspective on the content of the SAT.* (College Board Research Report No. 2003-03.) New York: College Board.

Lemann, N. (1999). *The big test: The secret history of the American meritocracy.* New York: Farrar, Straus and Giroux.

Lindquist, E. F. (1958). *The nature of the problem of improving scholarship and college entrance examinations.* Paper presented at Educational Testing Service invitational conference on testing problems. Princeton, NJ: Educational Testing Service.

Morgan, R. (1989). *Analysis of the predictive validity of the SAT and high school grades from 1976 to 1983.* (College Board Report No. 89-7.) New York: College Board.

National Association for College Admissions Counseling (NACAC). (2004). *National school counselor survey.* Alexandria, VA: Author.

National Association for College Admissions Counseling (NACAC). (2008). *Report of the Commission on the Use of Standardized Tests in Undergraduate Admissions.* Arlington, VA: Author.

Noeth, J., & Kobrin, J. (2007). *Writing changes in the nation's K–12 school system.* (College Board Research Report No. RN-34.) New York: College Board.

Princeton Review. (2009). *Prep for SAT subject tests.* Framingham, MA: Author. Retrieved July 26, 2009, from http://www.princetonreview.com/college/sat-subject-test-prep.aspx

Rothstein, J. (2004). College performance predictions and the SAT. *Journal of Econometrics, 121,* 297–317.

Sackett, P., Kuncel, N., Arneson, J., Cooper, S., & Waters, S. (2009). Does socioeconomic status explain the relationship between admissions tests and post-secondary academic performance? *Psychological Bulletin, 135,* 1–22.

University of California. (2002). *The use of admissions tests by the University of California.* Oakland, CA: UC Board of Admissions and Relations with Schools. Retrieved November 18, 2009, from http://www.universityofcalifornia.edu/senate/committees/boars/admissionstests.pdf

Venezia, A. (2000). Connecting California's K–12 and higher education systems: Challenges and opportunities. In E. Burr, G. C. Hayward, B. Fuller, & M. Kirst (Eds.), *Crucial issues in California education 2000: Are the pieces fitting together?* (pp. 153–176). Berkeley: Policy Analysis for California Education.

Zwick, R., Brown, T., & Sklar, J. C. (2004). California and the SAT: A reanalysis of University of California admissions data. *Research and Occasional Papers Series: CSHE.8.04.* Berkeley: Center for Studies in Higher Education, University of California. Retrieved November 18, 2009, from http://cshe.berkeley.edu/publications/publications.php?id=68

SAT Wars at the
University of California

JOHN AUBREY DOUGLASS

In 2001, University of California President Richard Atkinson, a psychometrician, asked why California's premier multi-campus research university should require the SAT for freshman admissions. The SAT dominates the market, and its purveyor—the Educational Testing Service (ETS)—claims that it is an important predictor of a student's success in America's colleges and universities. That's what it's all about, right?

But a university study initiated by Atkinson provided contradictory evidence. At least within the University of California (UC)—with some 150,000 undergraduates in 2001 scattered among nine undergraduate campuses—the SAT was *not* a very good predictor of performance. Grades in high school, along with some evaluation of a student's socioeconomic circumstance and achievements in that environment, proved to be a better predictor. Simply put, among an already relatively select group of students, evidence of a student's drive to learn and to be both academically and civically engaged in the years leading up to university enrollment is the best indicator of a student's future academic achievement at a place like Berkeley or UCLA—among the most selective institutions in the United States.

Opponents of the widespread use of the SAT have long claimed that the SAT promotes needless socioeconomic stratification. The test favors students from upper income families and communities, in part because they can afford a growing range of expensive commercially available test preparation courses and counseling.

Why should a public university require the SAT or any other test that does not actually test the knowledge of a student in subjects required by the university? Atkinson was not against tests. But he had a hard time rationalizing the use of standardized tests that have no demonstrable relationship to the specific subjects taught in high schools. The SAT, it is claimed, provides a proven indicator of academic "aptitude"—but it is telling that although *SAT* once explicitly stood for *Standardized Aptitude Test,* ETS decided some time ago to market it as simply the nondescript SAT.

A follow-up study by the University of California also demonstrated that subject tests, like the ACT, are only marginally better than the SAT. That means that subject-based tests, including a second array of tests marketed by ETS as the SAT II, are only philosophically better as an admissions requirement for the premier public university system in the United States. High school grades remain the best single measure of demonstrated academic achievement—a pretty good philosophical trump card.

Going Up Against the SAT

By requiring the SAT for admissions, the University of California has long sent a powerful message to schools and students that they need to prepare for the test. The modern infatuation with standardized testing, further promulgated by President George W. Bush's No Child Left Behind initiative, has slowly but surely altered the curriculum of our schools toward a test preparation culture. Some of that is fine—schools need to be held accountable and measures of accomplishment are necessary. But the sheer force of this testing culture has narrowed the idea of what education is all about.

In his speech before the American Council on Education at their 2001 meeting in Washington, DC, Atkinson, armed with an analysis of UC undergraduates, announced that he saw little reason for the University of California to require the SAT I reasoning test. Subject-based tests, such as the SAT II and ACT, revealed "mastery of subject matter rather than test preparation." For Atkinson, the focus on subject tests, and abandonment of the SAT I, would "help all students, especially low-income and minority students, determine their own educational destinies. And they will lead to greater public confidence in the fairness of the University of California's admissions process" (Atkinson, 2001).

As the largest multi-campus research institution in the nation, and one of the most prestigious and selective public universities, the loss of the University of California would have large market implications for ETS—many other major universities might follow, and California represents ETS's largest single market. In the end, however, Atkinson's threat to drop the SAT II prompted ETS to revise elements of the test and to add a new writing component. With those changes, many critics of ETS's mainstay test, including UC officials, were essentially forced into an extended period of reevaluating the worth of the revised SAT II—a process that continues today.

There is a great irony in the University of California's questioning of the efficacy of the SAT and, in some form, of all standardized testing.

Unbeknownst to university officials, including the university's faculty body, the Academic Senate, which has authority over admissions standards, these same conclusions had been reached and warnings issued some 40 years earlier by UC officials—a not too uncommon example of institutional amnesia.

In the late 1950s and early 1960s the university's faculty senate had carefully studied the possible adoption of the SAT and the ACT. The University of California had proven reluctant to adopt testing in the admissions process. Faculty leaders responsible for admissions thought grades and other indicators were good predictors, and had data to show it, and they worried about the possible impact of testing on lower income students and about the marginal utility of standardized tests.

The following discussion provides a brief historical review of the debate over the belated adoption of standardized tests in freshman admissions for the UC system, and discusses the shift over time in the use of the SAT and other tests at the University of California. A discussion of why and how UC has embraced the SAT and other tests provides a window into the behaviors and policy regimes adopted by major and highly selective public universities.

To help frame this story, four factors about the history of UC admissions need to be noted. Some of these factors are peculiar to California, but they have their roots in a common understanding of the role of public universities in society.

- UC admissions policies have the goal of creating requirements that guide students in their academic preparation for higher education and provide access to all segments of society.
- UC policies have historically stated that admissions requirements are calibrated to predict that those accepted, and those who subsequently enroll, will have a reasonable chance to succeed academically at the university and to graduate. Before 1960, under this rubric, the University of California admitted approximately the top 15% of all state high school graduates. After implementation of the 1960 Master Plan for Higher Education, that figure was reduced to the top 12.5%—a mandate that remains today.
- As part of a compact with the people of California, the University of California has historically enrolled all "UC Eligible" students who meet stated requirements (today including GPA in required courses and a sliding scale of test scores)—although not necessarily to the campus of their choice.
- An ancillary part of this social contract is that admissions requirements must be relatively clear and transparent—creating a set of standards and goals for prospective students.

A First Look at the SAT

In the late 1950s and extending into the 1960s, the University of California began a lengthy debate regarding the use of standardized tests. Many of the same issues discussed by supporters and opponents of testing today were vetted in that era—the socioeconomic biases of tests, their predictive value for collegiate success, and, most importantly, their proper use in the admissions process. Why did public universities adopt standardized testing? And how did this adoption influence the social contract of universities?

Until the late 1950s, few public universities required the SAT or other commercially available tests. Beginning in the 1930s and up to the 1960s, interest in the SAT by public institutions tended to focus on two rather narrow uses: (a) standardized tests were embraced as an alternative admissions criterion for out-of-state students and others who graduated from non-university-accredited high schools, and (b) by the 1950s, testing of a sample group of students after they enrolled in a university occasionally served as an analytical tool for assessing admissions criteria.

As late as 1959, the vast majority of clients for ETS remained along the Eastern Seaboard. ETS had opened a West Coast office in Berkeley in 1947, with the ambition to get the University of California and other public and private colleges and universities to adopt the test. ETS president Henry Chauncey successfully persuaded the College Board to establish the western outpost *and* to persuade the University of California to join the board as an institutional member—the first public university with a member on the board.

Normally, usage of the SAT by an institution was a prerequisite for membership on the board. Chauncey made an exception in the case of UC, in hopes of enticing California's state university into the fold and hence creating a potentially influential expansion of the market for standardized testing (Lemann, 1999). Chauncey aggressively marketed the tests, with an eye on the progress of ETS's rival, the purveyors of the ACT. ETS was beginning to make inroads in Michigan, Texas, and Colorado, but state universities in Illinois and Ohio were more interested in the subject-oriented tests offered by ACT. Chauncey's strategy was not very successful in California and elsewhere—at least initially. In 1951, for example, some 81,100 students took the SAT in the United States, the vast majority of these students located in the Northeast. Ten years later, the number taking the test nationally had jumped to 805,000. Yet the vast majority of test takers were still students from the Northeast, with some growth in the South and to a lesser degree the Midwest. After a more than 10-year campaign, few students in the Western states took the test (Hubin, 1988). One ETS official explained why California was reluctant. The "big problem," he noted, was that "UC was already selective and really with no need to adopt standardized tests" (Pearson, 1979). It already had what university faculty and academic leaders thought was a highly successful admissions process. University officials assessed this success largely by the high rates of academic success of students, both those admitted as freshmen and transfer students. In 1955, an estimated 62% of students who entered the Berkeley campus as freshmen completed their eighth semester and usually graduated. When including those who took a ninth semester, the graduation rate climbed to around 80%. Even in the 1950s, UC students often worked part-time and many did not attend the university for four solid years. Considering these variables, "This is a good record," noted a university report, matched by few other selective institutions at the time—public or private.

Nevertheless, by the late 1950s, a number of UC faculty and administrators showed new interest in the SAT and achievement tests, particularly for applicants for the freshman class. Grade inflation within the state's secondary schools was viewed as a growing problem. There was a sense that perhaps too many students were qualifying for university admission, especially at the freshman level. The problem might grow and the university might need new mechanisms to recalibrate admissions requirements—particularly with the expected flood of new students over the coming decades. Standardized testing could help manage future enrollment growth by altering and raising admissions standards. The SAT represented a general standard increasingly embraced by America's most prestigious institutions.

A state-sanctioned study on the future of California higher education completed in 1955 stated that the university should "experiment extensively with aptitude and achievement examination in combination with high school scholastic records in admitting freshmen" (Holy, Semans, & McConnell, 1955, p. 108). On the heels of the 1955 statewide study, a UC Academic Senate task force on admissions recommended quick adoption of the SAT as a requirement for all entering students. Yet the Academic Senate, and in particular the senate's Board of Admissions and Relations with Schools (BOARS), which was responsible for admissions policy, rejected the recommendation. Not only did yearly assessments of the academic success of admitted students buttress the sense that UC admissions practices were sound, but BOARS members had grave concerns regarding the validity of standardized tests in predicting the academic performance of university students. Studies in the 1950s, as today, consistently showed that the high school grade-point average (GPA) in required courses constituted the best predictor of scholastic success (BOARS, 1956).

Under the leadership of board chairman and UCLA professor Charles Nixon, BOARS outlined the possible use of standardized tests to university faculty, specifically the senate's legislative assembly. Nixon did not argue for the tests' immediate use in the admissions process. Rather, he and his fellow BOARS members thought the tests might become "a supplementary selective device" for determining UC Eligibility "if one becomes necessary." In the interim, BOARS stated that, at a minimum, test scores could provide "information about the student which is necessary for proper counseling" (BOARS, 1956). In early 1958, BOARS considered experimenting with the SAT. Charles W. Jones, a professor of English at Berkeley, replaced Nixon as the chair of BOARS, and he and other board members met with ETS representatives anxious to get the University of California into the fold. The university's new president, Clark Kerr, also urged a closer look at the SAT. Since 1953, when he was chancellor of the Berkeley campus, Kerr had served on the College Board. But he was cautious in his advocacy. With ETS's latest offer, he argued for the advantages of at least requiring the test; at a minimum it could be an analytical tool for assessing university admissions practices.

Jones and BOARS then approached the Academic Senate's legislative assembly, arguing that standardized tests be required for an experimental period of 2 years. BOARS would then initiate a major study on the validity of such tests as a predictor of university success. Only after the results were in would the senate consider the use of testing for setting admissions requirements. The assembly subsequently adopted Senate Regulation 256 in the spring of 1958. For the first time, with the entering class of fall 1960, students applying to the University of California would be required to take the SAT or similar exams identified by BOARS. In May of 1958, BOARS met with representatives of ETS to discuss the first large-scale use of the SAT and BOARS's plans to examine its potential merits. Anxious to gain the UC business, ETS agreed to administer the test at no cost to students. In late 1958, BOARS also completed a major study on the validity of the university's existing admissions criteria—an unprecedented review looking at data extending back before World War II. In reviewing the academic performance of students enrolled at Berkeley and UCLA, the study reiterated earlier findings: there was an extremely high correlation of student high school GPA with freshman performance at the University of California.

The 1958 analysis also indicated that admissions standards related to junior college transfers were generally successful. Between 1952 and 1956, 33,804 students entered the university, with 18,439 (or 54%) entering as advanced-standing students, largely junior-year transfers. The robust nature of the transfer function was an essential component of the California higher education system. As a result of California's pioneering community college sector, no other public or private university in the nation included such a high percentage of transfer students. The analysis of transfer students at the University of California showed good academic performance and persistence rates (BOARS, 1958).

In the post-war period, for the first time, junior-year transfer students outnumbered entering freshmen at the University of California. This was a shift first bolstered by the returning GI cohort and sustained until the immediate post–1960 Master Plan years. The robust nature of the transfer function from the 1930s into the 1950s attests to its vital role in promoting socioeconomic mobility in California. The transfer function, first envisioned by UC faculty, made California's higher education system unique— both in the high dependency on access through the community college and in the number of students who then matriculated to a public 4-year institution. The 1958 analysis by BOARS bolstered confidence in the University of California's existing admissions process and in its heavy reliance on grades as a predictor of collegiate academic success. Yet BOARS and its chairman, Charles Jones, kept an open mind on the potential uses of standardized testing. BOARS and the university needed to await the gathering of the test data. This would not occur until the first cohort of entering students took the test in 1960 and then completed their freshman year. A firm decision on adopting or rejecting standardized tests as anything other than an alternative route for access the university, or as an analytical tool, was 2 years away.

An Initial Rejection

By early 1961, in the wake of the 1960 adoption of California's Master Plan for Higher Education, the University of California sought to determine how to reduce the high school admissions pool. The Master Plan suggested dropping Special Action, as well as raising university admissions standards and adopting standardized tests for that purpose. Simply eliminating special admissions posed an administratively expedient remedy for pushing students to the community colleges, but there was considerable concern regarding the possible impact on disadvantaged students. Nonetheless, the pressure for the university to reduce access in the aftermath of the Master Plan agreement led BOARS, and the senate's legislative body, to reduce Special Action from around 10% of all UC admissions to a mere 2%.

But that would not be enough to meet a target of pushing some 50,000 students toward the community colleges over the next several years— students who would have been UC Eligible otherwise. An analysis of university test scores caused the board to reach a significant conclusion. "Extensive analysis of the data," BOARS chairman Charles Jones stated, and "careful and lengthy deliberation of the Board, leave the Board wholly convinced that the Scholastic Aptitude Test scores add little or nothing to the precision with which the existing admissions requirements are predictive of success in the University" (BOARS, 1962).

The board unanimously recommended ending the SAT requirement beginning with the class entering in the fall of 1962. Instead, BOARS sought to raise the GPA requirement in required courses. For the near term, the University of California had no plans to adopt the SAT. Supporting the conclusion of the board, the senate's representative assembly voted to repeal Senate Regulation 256 (BOARS, 1962).

The finding of BOARS was a major blow to ETS. Yet the university's faculty did not close the door completely on standardized tests. The board promised to launch a similar investigation into the possible future use of CEEB's (i.e., the College Board's) achievement tests, which purported to evaluate the knowledge level of students in specific academic subjects. These tests had been used in one form or another for admitting a small cohort of students from nonaccredited high schools or from out of state.

In February of 1964, the staff of Frank L. Kidner, dean of education relations, issued a report regarding the potential use of achievement tests. BOARS had asked two questions: "Can achievement test scores be utilized for the placement of students in freshman courses?" and "Does the use of the achievement test scores materially improve the accuracy of the prediction of first-year grade-point averages in the academic colleges on each campus?"

Edward W. Bowes, director of admissions, who reported to Kidner, was the main author of the study, and his conclusion echoed the findings of a 1963 analysis of the validity of the SAT. "The insistent question becomes, can any constructive use be made of the additional information which is supplied by the achievement scores?" His preliminary answer was that it probably could not (BOARS, 1965). Achievement tests unto themselves, Bowes noted, proved of marginal value in predicting academic success— although they were of slightly better value than the SAT. High school GPA remained the best indicator, Bowes stated. High school GPA explained 22% of the variance in university grades, whereas the achievement tests explained only 8%. He stated, however, that combining test scores and high school GPA appeared to offer a marginal improvement in predicting freshman grades, "though the superiority is admittedly slight." This conclusion warranted caution. The low level of predictive value of a student's high school GPA in required courses, he stated, "raises the question of the utility, or alternatively, the futility of the entire process" of predicting the collegiate success of a student based on grades.

Yet Bowes made a prophetic observation. Beyond actual prediction of a student's academic aptitude, there were other potential uses for standardized tests. For one, he noted, they could be a somewhat arbitrary tool for reducing eligibility—one that was less politically volatile than raising GPA requirements. This "added practical advantage" could reduce the complaints of students who came close to meeting the university's eligibility requirements but who were denied admission (BOARS, 1965). Bowes stated five potential uses for the achievement test:

* Admissions decisions
* Financial aid
* Academic placement, in lieu of a battery of university placement and qualifying examinations given during the first week of a semester
* Guidance counseling
* Academic planning

Bowes urged caution in interpreting his results, and BOARS took him at his word. While there were political advantages to using the SAT and achievement tests in regular admissions, the board concluded that that was not enough. Until there was a more concrete study that showed the predictive value of standardized tests—and ETS had no similar study to contradict the UC studies—then the issue could only be revisited at a later date.

The conclusions reached by BOARS contradicted the promotional efforts of the College Board and ETS. But the University of California also was running against the tide. Standardized tests were already being widely adopted by American public universities—with consequences not fully appreciated even today.

Inclusion or Exclusion?

So why did the University of California later require the SAT? The university would slowly adopt standardized tests, first for determining eligibility for admission to the university system beginning in 1968, and later in the process of selection at campuses such as Berkeley. The reason was not to improve the admissions process so as to admit the best students, but to use the test as a way to offer clear criteria for denying access to students.

The university had committed to a policy of accepting the top 12.5% of high school graduates based on grades in a specific set of college preparatory classes. But with grade inflation, UC had difficulties keeping to that quota, accepting students from the top 14–17% of the state's high school graduates.

Many state lawmakers and taxpayers groups criticized UC for taking on more students than agreed under the Master Plan, and therefore claiming more state funding than the institution deserved. Faculty, and specifically

Academic Senate leaders, wanted to take some action to raise admissions standards as they perennially complained about the remedial needs and academic abilities of students entering the university—a complaint that would increase as the state's demographics began to change rapidly, including substantial increases in immigrant groups in California. University officials, including succeeding UC presidents, had a different perspective. They had to deal with a growing contingent of lawmakers demanding that the University of California provide greater access to minority groups.

Yet how could officials reduce the number of students who were UC Eligible in a politically acceptable way? For senate leaders charged under the Board of Regents with primary responsibility for setting admissions standards, it was actually more politically charged to raise the mandatory GPA in required courses or to add additional course requirements—long the means of dealing with grade inflation—than to simply add the SAT to help cut the oversubscribed pool of applicants.

But UC would go slow in adopting the SAT. In 1968, UC first required the SAT, or as an alternative the ACT, for two purposes beyond the historical use of evaluating out-of-state students for admission:

- First, the tests would be used largely for diagnostic purposes, counseling, and course placement; they would not be used in making admissions decisions (UCOP, 1977). Undoubtedly, by requiring all freshman applicants to submit the standardized test scores, UC also would have the ability to integrate them into admissions decision-making if the need arose.
- Second, UC would use the tests in determining the eligibility of students with GPAs between 3.00 and 3.09—what amounted to less than 2% of all admissions.

Not until 1979 was the SAT used to assess whether or not a student was UC Eligible. That year, the chair of BOARS, Allan Parducci, a professor of psychology at UCLA, cited a number of indicators signaling an "alarming decline" in the preparation of students enrolling at the University of California. Their average test scores on the verbal portion of the SAT had dropped some 50 points in 6 years, more than twice the drop reported for the rest of the nation. He also reported that over that period the university increased its total freshman enrollment by 30%, while the absolute number of freshmen with high SAT scores dropped by 40%.

A similar decline was found in the less academically oriented high schools. Fewer than 10% of students at these schools were UC Eligible—schools where "a B average is often no guarantee of the ability to read a freshman text or even to do elementary arithmetic" (UCOP, 1977). Further,

TABLE 3.1 UC Eligibility Index, 2009

"a–g" GPA	Minimum UC Test Score total
California residents	
3.00–3.04	223
3.05–3.09	210
3.10–3.14	198
3.15–3.19	187
3.20–3.24	175
3.25–3.29	165
3.30–3.34	157
3.35–3.39	152
3.40–3.44	147
3.45 and above	143
Non-California residents	
3.40–3.44	147
3.45 and above	143

About the grade-point average: All campuses use the same method of cal-
culating a preliminary GPA for purposes of determining an applicant's
UC Eligibility. The GPA is calculated based on all "a–g" subjects completed in grades 10 and 11—including summer sessions—by assigning
point values to the grades a student earns, totaling the points, and
dividing the total by the number of "a–g" course units.

Test score total: For students who took the SAT Reasoning test, convert
their highest scores in Critical Reading, Math, and Writing from a single
sitting and their two highest SAT Subject Test scores from two different
subject areas equivalent to UC Scores. Then add the five UC Scores to
produce the UC Score Total (Critical Reading + Math + Writing + Subject
Test 1 + Subject Test 2).

yet another study indicated that UC was accepting students well above the
12.5% pool, despite the addition of more course requirements for freshman applicants.

Parducci successfully proposed to the Academic Senate, later with the
approval of the Board of Regents, to establish a new "Eligibility Index"
(see Table 3.1). The index combined an applicant's SAT scores and his or
her high school GPA in required courses on a sliding scale. Within the
index, GPA would be weighted more than six times as heavily as the SAT.
Grades remained the primary factor in determining eligibility under this
model. The index, however, not only created a new threshold regarding a
student's eligibility for acceptance to the University, but over time it could
be adjusted to account for grade inflation.

BOARS also increased the GPA requirements for new applicants marginally. In part to ease the introduction of the Eligibility Index, any student
who achieved a GPA of 3.1 in required courses (the 11 or so courses entitled

"a–g," for the seven subject areas required by the university) need only take the SAT, or ACT, test to become UC Eligible. GPA remained heavily weighted over SAT scores throughout the evolution of the Eligibility Index; not until around 2000 was a minimum combined score put into place for all applicants, regardless of their GPA.

Countervailing Force

In each instance in which the Academic Senate—now an apparent convert to standardized testing despite earlier analyses by BOARS in the early 1960s—elevated the use of standardized tests, university officials worried about the impact on lower income and underrepresented racial and ethnic groups. There was political pressure from a rising tide of Latino lawmakers, for instance, who demanded greater access for their constituents. As a countervailing force to fears over the greater exclusion of underrepresented groups who generally performed more poorly on standardized tests, UC presidents and their staff attempted to resurrect Special Action admissions—essentially, admissions for students not regularly deemed UC Eligible (Figure 3.1).

As noted previously, prior to 1960 UC had admissions policies that allowed for approximately 10% of all admissions to be Special Action, precisely in recognition of the varying quality of high schools and the adverse

FIGURE 3.1 Countervailing Force: Special Action Targets and Percentage of Total UC Systemwide Freshman Enrollment, 1960–1990

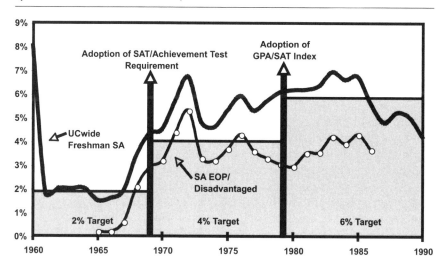

circumstances faced by many students who are from poor and underrepresented groups. Special Action also provided a path for California students with specialized abilities, including athletes, but in the past more commonly musicians, artists, and other academically promising individuals. In the period after World War II, to accommodate returning GIs, UC's Special Action admissions rose to some 40%.

As part of an effort to reduce enrollments at UC, the 1960 Master Plan called on the university to eliminate the Special Action category. But BOARS and Academic Senate leaders instead reduced the percentage target from 10% to just 2%. As senate leaders became more interested in limiting enrollment and meeting the Master Plan's top 12.5% edict, and essentially less concerned with socioeconomic inclusiveness, it was university administrators who became the champions of Special Action, making it a key component in the advent of Educational Opportunity Programs. When BOARS recommended requiring standardized tests of all applicants, and using scores for determining the eligibility of students at the margin of UC's GPA requirements, UC president Charles Hitch recommended that the Regents also increase Special Action to 4% of all admissions. The board approved this change under the assumption that each UC campus would have 4% of all freshman and transfer students admitted and enrolled under Special Action.

While some UC campuses used Special Action to expand opportunities for disadvantaged groups, many never filled the mandate given to them by the Board of Regents in 1979 to actually admit and enroll 6% of their total incoming class as Special Action. The Berkeley campus, for instance, enrolled fewer than 3% of new students as Special Action. This route, I would argue, has curiously not been used creatively by UC.

One reason for this relates to a major shift in UC admissions brought on by continued population growth and increased enrollment demand. By the 1980s, for the first time Berkeley and UCLA received many more UC Eligible applicants than they could enroll. Previously, students who were UC Eligible could enroll in virtually any campus they chose—with the exception of a few highly competitive programs such as engineering. Both Berkeley and UCLA were the first to use the SAT not so much as a way to identify talented students but as a rationale for denying them admission. UC Eligible students where then redirected to another UC campus.

An altered admissions process added to what became a deluge of applications to the most desired UC campuses: students who once submitted single UC applications, and noted their first, second, and third choices of campus, now had to apply to each campus of interest. The net result was a decentralization of admissions and a greater array of applications for each campus to review and select from. Berkeley, for instance, had a huge num-

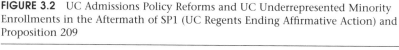

FIGURE 3.2 UC Admissions Policy Reforms and UC Underrepresented Minority Enrollments in the Aftermath of SP1 (UC Regents Ending Affirmative Action) and Proposition 209

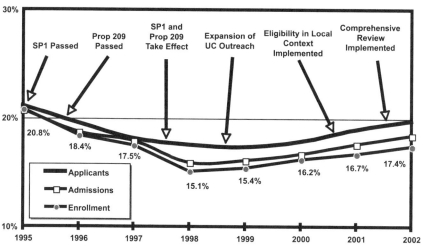

ber of highly qualified students to select from, yet it had reached a plateau in the number of new students that could be accepted each year at around 4500. At Berkeley and UCLA, academic leaders interested in diversity focused their attention on creating an admissions process that favored underrepresented groups who were UC Eligible as opposed to Special Action. What emerged was, essentially, a two-track admissions process: a regular admission track and an affirmative action track with different variables used for selection.

By the 1990s, not only did UC depend on standardized tests to determine UC Eligibility but the tests also became a factor in the selection process at most of the UC campuses (see Figure 3.2). Standardized test scores were extremely important for regular admissions and less so for affirmative action–designated students. This structured approach to increasing underrepresented students at UC, however, was the focus of attack by anti–affirmative action regents and by Governor Pete Wilson in his search for wedge issues that could bolster his planned campaign for the presidency. This led to regent Ward Connerly's successful proposal in 1995 for the board to end all use of race and ethnicity in admissions, despite opposition by UC president Jack Peltason, along with the various campus chancellors and the Academic Senate leadership. Shortly after, Proposition 209 was passed by voters and amended California's constitution with the same language barring affirmative action in all public agencies. This was the beginning of a campaign led by Connerly to extend the ban to other states via voter-approved initiatives.

In the essentially zero sum game of UC admissions, the university had feared large declines in underrepresented students without the tool of affirmative action. By 2001, UC was in the midst of a wide discussion on how best to rethink admissions policy. This included adding to the existing university mandate to accept students from the top 12.5% statewide pool of high school students a guarantee of admission for the top 4% of students from each high school class—as long as they took all the required courses—even if they had only minimal scores on standardized tests. This new policy, entitled "Eligibility in the Local Context" (ELC), did help to diversify the pool of UC Eligible students, and subsequent analysis has shown these students do as well, or nearly so, as students chosen via the statewide criteria. UC substantially expanded outreach efforts to schools with minority and poor students, and instituted new guidelines in the evaluation of UC Eligible students in the admission process entitled "Comprehensive Review." This essentially further elevated factors such as the socioeconomic background and circumstances of students, their engagement in extracurricular activities such as community service, and other personal variables.

As noted, Atkinson's gambit to possibly drop the SAT I brought national attention to the predictive validity and appropriate uses of standardized tests. What gave strength to Atkinson's stance was that he had sponsored and encouraged research on both the reasoning and subject tests within the University of California—a system that had some 150,000 undergraduates by 2001 and a data set on both the SAT I and SAT II tests and their equivalents dating back to the 1970s. Further, the Academic Senate was fully engaged in discussing the worth of the SAT I versus the SAT II subject tests, aligning with Atkinson and working closely with his analytical staff.

The response of ETS to UC's threat was clever: revise elements of the test—getting rid of the long-criticized use of analogies—and add a writing component formerly provided only as a subject test. For Atkinson and other UC leaders, it was a sort of compromise. Academic senate leaders, including the members of BOARS, agreed to continue to use the SAT I for a period and analyze its predictive validity in subsequent years, while renewing the possibility of dropping it. The New SAT, now a third longer with addition of the writing component, was introduced in 2005.

In the aftermath of Atkinson's gambit, a number of high-quality private undergraduate colleges—such as Bates, Bard, Connecticut College, Pitzer, and Bowdoin—with great fanfare dropped the SAT and the ACT as requirements for admissions. Thus far, however, no large and highly selective public or private university has followed suit.

Standing Back

As the value of higher education increases for the individual, and for society in general, the difficulties of allocating a scarce public resource will grow only more intense for universities. Because there are generally conflicting interests in setting and influencing admissions policies at selective public universities, such as the University of California, policy-making is inherently political.

Admissions policies are not simply rational policy solutions to identified problems. They are, in some form, a reflection of the internal and external politics that shape the policy behaviors of a university—particularly at highly selective public institutions with greater levels of accountability and expectations than their private counterparts. In the case of the University of California, requiring the SAT is not an independent variable but instead is part of a larger set of admissions requirements that, over time, policy-makers adopt or modify to fit perceived institutional goals.

Hence, the story of the use of standardized tests in UC admissions decisions reflects in part changing conditions and perceptions of different policymakers over time—beginning with the perceived need to adopt use of SAT I and SAT II scores in 1968, and then a fuller embrace of their use in 1979 to reduce the eligibility pool, followed by the threat to drop the SAT I in an effort to influence student behavior in high school and align admissions more closely with subject requirements, culminating in the decision to retain the SAT I and drop the subject tests as a means of expanding the pool of students who could be considered UC Eligible.

It is axiomatic that actual admissions policies and their administration at these selective institutions are extremely complicated and dynamic. A shift in policy for an expressed purpose does not always produce the desired effect. And large changes in admissions policies, such as the recently adopted 9+9–SAT II plan described on the next page, will create great volatility for admissions officers attempting to calculate how many students, once accepted, will actually enroll. University admissions is a policy realm that is built around longitudinal trends that help predict the pool of applicants and the behavior of students. This alone argues for marginal shifts in admissions policies over time as opposed to radical or large changes.

Finally, highly selective public universities may attempt to create relatively transparent admissions criteria, but in the end much of the decision-making is arbitrary. Berkeley, for instance, received more than 45,000 applications for fall 2010, almost all from students that were UC Eligible under the earlier admissions policies, a majority with 4.0 GPAs (inflated by honors and advanced placement courses). Yet only 14,000 or so would be accepted by Berkeley, some of whom would be accepted and enroll elsewhere. With a net enrollment target of around 4500 students, many highly qualified and talented students had to be rejected. This ratio of applications to actual admissions is similar at UCLA and UC San Diego, as well as a number of other UC campuses.

Exemplifying these broad observations, there is yet another turn in UC's use of standardized tests. In 2008, frustrated with the inability to declare UC Eligible a large group of California students who did not take the SAT II, a contingent of senate leaders on BOARS moved to eliminate the SAT II as a requirement, while keeping the SAT I with its new writing component. This recommendation was a significant reversal of the analysis and arguments made by president Atkinson and the Academic Senate, who favored SAT II subject tests yet maintained the SAT I requirement pending analysis of the test's predictive validity with the new writing component.

The chair of the Academic Senate's executive body, Michael Brown, a leading advocate for the proposal, stated that the UC campuses were not "getting that much out of it [the subject tests], and they are not getting information that they can't get in other ways" (Jaschik, 2008). Under the proposal, certain highly selective UC programs (such as engineering) that insisted there were benefits to requiring particular subject tests could recommend that students submit these test scores as well. BOARS then raised the 4% ELC (i.e., high school–specific) pool to 9%. But this also required, according to UC analysis, a rebalancing of the statewide pool. The plan called for reducing the statewide draw from the top 12.5% of all public and private high school graduates to the top 9%. Because many students would qualify under both the high school–specific and the statewide criteria, BOARS estimated that the new criteria would, combined, provide a possible UC Eligibility pool representing the top 10% of all high school graduates. This would allow for a 2.5% pool that could be evaluated on broader criteria (a revised version of Comprehensive Review) and selected under a process called "Entitled to Review." The Entitled to Review category expanded the definition of applicants eligible for a full admission review to include all who complete 11 of 15 required high school courses by the end of their junior year and achieve a GPA of at least 3.0.

On February 4, 2009, with the support of the university's new president, Mark Yudof, the UC Board of Regents approved the BOARS proposal, with the policy to go into effect for the entering class of 2012. "We believe that at end of the day, this is a positive step to making our university look more like the state of California," stated Yudof shortly after the vote (Keller & Hoover, 2009). I dub this the "9+9–SAT II policy"—9% UC Eligible by local high school, 9% statewide, and now eliminating the SAT II subject tests and only requiring the SAT I.

How this proposal developed and made its way into formal policy is yet another lengthy political story that lies beyond the scope of this chapter. It is a radical redefinition of what constitutes eligibility and, at this time, the likely results are somewhat unpredictable. Modeling of potential results indicates that this revision of UC admissions policies may not have the intended outcome—primarily an increase in underrepresented racial and ethnic groups, and improved access to lower income students.

I would argue that at highly selective universities and colleges, and where demand is extremely high, shifts in admissions policies should be pursued incrementally precisely because of the often unanticipated results. We will have to see how the new UC policy is implemented and then gauge its outcomes. Nevertheless, the 9+9–SAT II redefinition of UC Eligibility does provide a legitimate, if a bit worrying, vision for how the University of California can remain true to the concept of the top 12.5% pool (though redefined) and provide more flexibility at the campus level to choose from a much larger pool of students. It does hold the promise of reducing the relative role of standardized tests in the admission process, and it recognizes that academic talent comes in various forms and from various circumstances. The true impact of this more decentralized approach will undoubtedly cause some confusion among Californians and their lawmakers—at least initially. Unless the proposal suffers serious revision (a possibility as stakeholders absorb more fully its potential impact), one can imagine the new admissions regime opening opportunities to more underrepresented groups.

In a reminder about the difficulties of any change, small or large, in the admissions policies at highly selective public universities, UC president Mark Yudof noted that "There is no perfect admission system. But I believe the reforms contained in this new policy will make UC's admission process fairer while preserving our high academic standards. Most importantly, I believe it will produce a class that will be prepared to meet the rigors of a UC education and go on to meet the societal and workforce needs of California" (UCOP, 2009). He is not the first UC president to optimistically express the same sentiments.

Note

Sections of this chapter are adapted, with permission, from John Aubrey Douglass, *The Conditions for Admission: Access, Equity, and the Social Contract of Public Universities* (Stanford, CA: Stanford University Press, 2007).

References

Atkinson, R. C. (2001). *Standardized tests and access to American universities.* The 2001 Robert H. Atwell Distinguished Lecture, American Council on Education, Washington, DC. Retrieved from http://www.rca.ucsd.edu/comments/satspch.html

Board of Admissions and Relations with Schools (BOARS). (1956). [*Report.*] Minutes of the July 1956 meeting. Berkeley: University of California Academic Senate.

Board of Admissions and Relations with Schools (BOARS). (1958). *Report to the UC Academic Senate Representative Assembly.* Minutes of the October 28, 1958, meeting. Berkeley: University of California Academic Senate.

Board of Admissions and Relations with Schools (BOARS). (1962). *Report to the UC Academic Senate Representative Assembly.* Minutes of the May 22, 1962, meeting. Berkeley: University of California Academic Senate.

Board of Admissions and Relations with Schools (BOARS). (1965). *Progress report on the Fall 1963 Achievement Test Study.* Minutes of the February 25–26, 1965, meeting. Berkeley: University of California Academic Senate.

Holy, T. C., Semans, H. H., & McConnell, T. R. (1955). *A restudy of the needs of California in higher education.* Report to the University of California Board of Regents and the California State Board of Education. Sacramento: California State Department of Education.

Hubin, D. R. (1988). *The Scholastic Aptitude Test.* Unpublished doctoral dissertation, University of Oregon.

Jaschik, S. (2008, March 17). SAT subject tests face new scrutiny. *Inside Higher Ed.* Retrieved from http://www.insidehighered.com/news/2008/03/17/uc

Keller, J., & Hoover, E. (2009, February 5). U. of California to adopt sweeping changes in admissions policy. *Chronicle of Higher Education.*

Lemann, N. (1999). *The big test: The secret history of the American meritocracy.* New York: Farrar, Straus and Giroux.

Pearson, R. (1979). *Oral history transcript.* Interview conducted by Gary Saretzky. Educational Testing Service Oral History Program, ETS Archives. Princeton, NJ: Educational Testing Service.

University of California Office of the President (UCOP). (1977). *Final report of the Task Force on Undergraduate Admissions.* Oakland, CA: Author.

University of California Office of the President (UCOP). (2009, February 5). *UC Board of Regents approves changes to UC's policy on undergraduate admission requirements.* Press Release. Oakland, CA: Author.

Abolishing the SAT

CHARLES MURRAY

For most high school students who want to attend an elite college, the SAT is more than a test. It is one of life's landmarks. Waiting for the scores—one for Verbal, one for Math, and now one for Writing, with a possible 800 on each—is painfully suspenseful. The exact scores are commonly remembered forever after. So it has been for half a century. But events of recent years have challenged the SAT's position. In 2001, Richard Atkinson (2001), president of the University of California, proposed dropping the SAT as a requirement for admission. More and more prestigious small colleges, such as Middlebury and Bennington, are making the SAT optional. The charge that the SAT is slanted in favor of privileged students—"a wealth test," as Harvard law professor Lani Guinier calls it—has been ubiquitous (Zwick, 2004).

I have watched the attacks on the SAT with dismay. Back in 1961, the test helped get me into Harvard from a small Iowa town by giving me a way to show that I could compete with applicants from Exeter and Andover. Ever since, I have seen the SAT as the friend of the little guy, just as James Bryant Conant, president of Harvard, said it would be when he urged the SAT upon the nation in the 1940s.

Conant's cause was as unambiguously liberal in the 1940s as income redistribution is today. Then, America's elite colleges drew most of their students from a small set of elite secondary schools, concentrated in the northeastern United States, to which America's wealthy sent their children. The mission of the SAT was to identify intellectual talent regardless of race, color, creed, money, or geography, and give that talent a chance to blossom. Students from small towns and from poor neighborhoods in big cities were supposed to benefit—as I thought I did, and as many others think they did. But data trump gratitude. The evidence has become overwhelming that the SAT no longer serves a democratizing purpose. Worse, events have conspired to make the SAT a negative force in American life. And so I find myself arguing that the SAT should be abolished. Not just deemphasized, but no longer administered. Nothing important would be lost by so doing. Much would be gained.

To clarify my terms: Here, "SAT" will always refer to the Verbal and Mathematics tests that you have in mind when you recall your own SAT scores. They, along with the Writing test added in 2005, are now officially known as "reasoning tests" or SAT I (labels I will ignore). The College Board also administers 1-hour achievement tests in English literature, United States history, world history, biology, chemistry, physics, two levels of math, Chinese, French, German, Hebrew, Italian, Japanese, Korean, Latin, and Spanish. These are now called "subject tests" or SAT II (more labels I will ignore). I do not discuss the College Board's advanced placement (AP) tests that can enable students to get college credit, because they cannot serve as a substitute for either the SAT or the achievement tests. Not all schools offer AP courses, and the AP's 5-point scoring system conveys limited information.

The Value of the SAT

Nothing important would be lost by dropping the SAT. The surprising empirical reality is that the SAT is redundant if students are required to take achievement tests. In theory, the SAT and the achievement tests measure different things. In the College Board's own words from its website (www.collegeboard.com), "The SAT measures students' verbal reasoning, critical reading, and skills," while the achievement tests "show colleges their mastery of specific subjects." In practice, SAT and achievement test scores are so highly correlated that SAT scores tell the admissions office little that it does not learn from the achievement test scores alone.

The pivotal analysis was released in 2001 by the University of California (UC), which requires all applicants to take both the SAT and achievement tests (three of them at the time the data were gathered: reading, mathematics, and a third of the student's choosing). Using a database of 77,893 students who applied to UC from 1996 to 1999, Geiser and Studley (2004) analyzed the relationship among high school grades, SAT scores, achievement test scores, and freshman grades in college. Achievement tests did slightly better than the SAT in predicting freshman grades. High school grade-point average (GPA), SAT scores, and achievement test scores were entered into a statistical equation to predict the GPA that applicants achieved during their freshman year in college. The researchers found that achievement tests and high school GPA each had about the same independent role—that is, each factor was, by itself, an equally accurate predictor of how a student will do as a college freshman.

But the SAT's independent role in predicting freshman GPA turned out to be so small that knowing the SAT score added next to nothing to an admissions officer's ability to forecast how an applicant will do in college—the reason to give the test in the first place. In technical terms, adding the SAT to the other two elements added just one-tenth of a percentage point to the percentage of variance in freshman grades explained by high school GPA and the achievement tests.

But what about the students we're most concerned about—those with high ability who have attended poor schools? The California Department of Education rates the state's high schools based on the results from its standardized testing program for grades K–12. For schools in the bottom quintile of the ratings—hard as I found it to believe—the achievement tests did slightly *better* than the SAT in predicting how the test-takers would perform as college freshmen.

What about students from families with low incomes? Children of parents with poor education? Here's another stunner: after controlling for parental income and education, the independent role of the SAT in predicting freshman GPA disappeared altogether. The effectiveness of high school GPA and of achievement tests to predict freshman GPA was undiminished.

All freshman grades are not created equal, so the UC study took the obvious differences into account. It broke down its results by college campus (an A at Berkeley might not mean the same thing as an A at Santa Cruz) and by freshman major (an A in a humanities course might not mean the same thing as an A in a physical science course). The results were unaffected. Again, the SAT was unnecessary; it added nothing to the forecasts provided by high school grades and achievement tests.

Thorough as the Geiser and Studley (2004) presentation was, almost any social science conclusion can be challenged through different data or a different set of analyses. The College Board, which makes many millions of dollars every year from the SAT, had every incentive and ample resources to refute the UC results. But it could not. In 2002, the College Board published its analysis (Kobrin, Camara, & Milewski, 2002). The College Board's study disentangled some statistical issues that the UC study had not and used a different metric to express predictive validity, but its bottom line was effectively identical. Once high school GPA and achievement test scores are known, the incremental value of knowing the SAT score is trivially small.

The SAT Then and Now

Still reluctant to give up on the SAT, I wondered whether the College Board had been unwilling to make the best defense. Perhaps the SAT had made an important independent contribution to predicting college performance in earlier years, but by the time research was conducted in the last half of the 1990s, the test had already been ruined by political correctness. To see where this hypothesis comes from, a little history is required.

Originally, the point of the SAT—whose initials, after all, stood for Scholastic Aptitude Test—was to measure *aptitude,* defined by the dictionary as "inherent ability," rather than to measure academic achievement. But in the aftermath of the 1960s, the concept of aptitude became troublesome. The temper of the times meant that long-observed ethnic and class differences in mental test scores had to be interpreted as the fault of the tests that produced them. Like all other mental tests, the SAT persistently showed such differences; therefore, the SAT had to be a bad test, culturally biased in favor of upper-middle-class white kids.

The psychometricians at the College Board could provide ample data to refute the cultural bias charge (see literature reviews in Herrnstein & Murray, 1994; Jensen, 1980), but the College Board was run by people who were eager to demonstrate their own progressive credentials. They ran from the concept of aptitude as the Florentines fled the plague. In the 1980s, the College Board tried to make a semantic case for a difference between scholastic aptitude and intelligence. This was unsuccessful for the good reason that, operationally, there isn't any difference. In 1993, the College Board abandoned aptitude altogether and changed the name of the SAT to Scholastic Assessment Test. In 1994, it introduced major substantive changes to the SAT that were explicitly intended to link the test more closely to the curriculum.

Did the pre-1994 SAT measure something importantly different from what the post-1994 SAT had measured? Don't bother asking the College Board. The data for answering that question would require the College Board to reveal just how well the original and revised SATs measure the general mental factor g, the stuff of intelligence/aptitude, and the College Board does not want to acknowledge that the SAT measures g at all or, for that matter, that g even exists.

Seen from an outsider's perspective, the changes in 1993–1994 do not look particularly important. Twenty-five antonym items in the SAT Verbal were replaced with reading-comprehension items, on grounds that the antonym items could be compromised by students who memorized vocabulary lists. The math test saw some changes in the answer format. But samples of the new items appear to be plausible measures of g and not obviously inferior to the items they replaced. Despite the College Board's rhetoric about revamping the SAT to reflect curriculum, the changes in the test in 1993–1994 probably did not have much effect on the SAT's power to measure g—in the jargon, its g-loading. (I would not make the same statement about today's SAT, which has eliminated the highly g-loaded analogy items and added a writing component that carries with it a multitude of scoring problems.)

If I am wrong, and the pre-1994 SAT measured g much better than the SAT used for the UC study, then I hope some disaffected College Board psychometrician leaks that news immediately. I will thereupon join a crusade to restore the old SAT. But given the available information, I think it is probable that even analyses conducted prior to the revisions in the test would not have shown a major independent role for the SAT after taking high school transcript and achievement test scores into account. To put it another way, those of us who thought that the SAT was our salvation were probably wrong. Even coming from mediocre high schools, our scores on achievement tests would have conveyed about the same picture to college admissions committees as our scores on the SAT conveyed.

I know how counterintuitive this sounds (I am presenting a conclusion I resisted as long as I could). But the truth about any achievement test, from an AP exam down to a weekly pop quiz, is that the smartest students tend to get the highest scores. All mental tests are g-loaded to some degree. What was not realized until the UC study was just how high that correlation was for the SAT and the achievement tests. Before, studies of the relationship had been based on self-selected samples of students who chose to take achievement tests along with the SAT, and there was good reason to think those students were unrepresentative. But by requiring all applicants to take both the SAT and achievement tests, the University of California got rid of this problem—and the correlations were still very high.

After the College Board did all of its statistical corrections in its 2002 study and applied them to test-takers from California, it found, for example, that the correlation between the SAT Verbal and the Literature achievement test was +.83, while the correlation between the SAT Math and the Math IC achievement test was +.84 (Kobrin et al., 2002, Tables 5, 6).

Who Will Be Most Affected by Abolishing the SAT?

A high overall correlation between the SAT and achievement test scores does not necessarily mean that getting rid of the SAT will affect all types of students equally. But as one works through the scenarios, it seems likely that those who will be disadvantaged by eliminating the SAT are those who deserve to be disadvantaged. Start with motivated, high-ability students who go to truly bad schools, meaning the worst schools in the inner cities. The bright students' achievement test scores are likely to be depressed by the schools' dreadfulness, but even scores that are just fair will get the attention of an admissions office if the transcript shows As and the recommendations are enthusiastic. The nation's top colleges desperately want to increase their enrollment of inner-city blacks and Hispanics, and are willing to make large allowances for bad schooling to do so.

Next, let's turn to the much larger number of high-ability students who are in schools that are not awful, but mediocre—the typical urban or small-town public school. The curriculum includes all the standard college-prep courses, with standard textbooks. A few of the teachers are terrific, but most are no more than ordinary. The high-ability students in such schools who are playing the game, studying hard, have no problem at all if the SAT is eliminated. They have nearly straight As on their transcripts, which most college admissions offices treat as the most important single source of information. Their letters of recommendation are afire with zeal on their behalf. These students also do well on the achievement tests. A hard-working, high-ability physics student is likely to absorb enough physics from the textbook to do well on the physics achievement test despite a so-so teacher. In addition, high-ability kids who play the game have usually been reading voraciously—and in the process picked up a great deal of knowledge about history, literature, and culture on their own. This information has been gathered inefficiently, but high-ability students absorb knowledge like a sponge, no matter what schools they attend.

Now consider high-ability students in mediocre schools who do *not* play the classroom game. They are bored with their classes and sometimes get Bs and the occasional C, but they have active minds and are looking for ways to occupy themselves. They spend all their time on the debate team or writing for the high school newspaper, or in the drama department. By the end of high school, they have a long list of accomplishments studding their applications. One way or the other, by the end of high school, students in this category are very likely to have done things that will catch the attention of an admissions officer. And, again, their achievement test scores are high. These students are at least as intellectually curious as those who play the game. Their Bs do not mean they didn't absorb the substance of the coursework, and they too have typically encountered and retained large amounts of information outside school.

That leaves the worst case: high-ability students who are alienated by school and perhaps by life. They don't study, don't go out for the debate team, don't read on their own, don't even watch the Discovery Channel. It is possible for them nonetheless to achieve a high score on an individually administered IQ test, despite being hostile and uninterested. Arthur Jensen relates the time he was testing a sullen subject in a juvenile detention facility and came to the vocabulary item "apocryphal." The boy answered, "How the hell should I know? I think the whole Bible is [bunk]" (Jensen, 1980). In an individually administered IQ test, the examiner could score his answer as correct, but that same alienated boy is unlikely to get a high score on the SAT because no one, no matter how smart, gets a high score on the SAT without concentrating and trying hard over the course of three stressful hours. So keeping the SAT will not help most students in this category. They won't try hard, and their SAT scores will be mediocre despite their ability.

That leaves an extremely odd set of high-ability students who will be harmed by dropping the SAT—so alienated that they do nothing to express their ability in school, so completely walled off from independent learning that they do poorly on the achievement tests, and yet able to buckle down on the SAT and get a good score. I am not sure that getting a good score under such circumstances is even possible on the SAT Math—too many of the questions presuppose hard work in algebra class—but perhaps it could be done on the SAT Verbal. In any case, we are now talking about a very few students, and even for them it is not clear whether dropping the SAT introduces an injustice. Should such a student be given a slot that could have been filled by a less-talented student who is eager to give a competitive college his best effort? Being forced to go to an unselective college instead could well be the better outcome for all concerned.

Why Get Rid of the SAT?

If the SAT works just about as well as the achievement tests in predicting college success, what's the harm in keeping it? The short answer is that the image of the SAT has done a 180-degree turn. No longer seen as a compensating resource for the unprivileged, it has become a corrosive symbol of privilege. "Back when kids just got a good night's sleep and took the SAT, it was a leveler that helped you find the diamond in the rough," Lawrence University's dean of admissions told *The New York Times* recently. "Now that most of the great scores are affluent kids with lots of preparation, it just increases the gap between the haves and the have-nots" (Lewin, 2006).

If you're rich, the critics say, you can raise your children in an environment where they will naturally acquire the information the SAT tests. If you're rich, you can enroll your children in Kaplan, or Princeton Review, or even get private tutors to coach your kids in the tricks of test-taking, and thereby increase their SAT scores by a couple of hundred points. If you're rich, you can shop around for a diagnostician who will classify your child as learning disabled and therefore eligible to take the SAT without time limits. Combine these edges, and it comes down to this: if you're rich, you can buy your kids a high SAT score.

Almost every parent with whom I discuss the SAT believes these charges. In fact, the claims range from simply false, in the case of cultural bias, to not-nearly-as-true-as-you-think, in the case of the others. Take coaching as an example, since it seems to be so universally accepted by parents and has been studied so extensively. From 1981 to 1990, three separate analyses of all the prior studies were published in peer-reviewed journals (Becker, 1990; DerSimonian & Laird, 1983; Messick & Jungeblut, 1981). They found a coaching effect of 9–25 points on the SAT Verbal and of 15–25 points on the SAT Math. Briggs (2004), using the National Education Longitudinal Study of 1988, found effects of 3–20 points for the SAT Verbal and 10–28 points for the SAT Math. Powers and Rock (1999), using a nationally representative sample of students who took the SAT after its revisions in the mid-1990s, found an average coaching effect of 6–12 points on the SAT Verbal and 13–18 points on the SAT Math. Many studies tell nearly identical stories. On average, coaching raises scores by no more than a few dozen points, enough to sway college admissions in exceedingly few cases.

The scholarly literature on this topic is not a two-sided debate. No study published in a peer-reviewed journal shows average gains approaching the fabled 100-point and 200-point jumps reported anecdotally. I asked two major test preparation companies, Kaplan and Princeton Review, for such evidence. Kaplan replied that it chooses not to release data for proprietary reasons. Princeton Review did not respond.

But the coaching business is booming, with affluent parents being the best customers. If the payoff is really so small, why has the market judged coaching to be so successful? The answer is that parents are focused on seeing a high SAT score, not on thinking about what that SAT score might have been if they did nothing.

Most obviously, parents who pay for expensive coaching courses ignore the role of self-selection: the students who seem to profit from a coaching course tend to be those who, if the course had not been available, would have worked hard on their own to prepare for the test.

Then parents confuse the effects of coaching with the effect of the basic preparation that students can do on their own. No student should walk into the SAT cold. It makes sense for students to practice some sample items, easily available from school guidance offices and online, and to review their algebra textbook if it has been a few years since they have taken algebra. But once a few hours have been spent on these routine steps, most of the juice has been squeezed out of preparation for the SAT. Combine self-selection artifacts with the role of basic preparation, and you have the reason that independent studies using control groups show such small average gains from formal coaching.

It makes no difference, however, that the charges about coaching are wrong, just as it makes no difference that the whole idea that rich parents can buy their children high SAT scores is wrong. One part of the indictment is true, and that one part overrides everything else: the children of the affluent and well educated really do get most of the top scores. For example, who gets the coveted scores of 700 and higher, putting them in the top half-dozen percentiles of SAT test-takers? Extrapolating from the 2006 data on means and standard deviations reported by the College Board (2006, Table 11), about half of the 700+ scores went to students from families making more than $100,000 per year. But the truly consequential statistics are these: approximately 90% of the students with 700+ scores had at least one parent with a college degree; over half had a parent with a graduate degree.

In that glaring relationship of high test scores to advanced parental education, which in turn means high parental IQ, lies the reason that the College Board, politically correct even unto self-destruction, cannot bring itself to declare the truth: the test isn't the problem. The children of the well educated and affluent get most of the top scores because they constitute most of the smartest kids. They are smart because their parents are smart. The parents have passed their smartness along through parenting practices that are largely independent of education and affluence, and through genes that are completely independent of them.

The cognitive stratification of American society—for that's what we're talking about—was not a problem 100 years ago. Many affluent people were smart in 1907, but there were not enough jobs in which high intellectual ability brought high incomes or status to affect more than a fraction of really smart people, and most of the really smart people were prevented from getting those jobs anyway by economic and social circumstances (consider that in 1907 roughly half the adults with high intelligence were housewives).

From 1907 to 2007, the economic value of intellectual ability and socioeconomic status (SES) increased dramatically. The socioeconomic elite and the cognitive elite are increasingly one (Herrnstein & Murray, 1994). Imagine that, miraculously, every child in the country were to receive an education of equal quality. Imagine that a completely fair and accurate measure of intellectual ability were to be developed. In that utopia, a fair admissions process based on intellectual ability would fill the incoming classes of the elite colleges predominantly with children of upper-middle-class parents.

In other words, such a perfect system would produce an outcome very much like the one we see now. Harvard offers an easy way to summarize the revolution that accelerated after World War II. As late as 1952, the mean SAT Verbal score of the incoming freshman class was just 583. By 1960, the mean had jumped to 678 (Herrnstein & Murray, 1994). In eight years, Harvard transformed itself from a college with a moderately talented student body to a place where the average freshman was intellectually in the top fraction of 1% of the national population. But this change did not mean that Harvard became more socioeconomically diverse. On the contrary, it became more homogeneous. In the old days, Harvard had admitted a substantial number of Boston students from modest backgrounds who commuted to classes, and also a substantial number of rich students with average intelligence. In the new era, when Harvard's students were much more rigorously screened for intellectual ability, the numbers of students from the very top and bottom of the socioeconomic ladder were reduced, and the proportion coming from upper-middle-class backgrounds increased.

The other high-ranking schools have similar stories to tell. In a sample of 11 of the most prestigious colleges followed from the mid-1970s to the mid-1990s, Bowen, Kurzweil, Tobin, and Pichler (2006) found that the proportion of students in the top SES quartile rose from about a third to half of all students, while the share in the bottom quartile remained constant at one-tenth. And these were schools such as Princeton and Yale that get first chance to admit the scarce and sought-after candidates of high ability from poor backgrounds. When Carnevale and Rose (2003) expanded the definition of top-tier colleges to include 146 schools, fully 74% of the students came from families in the top SES quartile, while only 3% came from the bottom quartile. Ethnic diversity has increased during the last half century, but not socioeconomic diversity.

Because upper-middle-class families produce most of the smartest kids, there is no way to reform the system (short of disregarding intellectual ability altogether) to prevent their children from coming out on top. We can only make sure that high-ability students from disadvantaged backgrounds realize that the nation's best colleges yearn for their applications and that their chance of breaking out of their disadvantaged situations has never been better—in short, that the system is not rigged. Now, the widespread belief is that the system is rigged, and the SAT is a major reason for that belief. The most immediate effect of getting rid of the SAT is to remove an extremely large and bright red herring. But there are more good effects.

Getting rid of the SAT will destroy the coaching industry as we know it. Coaching for the SAT is seen as the teaching of tricks and strategies—a species of cheating—not as supplementary education. The retooled coaching industry will focus on the achievement tests, but insofar as the offerings consist of cram courses for tests in topics such as U.S. history or chemistry, the taint will be reduced.

A low-income student shut out of opportunity for an SAT coaching school has the sense of being shut out of mysteries. Being shut out of a cram course is less daunting. Students know that they can study for a history or chemistry exam on their own. A coaching industry that teaches content along with test-taking techniques will have the additional advantage of being much better pedagogically—at least the students who take the coaching courses will be spending some of their time learning history or chemistry.

The substitution of achievement tests for the SAT will put a spotlight on the quality of the local high school's curriculum. If achievement test scores are getting all of the parents' attention in the college admissions process, the courses that prepare for those achievement tests will get more of their attention as well, and the pressure for those courses to improve will increase.

The final benefit of getting rid of the SAT is the hardest to describe but is probably the most important. By getting rid of the SAT, we would be getting rid of a totem for members of the cognitive elite. People forget achievement test scores. They do not forget cognitive test scores. The only cognitive test score that millions of people know about themselves is the SAT score. If the score is high, it is seen as proof that one is smart. If the score is not high, it is evidence of intellectual mediocrity or worse. Furthermore, it is evidence that cannot be explained away as a bad grade can be explained away. All who enter an SAT testing hall feel judged by their scores.

Worse yet, there are few other kinds of scores to counterbalance the SAT. Of the many talents and virtues that people possess, we have good measures for quantifying few besides athletic and intellectual ability. Falling short in athletic ability can be painful, especially for boys, but the domain of sports is confined. Intellectual ability has no such limits, and the implications of the SAT score spill far too widely. The 17-year-old who is at the 40th percentile on the SAT has no other score that lets him say to himself, "Yes, but I'm at the 99th percentile in working with my hands," or "Yes, but I'm at the 99th percentile for courage in the face of adversity."

Conversely, it seems to make no difference that high intellectual ability is a gift for which its recipients should be humbly grateful. Far too many students see a high score on the SAT as an expression of their own merit, not an achievement underwritten by the dumb luck of birth. Hence the final reason for getting rid of the SAT: knowing those scores is too dispiriting for those who do poorly and too inspiriting for those who do well. In an age when intellectual talent is increasingly concentrated among young people who are also privileged economically and socially, the last thing we need are numbers that give these very, very lucky kids a sense of entitlement.

The Future of the SAT

How are we to get rid of the SAT when it is such an established American institution and will be ferociously defended by the College Board and a large test preparation industry? Actually, it could happen quite easily. Admissions officers at elite schools are already familiar with the statistical story I have presented. They know that dropping the SAT would not hinder their selection decisions. Many of them continue to accept the SAT out of inertia—as long as the student has taken the test anyway, it costs nothing to add the scores to the student's folder. In that context, the arguments for *not* accepting the SAT can easily find a receptive audience, especially since the SAT is already under such severe criticism for the wrong reasons. Nor is it necessary to convince everyone to take action at the same time. A few high-profile colleges could have a domino effect. Suppose, for example, that this fall Harvard and Stanford were jointly to announce that SAT scores will no longer be accepted. Instead, all applicants to Harvard and Stanford will be required to take four of the College Board's achievement tests, including a math test and excluding any test for a language used at home. If just those two schools took such a step, many other schools would follow suit immediately, and the rest within a few years.

It could happen, and it should happen. There is poignancy in calling for an end to a test conceived for such a noble purpose. But the SAT score, intended as a signal flare for those on the bottom, has become a badge flaunted by those on top. We pay a steep educational and cultural price for a test that no one really needs.

References

Atkinson, R. C. (2001). *Standardized tests and access to American universities*. The 2001 Robert H. Atwell Distinguished Lecture, 83rd Annual Meeting of the American Council on Education, Washington, DC. Retrieved from http://www.rca.ucsd.edu/comments/satspch.html

Becker, B. J. (1990). Coaching for the Scholastic Aptitude Test: Further synthesis and appraisal. *Review of Educational Research, 60*(3), 373–417.

Bowen, W. G., Kurzweil, M. A., Tobin, E. M., & Pichler, S. C. (2006). *Equity and excellence in American higher education*. Richmond: University of Virginia Press.

Briggs, D. C. (2004). Evaluating SAT coaching: Gains, effects, and self-selection. In R. Zwick (Ed.), *Rethinking the SAT: The future of standardized testing in university admissions* (pp. 217–234). New York: RoutledgeFalmer.

Carnevale, A. P., & Rose, S. J. (2003). *Socioeconomic status, race/ethnicity, and selective college admissions*. New York: The Century Foundation.

College Board. (2006). *2006 College-bound seniors: Total group profile report*. New York: College Entrance Examination Board.

DerSimonian, R., & Laird, N. M. (1983). Evaluating the effect of coaching on SAT scores: A meta-analysis. *Harvard Educational Review, 53,* 1–15.

Geiser, S., & Studley, R. E. (2004). UC and the SAT: Predictive validity and differential impact of the SAT I and SAT II at the University of California. In R. Zwick (Ed.), *Rethinking the SAT: The future of standardized testing in university admissions* (pp. 125–154). New York: RoutledgeFalmer.

Herrnstein, R. J., & Murray, C. (1994). *The bell curve: Intelligence and class structure in American life.* New York: Free Press.

Jensen, A. R. (1980). *Bias in mental testing.* New York: Free Press.

Kobrin, J. L., Camara, W. J., & Milewski, G. B. (2002). *The utility of SAT I and SAT II for admissions decisions in California and the nation.* New York: College Entrance Examination Board.

Lewin, T. (2006, August 31). Students' path to small colleges can bypass SAT. *New York Times.*

Messick, S., & Jungeblut, A. (1981). Time and method in coaching for the SAT. *Psychological Bulletin, 89,* 191–216.

Powers, D. E., & Rock, D. A. (1999). Effects of coaching on SAT I: Reasoning test scores. *Journal of Educational Measurement, 36*(2), 93–118.

Zwick, R. (2004). Is the SAT a "wealth test"? The link between educational achievement and socioeconomic status. In R. Zwick (Ed.), *Rethinking the SAT: The future of standardized testing in university admissions* (pp. 203–216). New York: RoutledgeFalmer.

PART II

New Techniques, Removing Test Bias, and Institutional Case Studies

5

College Admissions Assessments

New Techniques for a New Millennium

ROBERT J. STERNBERG

Standardized testing in the context of college admissions has been dominated in the United States by tests of knowledge and analytical thinking, such as the SAT and the ACT. Such tests measure some, but not all, of the skills needed for success in college and in life beyond college. In this chapter, I describe two projects—Rainbow and Kaleidoscope—that seek to expand the range of skills tested to include, but also go beyond, those measured in the currently used tests.

Measurement of the kinds of skills currently assessed by standardized tests has a long history. For roughly 100 years, since the work of Alfred Binet and Theodore Simon, testing to assess students' abilities has changed relatively little (see Binet & Simon, 1916). If any other technology had stayed about the same for 100 years, people would be amazed. Imagine if we had only telegraphs operated by Morse code, primitive telephones, no televisions, no computers, and no serious electrical appliances. That is a world hard to imagine; yet, in the field of testing the abilities of children and adults, that is the world in which we live.

It would not be fair to say that there have been no new developments. Howard Gardner (1983, 2006), Joseph Renzulli (1986), Robert Sternberg (2003b), and others (see Sternberg, 2000; Sternberg & Davidson, 2005) have proposed new models of abilities that go beyond conventional IQ. But the tests used to measure IQ have not changed much. They still measure the same basic construct of so-called "general ability" that Charles Spearman identified early in the 20th century (Spearman, 1927). Our late 20th- and early 21st-century efforts have addressed developing new kinds of tests to assess intelligence in broader ways than has been possible in the past. This chapter describes two of these efforts that apply in particular to college admissions testing.

When psychologists create a psychological test, generally they try to be quite specific about the psychological construct(s) the test measures. For example, they might refer to their test as a test of intelligence or personality or interests, or whatever. Thus, we have tests such as the Wechsler Adult Intelligence Scale (WAIS) or the Minnesota Multiphasic Personality Inventory (MMPI) or the Strong Interest Inventory (SII). There is an exception to this generalization, however.

Publishers of tests used for college admissions are somewhat vague about what their tests measure. Clearly, the tests are designed to predict college performance or, at minimum, first-year college grade-point average (GPA). But what is the psychological construct that predicts such performance? It appears to be very close to the intelligence construct that psychologists have tried to understand for many years (Frey & Detterman, 2004). Predictably, this conclusion has not been well received by those at the Educational Testing Service (e.g., Bridgeman, 2005), but the results seem to hold.

The basic conceptual framework my colleagues and I have used is one called the *theory of successful intelligence* (Sternberg, 1997, 1999b, 2005b, 2010a). The basic idea is that people in almost any walk of life need (a) *creative intelligence* to generate new and exciting ideas, (b) *analytical intelligence* to evaluate whether their (and others') ideas are good ideas, and (c) *practical intelligence* to execute their ideas and to persuade others of their value. In the most recent, augmented version of the theory, I have argued that they further need (d) *wisdom,* in order to ensure that their abilities are being used for some kind of common good that balances their own interests with other people's and institutional interests over the short and long terms (Sternberg, 2003b, 2010a) through the infusion of positive ethical values (Sternberg, 2009a, 2010b, 2011). According to the theory, these abilities are modifiable, to some degree, rather than fixed (Dweck, 1999; Sternberg, 1999a, 2003a; Sternberg & Grigorenko, 2007).

This framework suggests that conventional tests of abilities, dating back to Binet and Simon (1916) and Spearman (1927), are not fully adequate because they so heavily emphasize analytical (as well as memory-based) abilities to the near or total exclusion of creative and practical abilities. Such tests predict a large variety of performances (Herrnstein & Murray, 1994; Jensen, 1998; Schmidt & Hunter, 1998), but perhaps not at the highest level that can be achieved.

Many other theorists also have claimed that there are abilities beyond general intelligence (e.g., Ceci, 1996; Gardner, 1983, 2006; Guilford, 1967; Thurstone, 1938). Even within theories that postulate general intelligence, a widely accepted view is that abilities are hierarchically differentiated (e.g., Carroll, 1993; Cattell, 1971; Vernon, 1961; see essays in Sternberg & Grigorenko, 2002). So a view of broad measures of intelligence fits with many theories. Where the theories differ somewhat is in exactly which abilities are measured—in what kinds of abilities are considered meritorious—and in how important the abilities are considered to be beyond general intelligence (*g*).

School assessments, like standardized tests, often emphasize analytical and memory-based skills. For example, the SAT (used in the United States) measures, among other things, analysis of reading passages and solution of mathematics problems. The A-Levels (used in the United Kingdom) measure memory for knowledge learned in secondary school and basic analysis of this knowledge. These memory and analytical skills are precisely the abilities in which many children of the middle and upper middle classes excel, resulting in a fairly substantial correlation between test scores and socioeconomic class (Lemann, 1999; Soares, 2007; Sternberg, 1997). Of course, there are exceptions. But on the whole, the system of selective admissions based on tests is geared to favor these children, who have had opportunities that children of the working class may not have had.

The system also is stacked against children from the middle and upper middle classes who may be nontraditional learners. Thus, testing has the potential advantage of creating equity by admitting students because of their abilities and achievements, and the potential disadvantage of destroying equity by favoring, on bases other than abilities and achievements, some groups of students over others.

Success in life depends on a broader range of abilities than what conventional tests measure. For example, memory and analytical abilities may be sufficient to produce A grades in science courses, but they are probably not sufficient to produce outstanding research, even if they provide relevant benefits, such as deciding whether one's ideas are good ones (Lubinski, Benbow, Webb, & Bleske-Rechek, 2006). In particular, outstanding researchers must be creative in generating ideas for theories and/or experiments, analytical in discerning whether their ideas are good ones, and practical in getting their ideas funded and accepted by competitive refereed journals. Conventional tests thus may well be a good beginning to assessing mental abilities, but, over the years, they also seem to have become the end.

My work has undergone something of an evolution over time. In the earliest version of the theory of successful intelligence, called the *componential subtheory of intelligence* (Sternberg, 1977, 1980), I proposed that a set of information-processing components, collectively, formed what has come to be called general intelligence (*g*). For example, these components included inferring relations and later applying them. In a later version of the theory (Sternberg, 1984, 1985), I suggested that understanding intelligence only in terms of general ability—whether through factors or through processes—was inadequate because the construct was too narrow. I suggested instead a "triarchic" theory, according to which intelligence comprises both creative and practical as well as analytical abilities. A later version of the theory

(Sternberg, 1997) emphasizes that what matters most is not exactly the abilities one has, but rather how one capitalizes on strengths and compensates for or corrects weaknesses.

My colleagues and I have been involved in two related projects exploring whether broader quantitatively based assessments might be helpful in the university admissions process. The first of these projects is the Rainbow Project (Sternberg, 2008, 2009b, 2010a; Sternberg & the Rainbow Project Collaborators, 2006), the second, the Kaleidoscope Project (Sternberg, 2009b, 2010a; Sternberg, Bonney, Gabora, Karelitz, & Coffin, 2010; Sternberg & Coffin, 2010). My goal here is not to present the projects in detail, which is done elsewhere, but rather to discuss in outline new techniques for assessing mental abilities that assess a broader range of skills than do the SAT and ACT.

Supplementing Standardized Tests:
The Rainbow Project

The story of the Rainbow Project begins in the late 19th century, when British scientist Sir Francis Galton (1883) proposed a theory of intelligence based upon the notion that more intelligent people have keener sensory-motor capacities than do less intelligent ones. He expected the more intelligent, for example, to have keener eyesight, a firmer grip, greater ability to distinguish between different tones, and so forth. Based on this notion, Galton developed a test of intelligence based upon sensory-motor skills.

As is always true in science, investigators have different ideas about how a story should develop and how it should end. French scientists Alfred Binet and Theodore Simon disputed Galton's claims about the nature of intelligence and how to measure it. Intelligence, they argued, is a matter of higher level thinking and good judgment rather than sensory abilities (Binet & Simon, 1916). The tests they developed required people to demonstrate judgment, interpret proverbs, provide the meanings of words, and solve arithmetic problems, among other school-related skills. Their tests predicted school performance better than did Galton's and came, therefore, to serve as the basis for future intelligence test development. In fact, Binet and Simon's assessment device became the first IQ test. The term *IQ*, derived from the German word *Intelligenz-Quotient*, was coined by William Stern (1912), who suggested that intelligence tests could be scored by using a ratio of mental age divided by chronological age × 100.

An American psychologist, Lewis Terman of Stanford University, imported Binet and Simon's tests into the United States. He used them in his research and published a version and revisions (e.g., Terman & Merrill,

1937). The fifth edition of this test—called the *Stanford-Binet Intelligence Scale*—is in use today. Binet and Terman had created tests to measure the intelligence of individuals, one at a time. However, others were soon taking mental measurement in another direction. Researchers such as Carl Brigham (1923) were interested in group testing of individuals. Brigham was the inventor, in the early twentieth century, of what is today called the SAT.

The SAT has a long history. Originally, the initials were an acronym for Scholastic Aptitude Test. This name implied to many people that the test measured innate intellectual qualities, so the name was changed to Scholastic Assessment Test. Perhaps because this name was too vague, the test name was later changed to be simply the acronym. At present, SAT stands for nothing but itself!

One of the primary venues for assessing mental abilities is university admissions. When universities make decisions about selective admissions, the main quantitative information they have available to them typically is GPA in high school or its equivalent and scores on standardized tests (Lemann, 1999). Such assessments provide somewhat limited prediction of college success, broadly defined, but they also do little to enhance the diversity of a campus. Is it possible to create assessments that are psychometrically sound and that provide incremental validity over existing measures, without disadvantaging or ignoring the cultural and ethnic diversity that makes a university environment a place in which students can interact with and learn from others who are different from themselves? Can one create assessments recognizing that people's gifts differ and that many of the variety of gifts they possess are potentially relevant to university and life success (Sternberg & Davidson, 2005)? And can one do so in a way that is not merely a proxy for socioeconomic class (Golden, 2006; Kabaservice, 2004; Karabel, 2006; Lemann, 1999; McDonough, 1997; Soares, 2007) or for IQ (Frey & Detterman, 2004)?

The Rainbow Project (for details, see Sternberg & the Rainbow Project Collaborators, 2006; see also Sternberg, 2005a, 2006, 2008, 2009b; Sternberg & the Rainbow Project Collaborators, 2005; Sternberg, the Rainbow Project Collaborators, & the University of Michigan Business School Project Collaborators, 2004) is a first project designed to enhance university admissions procedures at the undergraduate level. The Rainbow measures were intended, in the United States, to supplement the SAT, but they can supplement any conventional standardized test of abilities or achievement, as well as high school GPA. In the theory of successful intelligence, abilities and achievement are viewed as being on a continuum—abilities are largely achieved (Sternberg, 1998a, 1999a)—so it is not clear that it matters greatly exactly what test is used, given that most of the tests that are used are highly g-loaded.

The SAT is a comprehensive examination currently measuring verbal comprehension and mathematical thinking skills, with a writing component recently added. A wide variety of studies have shown the utility of the SAT and similar tests as predictors of university and job success, with success in college typically measured by GPA (Hezlett et al., 2001; Kobrin, Camara, & Milewski, 2002; Schmidt & Hunter, 1998). Taken together, these data suggest reasonable predictive validity for the SAT in predicting undergraduate performance, although its incremental validity over high school GPA is generally quite small and it may also reduce the diversity of an entering class. Indeed, traditional intelligence or aptitude tests have been shown to predict performance across a wide variety of settings. But as is always the case for a single test or type of test, there is room for improvement. The theory of successful intelligence provides one basis for improving prediction and possibly for establishing greater equity and diversity, which is a goal of most institutions of higher education (Bowen, Kurzweil, & Tobin, 2006). The theory suggests that broadening the range of skills tested to go beyond analytic skills—to include practical and creative skills as well—might significantly enhance the prediction of undergraduate performance beyond current levels. Thus, the theory does not suggest *replacing,* but rather *augmenting,* the SAT and similar tests such as the ACT or the A-Levels in the undergraduate admissions process. A collaborative team of investigators sought to study how successful such an augmentation could be. Even if we did not use the SAT, ACT, or A-Levels, in particular, we still would need some kind of assessment of the memory and analytical abilities the tests assess.

In the Rainbow Project, data were collected at 15 schools across the United States, including 8 four-year undergraduate institutions, 5 community colleges, and 2 high schools. Data presented here are for 793 college freshmen.

The measure of analytical skills was provided by multiple-choice analytical items. The SAT also measures analytical skills, so our tests of analytical skills were merely further measures of the same psychological construct. Creative skills were measured by multiple-choice items and by performance-based items. One performance measure required writing two short stories based upon selections from among a list unusual titles, such as "The Octopus's Sneakers"; one required orally telling two stories based upon choices of picture collages; and the third required captioning cartoons from among various options. Open-ended, performance-based answers were rated by trained raters for novelty, quality, and task appropriateness. Multiple judges were used for each task, and satisfactory reliability was achieved (Sternberg & the Rainbow Project Collaborators, 2006).

Practical skills were assessed by multiple-choice items and by three situational judgment inventories: the Everyday Situational Judgment Inventory (Movies), the Common Sense Questionnaire, and the College Life Questionnaire, each of which taps different types of tacit knowledge. The general format of tacit-knowledge inventories has been described in Sternberg et al. (2000), so only the content of the inventories used in this study will be described here. The movies used in the Everyday Situational Judgment Inventory present everyday situations that confront undergraduate students, such as asking for a letter of recommendation from a professor who shows, through nonverbal cues, that he does not recognize the student very well. One then has to rate various options for how well they would work in response to each situation. The Common Sense Questionnaire provides everyday business problems, such as being assigned to work with a coworker whom one cannot stand, and the College Life Questionnaire provides everyday university situations for which a solution is required.

All materials were administered in either of two formats: in paper-and-pencil format or on the World Wide Web. No strict time limits were set for completing the tests, although the instructors were given rough guidelines of about 70 minutes per session. The time taken to complete the battery of tests ranged from 2 to 4 hours.

The analysis that follows is a conservative one that does not correct for differences in the selectivity of the institutions at which the study took place. In a study across so many undergraduate institutions differing in selectivity, validity coefficients will seem to be lower than is typical, because an A at a less selective institution counts the same as an A at a more selective institution. When the investigators corrected for institutional selectivity, the results described became stronger. But correcting for selectivity has its own problems (e.g., on what basis does one evaluate selectivity?), and so uncorrected data are used in this report. We also did not control for university major. Different universities may have different majors, and the exact course offerings, grading, and populations of students entering different majors may vary from one university to another, rendering control difficult.

When examining undergraduate students alone, the sample showed a slightly higher mean level of SAT than that found in undergraduate institutions across the United States. The standard deviation was above the normal 100-point standard deviation, meaning we did not suffer from restriction of range. Our means, although slightly higher than typical, are within the range of average undergraduate students.

Another potential concern is pooling data from different institutions. We pooled data because in some institutions we simply did not have large enough numbers of cases for the data to be meaningful.

Some scholars believe that there is only one set of skills that is highly relevant to school performance, what is sometimes called "general ability," or g (e.g., Jensen, 1998). These scholars believe that tests may appear to measure different skills, but when statistically analyzed, show themselves just to be measuring the single general ability. Does the test actually measure distinct analytical, creative, and practical skill groupings? Factor analysis addresses this question. Three meaningful factors were extracted from the data: practical performance tests, creative performance tests, and multiple-choice tests (including analytical, creative, and practical). In other words, multiple-choice tests, regardless of what they were supposed to measure, clustered together (see also Sternberg, Castejón, Prieto, Hautamäki, & Grigorenko, 2001, for similar findings). Thus, method variance proved to be very important.

The results show the importance of measuring skills using multiple formats, precisely because method is so important in determining factorial structure. The results show the limitations of exploratory factor analysis in analyzing such data, and also of dependence on multiple-choice items outside the analytical domain. In the ideal, one should control for method of testing in designing aptitude and other test batteries.

Undergraduate admissions offices are not interested, exactly, in whether our new tests predict undergraduate academic success. Rather, they are interested in the extent to which the tests predict school success beyond those measures currently in use, such as the SAT and high school GPA. To test the incremental validity provided by the Rainbow measures above and beyond the SAT in predicting GPA, a series of statistical analyses (hierarchical regressions) was conducted that included the items analyzed above in the analytical, creative, and practical assessments.

If one looks at the simple correlations, the SAT Verbal, SAT Math, high school GPA, and the Rainbow measures all predict first-year college GPA. But how do the Rainbow measures fare on incremental validity? In one set of analyses, the SAT Verbal, SAT Math, and high school GPA were included in the first step of the prediction equation because these are the standard measures used today to predict undergraduate performance. Only high school GPA contributed uniquely to prediction of undergraduate GPA. Inclusion of the Rainbow measures roughly *doubled* prediction (percentage of variance accounted for in the criterion) versus the SAT alone.

These results suggest that the Rainbow tests add considerably to the prediction achieved by the SAT alone. They also reaffirm the power of high school GPA in prediction, particularly, because it is an atheoretical composite that includes within it many variables, including motivation and conscientiousness.

Studying group differences requires careful attention to methodology and sometimes has led to erroneous conclusions (Hunt & Carlson, 2007). Although one important goal of the present study was to predict success in the undergraduate years, another important goal involved developing measures that reduce ethnic group differences in mean levels. There has been a lively debate as to why there are socially defined racial group differences, and as to whether scores for members of underrepresented minority groups are over- or underpredicted by the SAT and related tests (see, e.g., Bowen & Bok, 2000; Camara & Schmidt, 1999; Rowe, 2005; Rushton & Jensen, 2005; Sternberg, Grigorenko, & Kidd, 2005; Turkheimer, Haley, Waldron, D'Onofrio, & Gottesman, 2003). There are a number of ways one can test for group differences in these measures, each of which involves a test of the size of the effect of ethnic group. Two different measures were chosen: ω^2 (omega squared) and Cohen's D.

There were two general findings. First, in terms of overall differences, the Rainbow tests appeared to reduce ethnic-group differences relative to traditional assessments of abilities like the SAT. Second, in terms of specific differences, it appears that the Latino students benefited the most from the reduction of group differences. The black students, too, seemed to show a reduction in difference from the white mean for most of the Rainbow tests, although a substantial difference appeared to be maintained with the practical performance measures.

Although the group differences are not perfectly reduced, these findings suggest that measures can be designed that reduce ethnic and racial group differences on standardized tests, particularly for historically disadvantaged groups such as black and Latino students. These findings have important implications for reducing adverse impact in undergraduate admissions.

The SAT is based on a conventional psychometric notion of cognitive skills. Using this notion, it has had substantial success in predicting undergraduate academic performance. The Rainbow measures alone roughly doubled the predictive power of undergraduate GPA when compared with the SAT alone. Additionally, the Rainbow measures predict substantially beyond the contributions of the SAT and high school GPA. These findings, combined with encouraging results regarding the reduction of ethnicity-related differences, make a compelling case for furthering the study of the measurement of analytic, creative, and practical skills for predicting success in the university.

One important goal for the current study, and future studies, is the creation of standardized assessments that reduce the different outcomes between different groups as much as possible to maintain test validity. The measures described here suggest results toward this end. Although the group differences in the tests were not reduced to zero, the tests did substantially attenuate group differences relative to other measures such as the SAT. This finding could be an important step toward ultimately ensuring fair and equal treatment for members of diverse groups in the academic domain.

The principles behind the Rainbow Project apply at other levels of admissions as well. For example, Hedlund, Wilt, Nebel, Ashford, and Sternberg (2006) have shown that the same principles can be applied in admissions to business schools, also with the result of increasing prediction and decreasing ethnic-group (as well as gender) differences. Stemler, Grigorenko, Jarvin, and Sternberg (2006) and Stemler, Sternberg, Grigorenko, Jarvin, and Sharpes (2009) have found that including creative and practical items in augmented psychology, statistics, and physics advanced placement examinations can reduce ethnic-group differences on the tests. The same principles are being employed in a test for identification of gifted students in elementary school (Chart, Grigorenko, & Sternberg, 2008).

It is one thing to have a successful research project, and another actually to implement the procedures in a high-stakes situation. We have had the opportunity to do so. The results of a second project, Project Kaleidoscope, are described here.

The Kaleidoscope Project: Examining Intelligence Through Testing

Tufts University in Medford, Massachusetts, has strongly emphasized the role of active citizenship in education. It has put into practice some of the ideas from the Rainbow Project. In collaboration with Tufts' Dean of Admissions, Lee Coffin, we instituted Project Kaleidoscope, which represents an implementation of the ideas of Rainbow but goes beyond that project to include in its assessment the construct of wisdom (for more details, see Sternberg, 2007b, 2007c, 2010a; Sternberg et al., 2010; Sternberg & Coffin, 2010).

We placed on the 2006–2007 application for all of the more than 15,000 students applying to Arts, Sciences, and Engineering at Tufts, questions designed to assess *wisdom, analytical and practical intelligence, and creativity synthesized* (WICS), an extension of the theory of successful intelligence (Sternberg, 2003b). (The program was continued through 2010, but the data reported here are for the first year, for which we have more nearly complete data.)

WICS is a theory of that extends the theory of successful intelligence on the basis of the notion that some people may be academically and even practically intelligent but unwise, as illustrated in the case of corporate scandals such as those that have surrounded Enron, Worldcom, and Arthur Andersen, and in the case of numerous political scandals as well. Perhaps the Bernard Madoff scandal is the epitome of such failures of wisdom. The demise of Lehman Brothers, Bear-Stearns, and other investment banks also seems to have been due, in large part, to foolishness, in this case, in investments. Those responsible were smart, well-educated—and foolish. The conception of wisdom used here is that of the *balance theory of wisdom* (Sternberg, 1998b), according to which wisdom is the application of intelligence, creativity, and knowledge for the common good, by balancing intrapersonal, interpersonal, and extrapersonal interests, over the long and short terms, through the infusion of positive ethical values.

The questions were optional. Whereas the Rainbow Project was conducted as a separate high-stakes test administered with a proctor, the Kaleidoscope Project was done as a section of the Tufts-specific supplement to the Common Application. It was just not practical to administer a separate high-stakes test such as the Rainbow assessment for admission to one university. Moreover, an advantage of Kaleidoscope is that it got us away from the high-stakes testing situation in which students must answer complex questions in very short amounts of time under incredible pressure.

Students were encouraged to answer just a single question so as not to burden them excessively. Tufts University competes for applications with many other universities, and if its application was substantially more burdensome than those of our competitor schools, that would put Tufts at a real-world disadvantage in attracting applicants. In the theory of successful intelligence, successful intelligent individuals capitalize on strengths and compensate for or correct weaknesses. Our format gave students a chance to capitalize on a strength.

As examples of items, one creative question asked students to write stories with titles such as "The End of MTV" or "Confessions of a Middle-School Bully." Another creative question asked students what the world would be like if some historical event had come out differently, for example, if Rosa Parks had given up her seat on the bus. Yet another creative question, a nonverbal one, gave students an opportunity to design a new product or an advertisement for a new product. A practical question queried how students had persuaded friends of an unpopular idea they held. A wisdom question asked students how a passion they had could be applied toward a common good.

Creativity and practicality were assessed in the same way as in the Rainbow Project. Analytical quality was assessed by the organization, logic, and balance of the essay. Wisdom was assessed by the extent to which the response represented the use of abilities and knowledge for a common good by balancing one's own, others', and institutional interests over the long and short terms through the infusion of positive ethical values.

The goal of this work is to reconceptualize applicants in terms of aca-demic/analytical, creative, practical, and wisdom-based abilities, using the essays as one but not the only source of information. The objective is not necessarily to replace the SAT and other traditional admissions measures such as GPA and class rank with some new test. Tufts does not look only at test scores. In the admissions program, highly creative work submitted in a portfolio also could be entered into the creativity rating, or evidence of creativity through winning of prizes or awards. The essays were major sources of information, but if other information was available, the trained admissions officers used it.

We now have some results of the first year of implementation of the WICS assessment, and they are very promising. Applicants were evaluated for creative, practical, and wisdom-based skills, if sufficient evidence was avail-able, as well as for academic (analytical) and personal qualities in general.

Among the applicants who were evaluated as being academically quali-fied for admission, approximately half completed an optional essay. Doing these essays had no meaningful effect on chances of admission. However, *quality* of essays or other evidence of creative, practical, or wisdom-based abilities did have an effect. For those rated as an "A" (top rating) by a trained admissions officer in any of these three categories, average rates of acceptance were roughly double those for applicants not getting an A. Because of the large number of essays (more than 8000), only one rater rated each applicant, except for a sample to ensure that inter-rater reliabil-ity was sufficient, which it was.

Many measures do not look like conventional standardized tests but have statistical properties that mimic them. We were therefore interested in convergent-discriminant validation of our measures. The correlations of our measures with a rated academic composite that included SAT scores and high school GPA were modest but significant for creative, practical, and wise thinking. The correlations with a rating of quality of extracurricu-lar participation and leadership were moderate for creative, practical, and wise thinking. Thus, the pattern of convergent-discriminant validation was what we had hoped for.

The average academic quality of applicants in Arts & Sciences rose slightly in 2006–2007, the first year of the pilot, in terms of both SAT and high school GPA. (That increase has continued into the second and third years of the project.) In addition, there were notably fewer students in what before had been the bottom third of the pool in terms of academic quality. Many of those students, seeing the new application, seem to have decided not to bother to apply. Many more strong applicants applied.

Thus, adopting these new methods has not resulted in less qualified applicants applying to the institution and being admitted. Rather, the applicants who are admitted are *more* qualified, but in a broader way. Perhaps most rewarding were the positive comments from large numbers of applicants who felt our application gave them a chance to show themselves for who they are. Of course, many factors are involved in admissions decisions, and Kaleidoscope ratings were only one small part of the overall picture.

We did not get meaningful differences across ethnic groups, a result that surprised us, given that the earlier Rainbow Project reduced but did not eliminate differences. In the Rainbow Project, we got substantially better prediction than SAT alone (double) or SAT plus high school GPA (roughly 50% increase) and a decrease ethnic-group differences. In the Kaleidoscope Project, we essentially eliminated ethnic-group disparities—we did not see score differences between groups.

After a number of years in which applications to Tufts by underrepresented minorities were relatively flat in terms of numbers, in 2006–2007 they went up substantially. In the end, applications from African Americans and Hispanic Americans increased significantly, and admissions of African Americans were up 30% and of Hispanic Americans up 15%. Obviously, we cannot trace these results only to Kaleidoscope, as other factors may have been involved as well. On the whole, though, results of the Kaleidoscope Project exceeded even those of the Rainbow Project in showing that it is possible to increase academic quality and diversity simultaneously, and to do so in for an entire undergraduate class at a major university, not just for small samples of students at some scattered schools. Most importantly, the project sent a message to students, parents, high school guidance counselors, and others, that we believe that there is a more to a person than the narrow spectrum of skills assessed by standardized tests, and that these broader skills can be assessed in a quantifiable way.

After one year, we found that Kaleidoscope not only improved prediction of freshman GPA, but also that those who excelled in Kaleidoscope also excelled in extracurricular and leadership activities. So it was possible to improve the leadership profile of the school, as well as its ethnic diversity, without sacrificing its academic profile.

The Limitations of Assessments

There are many limitations of these studies that circumscribe the conclusions that can be drawn from them. A first limitation is that socioeconomic class is confounded with ethnicity. The reason we did not control for socioeconomic class is that we were unable to obtain the data that would have enabled us to do so. Thus, ethnicity differences may be attributable, in unknown measure, to socioeconomic class differences. A second limitation is that there were problematic methodological issues in both the Rainbow and the Kaleidoscope projects. In Rainbow, we used an incomplete design, meaning that not all students took all tests. This made the statistical analysis complex to the point where we would not recommend the use of this design by others. In Kaleidoscope, unlike in Rainbow, assessments were done without proctoring. Thus, we cannot be certain of the conditions under which the assessments were taken, or even that it was the applicant who took the assessment. A third limitation is that the new assessments require more time, resources, and money to score. We had to hire raters and train them. Although reliability was good, it could only be achieved with training. Schools would therefore have to decide that the additional information was worth the cost. Another limitation is that our follow-up data at this time are limited. For Rainbow, we have only first-year university grades. For Kaleidoscope, we have only first-year performance. To fully track these projects, we will be following up by measuring progress broadly—including nonacademic measures—during the 4 years the students are at the university. Lastly, in Kaleidoscope, there was the limitation of selection bias. Students who completed the essays were not a random sample of applicants: they chose to do extra work. However, because admission probabilities were not related to the fact of completing the essays, but only to the quality of essays for those who did complete them, the bias may not have been an important factor in the results.

The Argument for Broader Admissions Assessments

In sum, the augmented theory of successful intelligence appears to provide a strong theoretical basis for an expanded assessment of the skills needed for undergraduate success. There is evidence to indicate that it has good incremental predictive power and serves to increase equity. As teaching improves and university teachers emphasize more the creative and practical skills needed for success in school and life, the predictive power of the test may increase. Cosmetic changes in testing over the last century have made relatively little difference to the construct validity of assessment procedures. The theory of successful intelligence could provide a new opportunity to increase construct validity at the same time that it reduces differences in test performance between groups. It may indeed be possible to accomplish the goals of affirmative action through tests such as the Kaleidoscope assessments, either as supplements to traditional affirmative action programs or as substitutes for them.

Other modern theories of intelligence, such as those mentioned earlier in this chapter (e.g., Ceci, 1996; Gardner, 1983), may also serve to improve prediction and increase diversity. Moreover, other approaches to supplementing the SAT, and the Kaleidoscope tests, may be called for. For example, Oswald, Schmitt, Kim, Ramsay, and Gillespie (2004) have found autobiographical data and situational judgment tests (the latter of which we also used) to provide incremental validity to the SAT. Sedlacek (2004) has developed noncognitive measures that appear to have had success in enhancing the university admissions process.

The theory and principles of assessment described in this chapter can be extended beyond the United States (Sternberg, 2004, 2007a). We have used assessments based on the theory of successful intelligence on five continents and have found that the general principles seem to hold, although the content used to assess abilities needs to differ from one locale to another. At present, we are starting a collaboration with psychologists in Germany to determine whether the instruments used in the United States might, in suitable form, be useful there as well.

There is no question but that the methods used in the Rainbow Project, the Kaleidoscope Project, and related projects are at early stages of development. They do not have more than 100 years of experience behind them, as do traditional methods. What the results suggest is that an argument is to be made for broader assessments—that broader assessments are not synonymous with fuzzy-headed assessments. Such assessments can improve prediction and increase diversity, rather than trading off the one for the other. Broader assessments do not necessarily replace conventional ones. They supplement them. Our results show an important role for traditional analytical abilities in university success. But these are not the only abilities that matter, and they should not be the only abilities we measure.

Note

I am grateful to the Rainbow Project Collaborators and the Kaleidoscope Project Collaborators for making this research possible. Preparation of this chapter was supported by CASL–IES grant R305H030281, ROLE–NSF grant REC 440171, and REESE–NSF grant REC 0633952. The Rainbow Project was supported by the College Board, and the Kaleidoscope Project was supported by Tufts University.

References

Binet, A., & Simon, T. (1916). *The development of intelligence in children.* Baltimore: Williams & Wilkins. (Originally published in 1905.)

Bowen, W. G., & Bok, D. (2000). *The shape of the river: Long-term consequences of considering race in college and university admissions.* Princeton, NJ: Princeton University Press.

Bowen, W. G., Kurzweil, M. A., & Tobin, E. M. (2006). *Equity and excellence in American higher education.* Charlottesville: University of Virginia Press.

Bridgeman, B. (2005). Unbelievable results when predicting IQ from SAT scores. *Psychological Science, 16,* 745–746.

Brigham, C. C. (1923). *A study of American intelligence.* Princeton, NJ: Princeton University Press.

Camara, W. J., & Schmidt, A. E. (1999). *Group differences in standardized testing and social stratification.* (College Board Research Report No. 99-5.) New York: The College Board. Retrieved December 21, 2006, from http://www.collegeboard.com/research/home/

Carroll, J. B. (1993). *Human cognitive abilities: A survey of factor-analytic studies.* New York: World Book.

Cattell, R. B. (1971). *Abilities: Their structure, growth and action.* Boston: Houghton Mifflin.

Ceci, S. J. (1996). *On intelligence: A bioecological treatise on intellectual development.* Cambridge, MA: Harvard University Press.

Chart, H., Grigorenko, E. L., & Sternberg, R. J. (2008). Identification: The Aurora Battery. In J. A. Plucker & C. M. Callahan (Eds.), *Critical issues and practices in gifted education* (pp. 281–301). Waco, TX: Prufrock.

Dweck, C. S. (1999). *Self-theories: Their role in motivation, personality, and development.* Philadelphia: Psychology Press.

Frey, M. C., & Detterman, D. K. (2004). Scholastic assessment or *g?* The relationship between the Scholastic Assessment Test and general cognitive ability. *Psychological Science, 15,* 373–378.

Galton, F. (1883). *Inquiry into human faculty and its development.* London: Macmillan.

Gardner, H. (1983). *Frames of mind: The theory of multiple intelligences.* New York: Basic.

Gardner, H. (2006). *Multiple intelligences: New horizons.* New York: Perseus.

Golden, D. (2006). *The price of admission.* New York: Crown.

Guilford, J. P. (1967). *The nature of human intelligence.* New York: McGraw-Hill.

Hedlund, J., Wilt, J. M., Nebel, K. R., Ashford, S. J., & Sternberg, R. J. (2006). Assessing practical intelligence in business school admissions: A supplement to the Graduate Management Admissions Test. *Learning and Individual Differences, 16,* 101–127.

Herrnstein, R. J., & Murray, C. (1994). *The bell curve.* New York: Free Press.

Hezlett, S., Kuncel, N., Vey, A., Ones, D., Campbell, J., & Camara, W. J. (2001). *The effectiveness of the SAT in predicting success early and late in college: A comprehensive meta-analysis.* Paper presented at the annual meeting of the National Council of Measurement in Education, Seattle, WA.

Hunt, E., & Carlson, J. (2007). Considerations relating to the study of group differences in intelligence. *Perspectives on Psychological Science, 2,* 194–213.

Jensen, A. R. (1998). *The g factor.* Westport, CT: Praeger/Greenwood.

Kabaservice, G. (2004). *The guardians: Kingman Brewster, his circle, and the rise of the liberal establishment.* New York: Henry Holt.

Karabel, J. (2006). *The chosen: The hidden history of admission and exclusion at Harvard, Yale, and Princeton.* New York: Mariner.

Kobrin, J. L., Camara, W. J., & Milewski, G. B. (2002). *The utility of the SAT I and SAT II for admissions decisions in California and the nation.* (College Board Report No. 2002-6.) New York: College Board.

Lemann, N. (1999). *The big test: The secret history of the American meritocracy.* New York: Farrar, Straus and Giroux.

Lubinski, D., Benbow, C. P., Webb, R. M., & Bleske-Rechek, A. (2006). Tracking exceptional human capital over two decades. *Psychological Science, 17,* 194–199.

McDonough, P. M. (1997). *Choosing colleges: How social class and schools structure opportunity.* Albany: State University of New York Press.

Oswald, F. L., Schmitt, N., Kim, B. H., Ramsay, L. J., & Gillespie, M. A. (2004). Developing a biodata measure and situational judgment inventory as predictors of college student performance. *Journal of Applied Psychology, 89,* 187–207.

Renzulli, J. S. (1986). The three ring conception of giftedness: A developmental model for creative productivity. In R. J. Sternberg & J. E. Davidson (Eds.), *Conceptions of giftedness* (pp. 53–92). New York: Cambridge University Press.

Rowe, D. C. (2005). Under the skin: On the impartial treatment of genetic and environmental hypotheses of racial differences. *American Psychologist, 60*(1), 60–70.

Rushton, J. P., & Jensen, A. R. (2005). Thirty years of research on race differences in cognitive ability. *Psychology, Public Policy, and Law, 11,* 235–294.

Schmidt, F. L., & Hunter, J. E. (1998). The validity and utility of selection methods in personnel psychology: Practical and theoretical implications of 85 years of research findings. *Psychological Bulletin, 124,* 262–274.

Sedlacek, W. E. (2004). *Beyond the big test: Noncognitive assessment in higher education.* San Francisco: Jossey-Bass.

Soares, J. A. (2007). *The power of privilege: Yale and America's elite colleges.* Stanford, CA: Stanford University Press.

Spearman, C. (1927). *The abilities of man.* New York: Macmillan.

Stemler, S. E., Grigorenko, E. L., Jarvin, L., & Sternberg, R. J. (2006). Using the theory of successful intelligence as a basis for augmenting AP exams in psychology and statistics. *Contemporary Educational Psychology, 31*(2), 344–376.

Stemler, S., Sternberg, R. J., Grigorenko, E. L., Jarvin, L., & Sharpes, D. K. (2009). Using the theory of successful intelligence as a framework for developing assessments in AP Physics. *Contemporary Educational Psychology, 34,* 195–209.

Stern, W. (1912). *Psychologische Methoden der Intelligenz-Prüfung.* Leipzig, Germany: Barth.

Sternberg, R. J. (1977). *Intelligence, information processing, and analogical reasoning: The componential analysis of human abilities.* Hillsdale, NJ: Lawrence Erlbaum.

Sternberg, R. J. (1980). Sketch of a componential subtheory of human intelligence. *Behavioral and Brain Sciences, 3,* 573–584.

Sternberg, R. J. (1984). Toward a triarchic theory of human intelligence. *Behavioral and Brain Sciences, 7,* 269–287.

Sternberg, R. J. (1985). *Beyond IQ: A triarchic theory of human intelligence.* New York: Cambridge University Press.

Sternberg, R. J. (1997). *Successful intelligence.* New York: Plume.

Sternberg, R. J. (1998a). Abilities are forms of developing expertise. *Educational Researcher, 27*(3), 11–20.

Sternberg, R. J. (1998b). A balance theory of wisdom. *Review of General Psychology, 2,* 347–365.

Sternberg, R. J. (1999a). Intelligence as developing expertise. *Contemporary Educational Psychology, 24,* 359–375.

Sternberg, R. J. (1999b). The theory of successful intelligence. *Review of General Psychology, 3,* 292–316.

Sternberg, R. J. (Ed.). (2000). *Handbook of intelligence.* New York: Cambridge University Press.

Sternberg, R. J. (2003a). Teaching for successful intelligence: Principles, practices, and outcomes. *Educational and Child Psychology, 20*(2), 6–18.

Sternberg, R. J. (2003b). *Wisdom, intelligence, and creativity synthesized.* New York: Cambridge University Press.

Sternberg, R. J. (2004). Culture and intelligence. *American Psychologist, 59*(5), 325–338.

Sternberg, R. J. (2005a). Accomplishing the goals of affirmative action—with or without affirmative action. *Change, 37*(1), 6–13.

Sternberg, R. J. (2005b). The theory of successful intelligence. *Interamerican Journal of Psychology, 39*(2), 189–202.

Sternberg, R. J. (2006). How can we simultaneously enhance both academic excellence and diversity? *College and University, 81*(1), 17–23.

Sternberg, R. J. (2007a). Culture, instruction, and assessment. *Comparative Education, 43*(1), 5–22.

Sternberg, R. J. (2007b). Finding students who are wise, practical, and creative. *Chronicle of Higher Education, 53*(44), B11.

Sternberg, R. J. (2007c). How higher education can produce the next generation of positive leaders. In M. E. Devlin (Ed.), *Futures Forum 2007* (pp. 33–36). Cambridge, MA: Forum for the Future of Higher Education.

Sternberg, R. J. (2008). The Rainbow Project: Using a psychological theory of giftedness to improve identification of gifted children. In J. L. VanTassel-Baska (Ed.), *Alternative assessments with gifted and talented students* (pp. 147–156). Waco, TX: Prufrock Press.

Sternberg, R. J. (2009a). A new model for teaching ethical behavior. *Chronicle of Higher Education, 55*(33), B14–B15.

Sternberg, R. J. (2009b). The Rainbow and Kaleidoscope projects: A new psychological approach to undergraduate admissions. *European Psychologist, 14,* 279–287.

Sternberg, R. J. (2010a). *College admissions for the 21st century.* Cambridge, MA: Harvard University Press.

Sternberg, R. J. (2010b). Teaching for ethical reasoning in liberal education. *Liberal Education, 96*(3), 32–37.

Sternberg, R. J. (2011). Slip-sliding away, down the ethical slope. *Chronicle of Higher Education, 57*(19), A23.

Sternberg, R. J., Bonney, C. R., Gabora, L., Karelitz, T., & Coffin, L. (2010). Broadening the spectrum of undergraduate admissions. *College and University, 86*(1), 2–17.

Sternberg, R. J., Castejón, J. L., Prieto, M. D., Hautamäki, J., & Grigorenko, E. L. (2001). Confirmatory factor analysis of the Sternberg triarchic abilities test in three international samples: An empirical test of the triarchic theory of intelligence. *European Journal of Psychological Assessment, 17*(1), 1–16.

Sternberg, R. J., & Coffin L. A. (2010). Kaleidoscope: Admitting and developing "new leaders for a changing world." *New England Journal of Higher Education, 24*(Winter), 12–13.

Sternberg, R. J., & Davidson, J. E. (Eds.). (2005). *Conceptions of giftedness* (2nd ed.). New York: Cambridge University Press.

Sternberg, R. J., Forsythe, G. B., Hedlund, J., Horvath, J., Snook, S., Williams, W. M., Wagner, R. K., & Grigorenko, E. L. (2000). *Practical intelligence in everyday life.* New York: Cambridge University Press.

Sternberg, R. J., & Grigorenko E. L. (Eds.). (2002). *The general factor of intelligence: How general is it?* Mahwah, NJ: Lawrence Erlbaum.

Sternberg, R. J., & Grigorenko, E. L. (2007). *Teaching for successful intelligence* (2nd ed.). Thousand Oaks, CA: Corwin.

Sternberg, R. J., Grigorenko, E. L., & Kidd, K. K. (2005). Intelligence, race, and genetics. *American Psychologist, 60*(1), 46–59.

Sternberg, R. J., & the Rainbow Project Collaborators. (2005). Augmenting the SAT through assessments of analytical, practical, and creative skills. In W. Camara & E. Kimmel (Eds.). *Choosing students: Higher education admission tools for the 21st century* (pp. 159–176). Mahwah, NJ: Lawrence Erlbaum.

Sternberg, R. J., & the Rainbow Project Collaborators. (2006). The Rainbow Project: Enhancing the SAT through assessments of analytical, practical and creative skills. *Intelligence, 34,* 321–350.

Sternberg, R. J., the Rainbow Project Collaborators, & the University of Michigan Business School Project Collaborators. (2004). Theory based university admissions testing for a new millennium. *Educational Psychologist, 39*(3), 185–198.

Terman, L. M., & Merrill, M. A. (1937). *Measuring intelligence: A guide to the administration of the new revised Stanford-Binet tests of intelligence.* Boston: Houghton Mifflin.

Thurstone, L. L. (1938). *Primary mental abilities.* Chicago: University of Chicago Press.

Turkheimer, E., Haley, A., Waldron, M., D'Onofrio, B., & Gottesman, I. I. (2003) Socioeconomic status modifies heritability of IQ in young children. *Psychological Science, 14*(6), 623–628.

Vernon, P. E. (1961). *The structure of human abilities.* London: Methuen.

6

The SAT

Quantifying the Unfairness Behind the Bubbles

JAY ROSNER

The SAT has been called the best-known brand name in education in the United States. It is a test that is admired and feared, praised and criticized. The acronym SAT originally stood for Scholastic Aptitude Test, and then for a short while it stood for Scholastic Assessment Test. Although that change was prompted by an attempt to abandon any connection between the test and the concept of aptitude, the new moniker could have been hatched in Firesign Theater's Department of Redundancy Department. The new "Assessment Test" name did not last very long; however, the SAT itself continues to do quite well, with increasing numbers of students taking it every year despite an expanding test-optional movement by colleges.

A common criticism of the SAT is that it is culturally biased. Females score lower than males on SAT Math by about 35 points (approximately ⅓ of a standard deviation, which is about 100 points on SAT Math or SAT Critical Reading). Latinos score about ⅔ of a standard deviation lower than whites, and African Americans score about 1 standard deviation lower than whites on both the Math and the Critical Reading tests. Supporters of the SAT who do not attribute performance disparities to genetic pools argue that these score gaps result from differences in wealth, income, parental education, or quality of schools attended. Critics of the SAT, while acknowledging these group differences in resources and access to relevant cultural capital, argue that the SAT adds to the gaps because of its structure and content.

The SAT could exacerbate group differences if its questions systematically benefit one group over another. In the past, critics used to cite the famous SAT verbal analogy "oarsman::regatta" to demonstrate the obvious skewing of SAT content. Yet in recent years there has been only the occasional SAT question that appears biased on its face. Critics have had to argue backward, claiming disparate SAT scores prove test unfairness—and that is a compelling argument primarily to those who already accept the conclusion. Is there anything new that can be said about the relative social neutrality and fairness of the SAT?

There is a substantial body of relatively unexamined evidence pertinent to test fairness that permits us to move the discussion forward. Unfortunately, it is kept in the vise grip of the test developers, the Educational Testing Service (ETS) and the College Board; it is nearly impossible to obtain this evidence. The information is called "item level data," and it details the performance of each individual SAT "item," which is the word used by test developers to refer to an SAT question. This chapter is based upon two sets of ETS's item level data from two different years of actual SAT tests. The data permit a discussion of SAT content that is quantified, based upon characteristics of individual test questions, which allows us to evaluate the group performance impact of question selection in the testing process.

Questions do not just randomly appear on the SAT. ETS uses a careful, deliberate process to choose questions. To understand the question selection process one needs to be familiar with the concept of *pretesting*. New questions are written and reviewed, and then placed in an unscored (also called variable, or experimental) section on an actual, official SAT form. Tens of thousands of students answer these new questions, and ETS then analyzes the results from those students.

Those unfamiliar with the SAT may wonder why students would expend time and energy answering questions that do not contribute to their SAT scores. Students do not know which section is the unscored section on an SAT—it looks just like a scored section. Students answer the questions on the unscored section because it could be a scored section. There is some deception involved, although to be fair to ETS, students are notified of the existence of the unscored section in material they read before they take the SAT. Therefore, students treat the unscored section seriously because they do not know which one it is, and ETS gets informative pretesting data as a result.

After ETS has had a chance to analyze the data from students' answers to the new questions on the unscored section, it then decides whether each new question is performing sufficiently well to be considered for future use on a scored section of the SAT. If the question "passes" its pretest and generates acceptable answering data for ETS, the question will be selected for future use on a scored section. If the question "fails" its pretest by generating unacceptable data, it is either rejected for future use or modified. If modified, it is placed in subsequent unscored section for ETS to determine whether it will "pass" its pretest in modified form.

SAT Math Question Selection: Impact by Gender

As stated previously, females score about 35 points lower, on average, than males do on SAT Math. This has been the case for decades. Professor Janet Hyde (Hyde, Lindberg, Linn, Ellis, & Williams, 2008), in a 2008 study concluding that girls now perform as well as boys on the most widely used standardized math tests, hypothesized that this persistent SAT Math gender difference is a result of more females from a wider ability range taking the SAT than males; however, where populations of test takers are relatively equal (as in Maine, which requires all of its high school graduates to take the SAT), the average gap is reduced by only about half. A troubling SAT Math gap remains between genders; furthermore, on SAT Math there are many more highly scoring males than females.

Sample SAT Question #1

Suppose that all of the questions on the Math section of the SAT were selected in such a manner that females did better than males on 99% of the questions chosen to appear on scored sections of the test.

First, could this even be done? Second, would it be fair to skew the selection of SAT math questions in such a way to favor females? There has been considerable controversy in recent years on the subject of women and math/science achievement. Former Harvard President Lawrence Summers created a firestorm in academia in 2005 by volunteering his opinion that there were more male than female scientists because of innate differences between men and women, and not because of discrimination against women. Perhaps the SAT can add to our understanding of this topic.

Let's start by looking at an SAT question (College Board, 2000a):

$$\frac{4K8}{3} = m$$

In the equation above, K is a digit in the three-digit number $4K8$, and m is a positive integer. Which of the following could be the digit K?

    (A) 1
    (B) 3
    (C) 4
    (D) 5
    (E) 7

This is an actual SAT math question that appeared on the test administered in October 2000. The correct answer to this "three-digit number" question is (B) 3. There are much more important issues here than the correct answer:

namely, Who is getting this question correct? Are high school boys doing better on this question than high school girls, or vice versa?

For convenience, let's divide SAT math questions into three categories:

1. *Male* questions are items for which correct answers are given by a higher percentage of males than females,
2. *Female* questions are items for which correct answers are given by a higher percentage of females than males,
3. *Neutral* questions are items for which correct answers are given by exactly the same percentages of males and females.

How can anyone possibly know whether any question is a male question, a female question, or a neutral question? The process for determining this is actually quite simple. Students indicate their gender when they sign up for the SAT, on a form called the Student Descriptive Questionnaire. One of the many things the ETS can tabulate after pretesting a question is which gender is better at getting the question correct.

So, is the "three-digit number" question given here a male question or a female question? It is *not* a neutral question. It is either a male question or a female question. Before reading on, you are invited to take a few moments to try to guess whether this question is a male question or a female question.

A slightly higher percentage of females than males answer it correctly: 88% of females answered it correctly on the October 2000 SAT, as compared to 87% of males. Yes, this 1% difference is very small and arguably insignificant, but the importance of this very small gap will be revealed later.

Back to the sample SAT question posed earlier: What if all the questions on the Math section "favored" females in the same way as this question does, albeit by larger differences? What if we pretested, sorted, and picked through questions until we came up with a lot of math questions that favored females, and then put together an SAT that included, say, 99% female math questions?

Many would see that as skewing the Math part of the SAT in a deeply unfair manner, biasing it in favor of females. They would object to females being given an advantage of having nearly every question rigged in their favor. Certainly some women (and men) would feel quite differently and would favor skewing the Math section of the SAT in this manner to help counter decades of educational unfairness to young women in math and math-related fields.

One argument in favor of slanting the SAT in favor of females in this way is a "reparations" argument. Females have a history in the United States of first being excluded and then being discouraged from high-level academic achievement in the STEM (science, technology, engineering, and math) fields. Designing the SAT Math section so that it benefits females over males could be seen as an appropriate counterbalance to prior unfairness, a kind of compensation for past injustice. Our judicial system often works this way—where injury has been caused, courts can order changes to produce a remedy to rectify the harm and compensate for it.

The counterargument is that skewing the SAT in favor of any group is academically unjustifiable. If the SAT were designed to benefit females, many would complain that it would introduce a fundamental unfairness into college admissions, an unfairness benefiting females in an unjust manner.

If just the thought of this troubles you, please be assured that this particular skewing of the SAT (by choosing math questions so 99% of them favor females) does *not* currently exist. Let's examine just how the Math section of the SAT actually operates with respect to gender.

Two data sets purchased from ETS permit us to shed light on this issue: one data set is from the October 1998 SAT, and the other is from the October 2000 SAT. The "three-digit number" question above appeared on the October 2000 SAT. ETS provided item level data on all the test answers supplied by 100,000 randomly chosen test takers who took that SAT on each of those two dates (a total of about 400,000 students take the test every October), which constitutes a robust, representative sample of all the test takers on that date. ETS also provided those same students' answers to questions about their race, gender, and ethnicity. These data were tabulated in a way that permits us to determine the percentage of males and the percentage of females answering each question correctly.

In 1998 and in 2000, each SAT consisted of 138 test questions: 60 math questions and 78 verbal questions. The test was modified somewhat in 2005, and the numbers of these questions have decreased slightly, to 54 math questions and 67 verbal (now called critical reading) questions on the test today; however, 49 "writing" bubble-in (i.e., no writing involved) questions have been added since 2005, along with a 25-minute essay, so the SAT is now significantly longer than it had been previously.

For the purpose of this analysis, ETS has maintained that scores for the Verbal (or Critical Reading) and Math sections obtained after the modifications in 2005 are fully comparable with scores obtained prior to 2005, so it is reasonable to assume that the way questions are selected has not changed significantly since 2005.

For the actual SATs given in October 1998 and October 2000, let us explore how gender was reflected in the nature of the math questions, specifically the issue of how many female-slanted questions there were and how many male-slanted questions there were. Each of the two tests (from 1998 and 2000) included 60 math questions, so the total number of math questions in the combined data sets is 120.

Do the Questions Pass the Fairness Test?

I invite you to try to guess the number of *female-skewed questions* among the 120 total math questions analyzed. Here are some hints:

1. Of the 120 math questions, 3 questions were neutral questions. These 3 math questions were each answered correctly by exactly the same percentage of females and males. Removing these 3 questions from the 120 total, there are 117 remaining math questions that are either female questions or male questions.
2. Recall that, on average, males score higher than females on SAT Math. Therefore, one might assume that there would be more male-preference questions than female-preference questions among the 117 remaining math questions, and this assumption is correct.
3. One may infer that since half of 117 is 58.5, the number of male questions would be at least half, and the number of female questions would be less than half, or fewer than 58.

How many of the 117 non-neutral SAT math questions were female skewed? Please pause a moment, and guess the number before reading on.

What the Data Show

Of the 117 math questions that were either male- or female-skewed questions, only one was a female question—and that was the "three-digit number" question discussed earlier. In other words, out of 117 math questions, 116 were male-slanted questions.

Extrapolating from the information presented earlier, one might assume that because the "three-digit question" generates a tiny 1% difference between the correct female and the correct male answering percentages, then all the differences may be as tiny, and this all becomes much ado about very little. On the contrary, the male–female answering percentage differences, or gaps, are not all tiny. In fact, they are quite substantial, ranging all the way up to 18%, with an average difference of about 7%. Figure 6.1 sets forth the percentage gaps for all the math questions on these two SATs, representing a simple subtraction of the female correct answering percentage from the male correct answering percentage.

Recall sample SAT Question #1 from earlier, where the reader was asked to consider an SAT Math section in which 99% of the questions were chosen to favor females over males. Let's now consider the opposite. Suppose that all the questions on the Math section of the SAT were selected in such a manner that *males* did better than *females* on 99% of the questions chosen to appear on scored sections of the test.

FIGURE 6.1   Gender Gap for All Math Questions on October 1998 and October 2000 SAT Exams

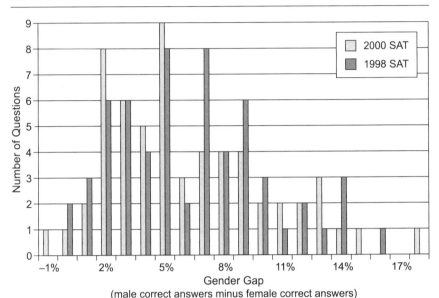

Gender Gap
(male correct answers minus female correct answers)

We can say with assurance, based upon the two robust data sets from 1998 and 2000, that it is not only possible to have a test where 99% of the math questions advantage one gender over the other, but that it has been done and continues to be done on every SAT, year in and year out. Is this fair? It would appear to be in the self-interest of males to say yes; however, many of us have daughters, and female partners, and an affinity for justice and equity, so a lot of males will find this to be profoundly unfair. Females may be less divided on this subject.

SAT Question Selection: Impact by Ethnicity

Since we have discussed SAT math questions and gender a bit, let us now switch gears and look at an SAT verbal question and ethnicity. The first example that follows concerns the test score gap between ethnic groups, so please recall that there is approximately a ⅔ standard deviation difference (about 67 points on the Math section and 67 points on Critical Reading) between the SAT scores of whites and Latinos.

Sample SAT Question #2

Consider the following "security blanket" question (College Board, 2000b):

> At bedtime the security blanket served the child as _____ with seemingly magical powers to ward off frightening phantasms.
>
> (A) an arsenal
> (B) an incentive
> (C) a talisman
> (D) a trademark
> (E) a harbinger

The correct answer is (C) a talisman. With the correct answer in mind, we are ready to tackle much more significant concerns: namely, Who answered this question correctly? Why was this question was chosen to appear on the SAT?

When students register for the SAT, they are asked to provide information on their gender and race/ethnicity. When the SAT containing this "security blanket" question was administered, there were four categories from which Hispanic students could choose to describe themselves. Of the four categories, the "Mexican-American" category was chosen by most Hispanic test takers. Because combining the categories introduces both mathematical and logistical complications, only the Mexican American category will be used in this discussion. Offense is not intended to anyone who objects to what appears to be the use of the Mexican American category as a proxy for ethnicity.

The comparison here will be directly between the performances of white students and Mexican American students. In a manner similar to the "three-digit question," the reader is challenged to determine whether this "security blanket" question is a white question or a Mexican American question. Who is doing better on this question? Do white students answer this question correctly more often, or do Mexican American students answer this question correctly more often when compared to white students?

As earlier, let's divide SAT questions into three categories:

1. *White* questions are items for which correct answers are given by a higher percentage of white students than Mexican American students.
2. *Mexican American* questions are items for which correct answers are given by a higher percentage of Mexican American students than white students.

3. *Neutral* questions are items for which correct answers are given by exactly the same percentages of white students and Mexican American students.

So, is the "security blanket" question a white question or a Mexican American question?

This question was answered correctly by 49% of Mexican American students and 46% of white students. The difference, or gap, in this case is 3%, which admittedly is not large. But at stake here is the cumulative effect of multiple questions being on a test that advantage or disadvantage one ethnic group over another. How large is the ethnic question gap problem?

Going back to the 1998 and 2000 SATs referred to earlier, let us explore how ethnicity was reflected in the nature of the verbal and math questions. There were 78 verbal questions and 60 math questions on each of the two tests (from 1998 and 2000), so the total number of verbal and math questions in both data sets is 276.

Do the Questions Pass the Fairness Test?

This time, I encourage you to try to guess the number of *Mexican American questions* among the total 276 verbal and math questions analyzed. Here are some hints:

1. Of the 276 verbal and math questions, 1 question is a neutral question. There are 275 remaining verbal and math questions that are either Mexican American questions or white questions.
2. On average, whites score higher than Mexican Americans on the SAT Verbal and Math sections. Therefore, there would be more white questions than Mexican American questions among the 275 remaining verbal and math questions.
3. So, since half of 275 is 137.5, the number of white questions would be at least half, and the number of Mexican American questions would be less than half, or fewer than 137.

How many of the 275 non-neutral SAT questions were Mexican American questions? As before, kindly stop and make a guess before proceeding.

What the Data Show

Of the 275 verbal and math questions, only one is a Mexican American question! And that was the "security blanket" question from earlier. Before delving into the remaining 274 white verbal and math questions, we should stir into the mix the issue of race.

SAT Question Selection: Impact by Race

As with ethnicity, we will look at racial effects by contrasting the differences between two racial groups: blacks and whites. As mentioned earlier, on the SAT blacks score about 1 standard deviation lower than whites (about 100 points on math questions and 100 points on verbal/critical reading questions).

Sample SAT Question #3

Here is another SAT verbal question, the "actor's bearing" question (Marcus, 1999):

> The actor's bearing on stage seemed _____; her movements were natural and her technique _____.
>
> (A) unremitting . . . blasé
> (B) fluid . . . tentative
> (C) unstudied . . . uncontrived
> (D) eclectic . . . uniform
> (E) grandiose . . . controlled

The answer is (C) unstudied . . . uncontrived. As before, we'll tackle the more important issues: namely, Who answered this question correctly? Were there racial differences in response to this question?

The comparison here will be directly between the performances of white students and black students. In a manner similar to the "three-digit question" and the "security blanket" questions above, the reader is challenged to determine whether this "actor's bearing" question is a white question or a black question. Who is doing better on this question? Do white students answer this question correctly more often blacks, or do black students answer this question correctly more often than whites?

As earlier, let's divide SAT questions into three racial categories:

1. *White* questions are items for which correct answers are given by a higher percentage of white students than black students.
2. *Black* questions are items for which correct answers are given by a higher percentage of black students than white students.
3. *Neutral* questions are items for which correct answers are given by exactly the same percentages of white students and black students.

So, is the "actor's bearing" question a white question or a black question?

The "actor's bearing" question is a *black* question, with 8% more blacks than whites answering it correctly.

Again, going back to the 1998 and 2000 SATs, we can examine how race was reflected in both the verbal and the math questions. There were 78 verbal questions and 60 math questions on each of the two tests (from 1998 and 2000), so the total number of verbal and math questions in both data sets is 276.

Do the Questions Pass the Fairness Test?

Finally, I invite you to try to guess the number of *black questions* among the total 276 verbal and math questions analyzed. Here are some hints:

1. Of the 276 verbal and math questions, there are no neutral questions.
2. On average, whites score higher than blacks on the SAT Verbal and Math sections. Therefore, there are more white questions than black questions in the pool of 276 verbal and math questions.
3. Since half of 276 is 138, the number of white questions would be at least half, and the number of black questions would be less than half, or fewer than 138.

How many of the 276 SAT questions were black questions? Once again, please guess the number before reading further.

What the Data Show

Of the 276 verbal and math questions, there were zero black questions. Each and every one of the 276 questions were white questions in this white/black comparison.

What about the "actor's bearing" black question that appears above? Why doesn't that appear in the tally? I apologize for sandbagging the reader. The "actor's bearing" question, although a black question, never appeared on a scored section of the SAT. Apparently it was rejected because a higher percentage of blacks than of whites answered that question correctly in the pretesting phase. The data set forth above relative to that question were pretesting data, not data from a scored section. So, black questions do exist, but it appears that none ever make it onto a scored section of the SAT. Black students may encounter black questions, but only on unscored sections of the SAT.

Why Are Questions Chosen in This Manner?

Through the pretesting process the test developer obtains gender, ethnicity, and race data about all items that appear in unscored sections *before* the questions are chosen to appear on scored SAT sections. The breakdowns described—of the numbers of female questions, Mexican American questions, and black questions that appear on scored sections—are not happenstance. On the contrary, all of the selected questions were chosen after careful pretesting and after the pretesting data were analyzed by the test developer, ETS.

In a very short article that appeared several years ago, I endeavored to clearly describe why and how this happens, in the fewest words possible:

> Each individual SAT question ETS chooses is required to parallel the outcomes of the test overall. So, if high-scoring test-takers—who are more likely to be white (and male, and wealthy)—tend to answer the question correctly in pretesting, it's a worthy SAT question; if not, it's thrown out. Race and ethnicity are not considered explicitly, but racially disparate scores drive question selection, which in turn reproduces racially disparate test results in an internally reinforcing cycle. (Rosner, 2003, p. 24)

The process described above is point bi-serial correlation, a key methodology used by psychometricians to construct admission tests such as the SAT, ACT, GRE, LSAT, GMAT, MCAT, and many other bubble tests. Put another way, the profile of the answering cohort for each individual question should parallel the answering cohort of the test overall. If you are a psychometrician designing a test, you want the students who are adept at the test to tend to answer the questions correctly, and the students who are not adept at the test to tend to answer incorrectly.

The data cited above demonstrate that 99% of SAT math questions chosen to appear on scored sections have to be answered correctly by a higher percentage of males than females, a higher percentage of whites than Mexican Americans, *and* a higher percentage of whites than blacks, *simultaneously*. It may or may not be an easy task to accomplish this, but ETS certainly prides itself on its extensive process that creates this result.

Discussions of these data sets are met with a range of reactions. Often, a concern is expressed as to what ETS has to say about this kind of analysis. ETS's primary contention on fairness is that their Differential Item Functioning (DIF) process ensures that all the SAT questions are chosen in a fair manner. The results of DIF are set forth in the analysis above, since the specific questions used above (except for the one question from pretesting) "passed" the DIF process, as did all of the rest of the 276 questions in the two data sets.

ETS appears to be safe in continuing to use these question selection methods. Why? It is hard to imagine anyone powerful enough to confront ETS effectively on this topic, let alone get additional item level data. Admissions officers from universities requiring the SAT could request item level data, but challenging ETS by merely asking this question might be threatening to anyone who wants to continue a career in admissions.

ETS should be required to make item level data available to anyone who requests it, at fees that were applicable ($500 per test) when the data were last available to the public (up until about 2002). Withholding item level data appears to be both ETS's prerogative and policy in the absence of pressure to release the data. Any college could, and should, make the ability to obtain item level data a condition of that college requiring students to submit SAT scores. Perhaps there is a college (or a consortium of colleges) that has the courage to do so.

I have been denied additional SAT item level data, and I am aware of university deans who have asked and have been refused item level data by another admissions test developer. By the way, the "actor's bearing" question was a rejected question provided by ETS to a newspaper reporter. It appeared in a sidebar to an article about the fairness of the SAT. The publicly available data on rejected SAT questions are limited to partial data on about a dozen questions given by ETS to a few reporters, so no study of rejected questions is possible.

Another common reaction to the findings I have described is the suggestion that someone should litigate against ETS on the basis of this kind of analysis. I served on the legal team for what might be the only two successful lawsuits brought by individual students against ETS, and both were long, expensive, and painful despite the victories attained. The annual revenues of ETS, when last checked, were approaching one billion dollars, so anyone who considers suing without substantial resources to spend is not being realistic. It might be interesting if several thousand students, when signing up for the SAT, first demanded a test that did not contain 99% white questions, and then later filed cases in their local small claims courts demanding a refund of their test fees based upon the nature of the test they were provided.

On a related note, several states currently forbid the use of affirmative action in state university admissions through legal provisions that usually read like this:

The state shall not discriminate against, or grant preferential treatment to, any individual or group on the basis of race, sex, color, ethnicity, or national origin in the operation of public employment, public education, or public contracting. (California Constitution, Sec. 31 (a))

Does the structure of the SAT, with 99% of questions favoring whites over blacks and Mexican Americans, constitute "preferential treatment" for whites when state universities require the SAT for admissions? How about the LSAT, or other admissions tests?

Unfortunately, there is no national regulatory body that regulates the high-stakes world of admissions testing. And, in this era when credit default swaps and derivatives may become subject to meaningful regulation, perhaps it is finally time to subject admissions testing to regulatory scrutiny.

Note

I thank Professor Martin Shapiro of Emory University in Atlanta, whose generous assistance has been invaluable.

References

College Board. (2000a). *October 2000 SAT,* section 1, question number 6. New York: Author.

College Board. (2000b). *October 2000 SAT,* section 2, question number 7. New York: Author.

Hyde, J. S., Lindberg, S. M., Linn, M. C., Ellis, A. B., & Williams, C. C. (2008). Gender similarities characterize math performance. *Science, 321*(5888), 494–495.

Marcus, A. D. (1999, August 4). To spot bias in SAT questions, test maker tests the test. *Wall Street Journal.*

Rosner, J. (2003, April 14). On white preferences. *The Nation,* p. 24.

7

The SAT as a Predictor of Success at a Liberal Arts College

KEVIN RASK and JILL TIEFENTHALER

Confidence in the SAT has declined in recent years. From the increase in testing time resulting from addition of a writing component in 2005 to the scoring scandal in 2006 to the recent increase in the number of colleges that do not require the SAT for college admissions, the test that was once widely accepted as an objective measure for comparing college applicants is increasingly under fire. The chief complaint against the SAT is that it is not the best predictor of college success but is highly correlated with parental education and income and, therefore, contributes to perpetuating the inequality in higher education. This criticism comes at a time when highly selective colleges are being called on to address the fact that the vast majority of their students continue to come from families of high socioeconomic status.

The debate over the SAT continues in the higher education community, and selective institutions are divided on the weight it should be given in admissions decisions. While some schools are dropping the SAT because of its potential bias, others are giving it increased weight in admissions decisions. Drew University president Robert Weisbuch wrote that his institution dropped the SAT in 2006 to improve the applicant pool and encourage high-quality students of color to apply, and also because it showed little correlation with student performance (Weisbuch, 2005). Many college presidents at top liberal arts institutions apparently agree. Bates, Bowdoin, Hamilton, Holy Cross, Smith, and Middlebury have all made the SAT optional in recent years. In 2008, Wake Forest University became the first top-ranked university to go test-optional, followed by New York University in 2009. However, most selective colleges continue to require the SAT and some are even giving it more weight in admissions decisions. For example, a few years ago Towson University announced an experimental program to enroll more young men who score higher on the

SAT but have lower high school grades than those admitted under Towson's regular standards (Wilson, 2007).

The growing debate on the SAT makes it clear that research is needed to examine the efficacy of the test. Is the SAT a good measure of student ability? Is it equally predictive across race, gender, and socioeconomic status? Are there other variables available in the admissions file that can be used instead? Perhaps variables that are less correlated with socioeconomic status? The work described in this chapter employs improved econometric techniques and a rich data set from a highly selective liberal arts college to build on the literature that examines the usefulness of the SAT in predicting college performance.

We analyzed data from a 17-year panel following students through their college careers. In this chapter we present descriptive summaries of our source data, and then provide results of modeling studies evaluating the relationships of college GPA with various types of information readily available in admissions files. Modeling results are given for the study group as a whole and for subgroups delineated by gender, race, and financial factors. We look at the explanatory power of the SAT score alone and in conjunction with other academic and personal data. For two models, we also examine predictive power by subgroup to determine whether the SAT predicts college GPA better for some groups than for others. For example, if SAT prep courses do give wealthy students an advantage (as many believe), it is likely the SAT score will have less predictive power for wealthy students than for aided students. Also, some argue that the SAT is biased against women; if that is the case, the SAT score may have more predictive power for men than for women.

All previous work has relied on the reported college GPA as the measure of success. However, this variable may be a biased indicator, because the student's choice of major dramatically impacts GPA. If weaker students are drawn to less demanding courses or majors, or less ambitious students are drawn to courses or majors with relative grade inflation, measures of student performance in those classes will lose some of their predictive power. To eliminate this potential bias, we converted the raw GPA to a z-scored GPA that uses a person's relative rank in a course as the indicator of performance and, therefore, severs the link between course choice and the nominal grade.

Our data are derived from student cohorts entering in fall 1992 through fall 2008. We initially looked at two main samples: (a) the total sample, which was used to examine first-year GPA; and (b) the graduated sample, a somewhat smaller sample consisting only of graduates, which was used for models of graduating GPA. To be included in the total sample, students had to complete their first year; to be included in the graduated sample,

TABLE 7.1 Descriptive Statistics for Graduated Sample and Total Sample

Group	Mean	75th percentile	25th percentile
GPA	3.16 / 3.11	3.44 / 3.43	2.91 / 2.87
SAT	1292 / 1299	1370 / 1380	1230 / 1230
Female	51.7% / 50.9%		
Minority	8.5% / 9.8%		
Financial aid	43.7% / 40.6%		

Note: Data are reported as Graduated / Total. Numbers of observations: 8529 / 11,724.

they had to graduate by the spring of 2008. The two samples are similar in their characteristics, except for the smaller number and higher GPA in the graduated sample (see Table 7.1). Because our findings were largely similar for the two samples, here we report modeling results based solely on the graduated sample.

The Explanatory Power of the SAT

Of primary interest in this study is the relationship between one's SAT score and one's college GPA. Figure 7.1 illustrates simple scatter diagrams for these variables. From both plots it is clear that there is a relationship between the two factors. These are the kinds of scatter diagrams that lead to correlation coefficients like those reported in both the psychology and the economics literature.

However, it is also clear from these figures that there are two important characteristics of the relationship. First, it is very imprecise. There is significant scatter—that is, high variance—whether you are looking at graduat-

FIGURE 7.1 College GPA versus Total SAT Score

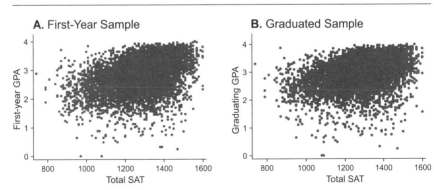

FIGURE 7.2   Graduating GPA for Those with 1200 and 1400 Total SAT Scores, Graduated Sample

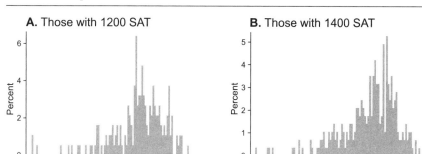

ing GPA or first-year GPA. The second important feature of these graphs is that the slope is very flat. The plots are upward sloping, signifying the positive relationship between the two variables. However, the actual difference between the average GPAs of people with quite different SAT scores is not very large. Figure 7.2 takes vertical slices out of Figure 7.1B (graduated sample) at two points—SAT scores of 1200 and 1400—to further illustrate these issues. It is clear that the average GPA for those with a 1200 SAT is less than that for those with a 1400. However, the variability is also clear. There is a significant portion of 1200 SAT people with GPAs between 2.0 and 3.0, just as there is for the population with 1400 SAT. These issues of variability and slope are explored more formally in the discussion that follows.

We evaluated the marginal explanatory power of the SAT through a series of GPA equations that used readily available admissions information. Because SAT scores, high school grades (HSGPA), and advanced placement (AP) credits overlap to some extent in what they measure, our strategy was to use multivariate regression analysis to examine the independent explanatory power of each. Here we report the R^2 from the equations as the measure of the proportion of variance across GPAs explained by the factors in each model. The models range from simple regressions with SAT score or HSGPA, for example, to multiple regressions that add sociodemographic characteristics.

Table 7.2 presents the R^2 from seven models. In column 1 the results from a simple model of graduating GPA versus SAT score are reported. In the full sample, the SAT explains 15% of the variability in graduating GPA. Similarly, HSGPA explains 17% and AP credits 11% (columns 2 and 3). The significant overlap in these measures of academic ability is evident in column 4, which contains the results from a multiple regression model that

TABLE 7.2 R^2 (%) from Ordinary Least Squares (OLS) Models of Graduating GPA and Academic and Sociodemographic Characteristics

Group (n)	(1) SAT	(2) HSGPA	(3) AP credits	(4) All acad	(5) (4) – SAT	(6) Full model	(7) (6) – SAT
Full sample (8362)	15	17	11	27	22	31	28
Men (3973)	19	14	12	27	21	28	23
Women (4389)	16	15	12	27	22	27	24
White (7637)	12	16	11	24	22	28	25
Minority (1013	15	12	8	23	17	28	20
Full-pay (4667)	6	12	9	19	17	24	22
Aided (3695)	25	21	14	35	27	38	33
Aided							
Parent income, Q1	23	25	12	38	30	43	38
Parent income, Q2	25	21	14	35	27	38	33
Parent income, Q3	21	21	13	32	26	36	31
Parent income, Q4	18	21	15	31	28	35	31

controls for all three factors. In total, those three factors explain 27% of the variability for the full sample. To demonstrate the marginal benefit of the SAT score, column 5 contains the results for the model shown in column 4 after dropping SAT from the equation. For the full sample, the R^2 goes from 27% down to 22%, a loss of 5 percentage points of explanatory power. To further investigate the overlap, we evaluated a more complete model that included race, gender, and region of the country, in addition to the academic factors. This "full" model explains 31% of the variability in the full sample. Finally, dropping the SAT from the full model gives the results in column 7, where we lose 3 percentage points of explanatory power by not knowing someone's SAT in the admissions process.

Looking at the various subgroups reveals significant heterogeneity among the influences (Table 7.2). The biggest difference is among aided and full-pay students. For full-pays the SAT on its own explains 6% of the variability in GPA. When more inclusive models are estimated, the marginal explanatory power of the SAT for full-pays drops by 2 percentage points. The SAT holds a little more predictive power for men than for women; however, the marginal explanatory power of the SAT is similar across gender. In terms of race, the SAT holds more marginal explanatory power for minorities when compared with whites. For the full model, dropping the SAT from a GPA equation leads to an 8 percentage point drop in R^2 for minorities, while the effect for whites is only 3 percentage points. The link between SAT and income is also evident in the lower panel of Table 7.2. While the marginal explanatory power is largely similar across the aided income quartiles, the total explanatory power of the GPA equations is larger for the lower income quartiles. The results in Table 7.2 illustrate quite vividly what Carl Brigham, the man responsible for development of the original SAT, came to realize not long after it began to be widely used. Lemann (1999) reports that in an unpublished manuscript Brigham wrote that the standardized testing movement was based on

> one of the most glorious fallacies in the history of science, namely, that the tests measured *native intelligence* purely and simply without regard to training or schooling. . . . The test scores very definitely are a composite including schooling, family background, familiarity with English, and everything else. (p. 34)

Predicting College GPA Based on the SAT

Evaluating explanatory power is one way to investigate the usefulness of the SAT in the admissions process. Examining the actual differences in GPA across students gives one a sense of the magnitude of the impact of SAT differences on expected academic outcomes. From the multivariate regression models we can confidently assert that SAT scores are positively correlated with both first-year and graduating GPAs. An important policy question that arises from this conclusion is, What is the expected difference in GPA when comparing applicants with different SATs? For example, two applicants look similar on paper, but one has an 1100 SAT score and another has a 1200. What is our best guess at the likely difference in their college GPAs?

Table 7.3 displays the slope estimates from our GPA models that include the SAT. Column 1 contains simple regression results, and the changes from column 1 to columns 2 and 3 illustrate the bias inherent in univariate analysis. Because of the correlation between SAT score and HSGPA, models with the SAT as the only explanatory variable suffer from omitted variables bias, because some of the effect of high school grades is being

TABLE 7.3 $\widehat{\beta}_{SAT}$ from OLS Models of Graduating GPA

Group	(1) SAT	(2) All acad	(3) Full model
Full sample	0.0013	0.0008	0.0008
Men	0.0015	0.0010	0.0009
Women	0.0012	0.0008	0.0007
White	0.0012	0.0007	0.0008
Minority	0.0011	0.0008	0.0008
Full-pay	0.0009	0.0004	0.0005
Aided	0.0015	0.0010	0.0010

attributed to the SAT. When the other main factors are accounted for (columns 2 and 3), the results are remarkably stable across specifications. For the full sample results from the full model, the β estimate of 0.0008 implies that the expected difference in GPA between our hypothetical applicants with 1100 and 1200 SAT scores is 0.08. To put this in some context, estimates of the gender difference in GPA in these models—the average amount that a woman's GPA differs from a man's, holding the other included factors constant—are around 0.17. That is more than double the effect of a 100-point difference in SAT score. Stated in another way, it takes about a 200-point difference in SAT scores to erase the gender deficit that men face in college GPA.

How Much Do Differences in SAT Scores Really Matter?

The results from the previous section highlight the average difference in estimates of college GPA based upon differences in SAT scores. In this section, we use the error inherent in average GPA to illustrate the confidence with which we can identify differences in applicants' academic outcome based upon their SAT scores. For example, in Figure 7.2 we illustrated a broad range of college academic outcomes from those with 1200 and those with 1400 SAT scores. Looking at the ranges, there is significant overlap in GPA between these two groups of students. In this section, we formalize this comparison by examining 95% confidence intervals for GPA from a set of SAT scores. We begin with all those with a score of 1000 and then increment it by 50 until we reach the final group, those with an SAT score of 1500. Table 7.4 shows the average graduating GPA for each group. It is

TABLE 7.4   Mean Graduating GPA and 95% Confidence Intervals by SAT Group

SAT group (n)	Mean GPA	Lower limit	Upper limit
1000 (31)	2.58	2.43	2.74
1050 (62)	2.71	2.58	2.84
1100 (74)	2.77	2.65	2.88
1150 (97)	2.81	2.71	2.92
1200 (202)	2.95	2.88	3.02
1250 (289)	3.11	3.07	3.15
1300 (518)	3.16	3.12	3.19
1350 (424)	3.19	3.15	3.23
1400 (305)	3.28	3.23	3.33
1450 (172)	3.28	3.21	3.35
1500 (77)	3.39	3.28	3.50

clear that as the SAT score increases, the average GPA also increases, from 2.58 to 3.39 for the range illustrated here. However, looking at the lower and upper limits of a 95% confidence interval around each mean, we can see that the mean GPA for people with a 1000 SAT is indistinguishable from the GPA those with an 1150. The upper limit (2.74) for those with a 1000 is higher than the lower limit (2.71) for those with an 1150. This example is the broadest range where outcomes are statistically identical at the 95% level, but other groups are identical in ranges of 50 or 100 points.

The results in Table 7.4 suggest that admissions officers should not let modest differences in SAT scores unduly influence their decisions. Evaluations and groupings should be made between applicants with 100- to 200-point differences rather than between those with 10- or 20-point differences. One should consider groups with broader ranges of scores as applicants likely to have equivalent college academic outcomes.

The SAT Is a Poor Predictor of Academic Success in College

The SAT, long considered an objective measure for comparing college applicants, has come under increased scrutiny in recent years. The debate centers around the question of how useful the SAT is in predicting college success and what role the test plays (or should play) in limiting access to higher education. Using improved econometric techniques and a rich data set from a highly selective liberal arts college, we examined the usefulness of the SAT in predicting college performance, as judged from a z-scored GPA based on the student's relative rank in each course. For the study group as a whole and for subgroups delineated by gender, race, and financial factors, we examined the explanatory power of the SAT score alone and in conjunction with other academic and personal data, as well as the predictive power of the SAT for projecting college academic outcomes.

The results indicate that the SAT increases the explanatory power of a model based on academic plus personal data, but only marginally—by 3 percentage points (increasing R^2 from 28% to 31%). In addition, we found that the SAT has more predictive power for certain groups—men (relative to women), minority students (relative to white students), and aided students (relative to students receiving no financial aid). We also found that it takes large differences in SAT scores (more than 100 points) to generate meaningful differences in the predicted college GPA.

In summary, our results show that the SAT adds only marginally to the total predictive power of a model that takes into account other academic and personal data readily available in an applicant's admissions file. In future work examining the usefulness of the SAT in college admissions, these marginal gains in predictive power should be evaluated against the costs—sociological, psychological, and financial—of the SAT. Further, we found that the SAT has more predictive power in explaining college GPA within certain groups than it does across all students. For example, the SAT is much more valuable in predicting college success for students on financial aid than it is for students who do not receive need-based aid. This finding suggests that it is likely that students from high-income families benefit from test preparation, which elevates their SAT score independent of other academic considerations, thus diminishing the value of the test in predicting their college performance.

Our results also indicate that caution should be used when comparing small differences in SAT scores in making college admissions decisions. We found that it takes large changes in SAT scores to generate meaningful increases in the college GPA. For example, for two otherwise identical applicants with SAT scores of 1100 and 1200, the student with the 1200 is predicted to have a 0.08 higher graduating GPA. In these types of equations the gender difference in GPA is more than double this SAT difference, with women outperforming men by a GPA of about 0.17. Therefore, colleges that choose to use the SAT for evaluating applicants for admissions should be very careful not to make their decisions on the basis of small differences in SAT scores.

References

Lemann, N. (1999). *The big test: The secret history of the American meritocracy.* New York: Farrar, Straus and Giroux.
Weisbuch, R. A. (2005, November 11). Pacing myself. *Chronicle of Higher Education.* Retrieved from http://chronicle.com/article/Pacing-Myself/44984/
Wilson, R. (2007, January 26). "Towson U. gives men with low grades a chance at college." *Chronicle of Higher Education.* Retrieved from http://chronicle.com/article/Towson-U-Gives-Men-With-Low/25926/

8

The New SAT and Academic Performance at a Flagship Public University

CHRISTOPHER CORNWELL, DAVID B. MUSTARD,
and JESSICA VAN PARYS

The College Board first released the SAT in 1926, but the test did not gain widespread use in college admissions until the 1960s. By 2006, more than 90% of 4-year colleges and universities incorporated the SAT (or the rival ACT) in their admissions decisions (Zwick, 2007). The nearly universal adoption of standardized tests as screens in college admissions is usually justified by reference to their capacity to predict student academic performance, but their predictive prowess is not uncontroversial. Criticisms raised by researchers in the President's office of the University of California, recounted in earlier chapters of this book, led the tests' creators to release a new version of the SAT in 2005.

With the New SAT, the College Board dropped analogies in the Verbal (now called Critical Reading) section in favor of more reading comprehension questions, replaced quantitative-comparison with free-response questions in the Math section, and altered the Math section's content to include Algebra II. More significantly, a new section was added to test writing skills. The Writing section is divided into two parts: the first contains multiple-choice questions designed to test grammar usage and the second prompts a short essay to demonstrate the capacity for effectively communicating and supporting ideas. The addition of the Writing section increased the maximum score from 1600 points to 2400 points (800 points per section).

We were the first to offer an independent scholarly evaluation (Cornwell, Mustard, & Van Parys, 2008) of the New SAT rolled out in 2005. In this chapter, we summarize our initial findings and extend our analysis to assess the relevance of the new test to a public university's ability to predict the academic performance of youths broken down by gender and race.

The University of Georgia (UGA) is an interesting case study because, like other flagship public universities, it is very selective and attracts students with strong test scores. Its current position among flagship institutions (18th in the 2011 *U.S. News and World Report* rankings) has been established since the introduction of the state's popular HOPE Scholarship in 1993. The scholarship pays the full tuition at any public college or university in Georgia for any student who graduates from a Georgia high school with a B average and has contributed to a steady rise in selectivity.

The University of Georgia's 2006 Freshman Class

In fall 2006, with the first New SAT cohort, approximately 4300 first-year students enrolled at UGA. We included in our analysis only "typical" first-time freshmen—students who enrolled in their first course at UGA in the fall of 2006. From student-record data, we obtained information on college academic performance, high school achievement, personal characteristics, parental education, and high school attended. Tables 8.1 and 8.2 provide some perspective on the statistical composition of UGA's 2006 freshman class.

TABLE 8.1   Mean Characteristics of UGA'S 2006 Freshman Class: College Performance and High School Achievement (standard deviations in parentheses)

	White	Black	Female	Male
College performance				
First-year GPA	3.19	2.75	3.18	3.10
	(0.58)	(0.69)	(0.58)	(0.64)
Hours earned	26.36	26.09	26.65	26.12
	(4.68)	(5.21)	(4.55)	(4.93)
High school achievement				
SAT Writing	607.73	541.83	601.88	597.88
	(72.55)	(64.93)	(73.37)	(75.83)
SAT Critical Reading	614.64	555.90	603.23	613.95
	(72.83)	(65.28)	(74.72)	(74.46)
SAT Math	620.77	537.24	601.53	637.44
	(69.19)	(69.29)	(70.66)	(71.95)
High school GPA	3.78	3.62	3.80	3.73
	(0.30)	(0.31)	(0.29)	(0.32)
AP credits	8.20	3.37	7.52	8.71
	(8.98)	(5.30)	(8.26)	(9.86)
Observations[a]	3439	306	2719	1590

[a] These are the total observations for each group, not each variable. Not everyone has a valid observation for every variable. For example, a few students have missing observations on first-year GPA or earned credit hours.

TABLE 8.2   Mean Characteristics of UGA'S 2006 Freshman Class: Personal Characteristics and Parental Education (standard deviations in parentheses)

	White	Black	Female	Male
Personal characteristics				
Female	0.62	0.75		
	(0.48)	(0.43)		
Black			0.09	0.05
			(0.28)	(0.21)
Georgia resident	0.83	0.95	0.84	0.87
	(0.37)	(0.23)	(0.37)	(0.33)
U.S. citizen	0.99	0.93	0.96	0.96
	(0.11)	(0.25)	(0.19)	(0.20)
Parental education				
Father: At least a B.A.	0.87	0.72	0.84	0.87
	(0.33)	(0.45)	(0.37)	(0.34)
Mother: At least a B.A.	0.85	0.77	0.83	0.83
	(0.35)	(0.42)	(0.38)	(0.37)
Observations	3439	306	2719	1590

The top section of Table 8.1 lists first-year college GPA and credit hours earned for whites and blacks and for females and males. First-year GPA is a common target in the prediction exercise admissions officials carry out with each applicant. Table 8.1 shows that among the students in the 2006 freshman class, whites earned higher average GPAs with lower variance than blacks. The difference in mean performance was almost half a grade point. The same pattern prevailed for females with respect to males, although the differences were smaller. In terms of credit hours, all groups averaged over 26, which is 4 credits shy of a full academic-year load. However, whites and females completed slightly more credits, with females earning the greatest number.

The bottom section of Table 8.1 reports average SAT scores, high school GPA, and advanced placement (AP) credits for the class. The mean SAT scores of whites were more than 600 on each section, roughly 60 points higher than those of blacks on the Writing and Verbal sections and 80 points higher on the Math section. There is also a large racial gap in AP credits, with whites receiving about two and a half times as many as blacks. The racial differences in high school GPA are somewhat smaller. Males outperformed females on the Verbal and Math sections of the SAT, and scored an average of only 4 points lower on the Writing section. Females had higher average high school GPAs, but slightly fewer AP credits.

The race and gender breakdown given in the top section of Table 8.2 reveal that the 2006 freshman class was well over 60% female, less than

10% black, and overwhelmingly citizens of the United States and residents of Georgia. Among blacks, the predominance of females was significantly greater. Three-quarters of black students were women compared with 62% of whites. Blacks were also more likely to be Georgia residents. Parental education differed by race: at least 85% of white students had a parent with a college degree, while no more than 77% of black students did. There was essentially no difference in parental education by gender.

In sum, the typical member of the 2006 UGA freshman class was an academically high-achieving, white, female Georgia resident whose parents went to college. On average there were notable racial disparities in high school achievement and first-year college GPA. There has been little variation in this profile at UGA over the last 15 years, except that SAT scores and high school GPAs have steadily risen.

An Overview of the Empirical Analysis

The justification for using standardized tests in college admissions has evolved, but currently rests on the finding that they predict first-year grades. A common approach to appraising the value of the test is to fit a regression model of first-year college GPA in terms of the high school achievement measures in the bottom section of Table 8.1 and to use the estimated regression to predict first-year GPA. We will proceed similarly, also taking personal characteristics, parents' education, and high school attended into account.

Empirical Findings

Predicting Performance for the Entire Class

As others have found, we see that SAT Math (SATM) and SAT Verbal (SATV) scores contribute statistically significantly to the explanation of first-year GPA, conditional on high school GPA, AP credits, and the personal and family background characteristics given in Table 8.2. On average, an extra 100 SATM points predicts an additional 0.057 GPA points; the same rise in SATV predicts an additional 0.065 GPA points. High school GPA and AP credits also enter statistically significantly, with a point of high school GPA translating into about 0.82 college GPA points, and each three-credit AP exemption corresponding to about 0.027 college GPA points.

To get some perspective on what a 100-point change in an SAT score and a 1-point change in high school GPA means, consider that 1 standard deviation in each test section's score is about 75 points and 1 high school

GPA point is about 3 standard deviations. A 1 standard deviation change in AP credits is about 9. (See Table 8.1.) So, in terms of standard deviation increases, the SATV (SATM) effect is 0.049 (0.043) extra college GPA points, the AP credits effect is about 0.08 more college GPA points, and the high school GPA effect is an additional 0.25 college GPA points. On these grounds, it is fair to say that high school GPA is indeed the strongest predictor of college grades.

We find that introducing the SAT Writing (SATW) score weakens and diminishes the effect of SATV to 0.028 and reduces the effect of SATM to 0.045, leaving the effect of the SATW as the largest of the three. Increasing SATW by 100 points predicts a 0.071-point higher first-year college GPA. Including SATW does not change the high school GPA and AP credit effects. Finally, we demonstrate the empirical importance of controlling for the high school attended. Doing so causes the influence of SATM to disappear, increases the effect of high school GPA by 10%, decreases the effect of AP credits, and raises the regression R^2 by 50%; however, the effects of SATV and SATW remained essentially unaffected.

When first-year earned credit hours are used as a performance measure, we find that of the three test scores, only SATW enters the regression significantly. An extra 100 SATW points translates into an average of 0.54 more earned credit hours. High school GPA is an even stronger predictor of first-year credit hours. Earned credit hours are shown to rise by 3.6 (more than a full course) for every point of high school GPA. AP credits also matter, but the effect is small: one course exemption predicts only a 0.11 credit increase. The small impact of AP credits is not surprising because for some students AP credit is an opportunity take more (and different) courses, while for others it is a mechanism to lighten course loads.

Predicting Performance by Race and Gender

Tables 8.3 and 8.4 distinguish racial and gender differences in the relationship between college performance and SAT scores. Table 8.3 reports our findings for first-year college GPA; Table 8.4 provides the results for earned credit hours. Each column of each table gives the estimated coefficients of the SAT and high school achievement variables (with their standard errors) from regressions of the first-year college GPA or earned hours on those measures, controlling for the variables in Table 8.2 and high school attended.

First, consider the racial differences shown in Table 8.3. Two observations stand out: SAT scores do not appear to aid, and high school GPA matters much more, in predicting the success of blacks. No SAT coefficient estimate is statistically significant for blacks, although the SATV effect is

TABLE 8.3 The Relationship Between First-Year College GPA and SAT Scores, by Race and Gender (standard errors in parentheses)

Variable	White	Black	Female	Male
SAT Writing (in 100s)	0.071*	0.023	0.062*	0.064†
	(0.020)	(0.105)	(0.022)	(0.033)
SAT Verbal (in 100s)	0.026	0.111	0.031	0.011
	(0.021)	(0.106)	(0.023)	(0.032)
SAT Math (in 100s)	0.006	−0.003	0.035	−0.056†
	(0.020)	(0.089)	(0.022)	(0.033)
High school GPA	0.877*	1.235*	0.919*	0.873*
	(0.053)	(0.248)	(0.061)	(0.078)
AP credits	0.007*	0.020	0.007*	0.009*
	(0.001)	(0.015)	(0.002)	(0.002)
Observations	3435	306	2716	1589
R^2	0.49	0.71	0.57	0.55

Notes: We also included in each regression the variables in Table 8.2 and the high school attended. * indicates statistical significance at the 5% level; † indicates significance at the 10% level.

perhaps too large to be entirely dismissed. For whites, as in the overall sample, SATW enters with the strongest influence: a 100-point increase corresponds to 0.07 more college GPA points. The estimated coefficient of high school GPA for black students is 40% higher than for whites. An extra high school GPA point translates into an additional 1.23 college GPA points for blacks, but only 0.88 points for whites. One other noteworthy finding that may not stand out quite as clearly is that the fit of the regression for blacks is much higher, with an R^2 of 0.71 versus 0.49 for whites. Most of this difference is traced to the importance of knowing where a student attended high school. Without the high school controls, the R^2 values are much more similar: 0.37 for blacks and 0.31 for whites. The obvious implication is that there is much greater variance in the quality of the high schools blacks attended. Finally, AP credits do not enter the black regression significantly, but the size of the coefficient is three times that of whites, perhaps reinforcing the point about high school quality.

Next, turn to the gender-specific results. With one exception, the estimated effects of SAT scores, high school GPA, and AP credits are very similar for females and males, and the magnitudes of the regression coefficient estimates are on par with those reported from the combined sample. The one exception is SATM, whose coefficient is estimated to be 0.035 for females and −0.056 for males. Neither is very precise, but the male coefficient estimate is significant at the 10% level. The difference is likely

TABLE 8.4   The Relationship Between First-Year Earned Credit Hours and SAT Scores, by Race and Gender (standard errors in parentheses)

Variable	White	Black	Female	Male
SAT Writing (in 100s)	0.570*	0.037	0.558*	0.554†
	(0.194)	(0.993)	(0.194)	(0.314)
SAT Verbal (in 100s)	−0.193	−0.156	−0.237	−0.514
	(0.192)	(0.916)	(0.200)	(0.320)
SAT Math (in 100s)	0.235	−0.016	0.244	−0.188
	(0.167)	(0.896)	(0.184)	(0.283)
High school GPA	3.277*	5.439*	3.572*	3.666*
	(0.463)	(2.459)	(0.579)	(0.639)
AP credits	0.024†	0.172	0.041*	0.041*
	(0.014)	(0.121)	(0.016)	(0.020)
Observations	3443	306	2722	1592
R^2	0.39	0.57	0.46	0.44

Notes: We also included in each regression the variables in Table 8.2 and the high school attended. * indicates statistical significance at the 5% level; † indicates significance at the 10% level.

explained by males with higher SATM scores tending to select into more quantitative courses, which produce lower average GPAs. While almost 65% of UGA undergraduates are female, men outnumber women in business, mathematics, statistics, and most of the "hard" sciences.

The same basic pattern of racial and gender differences is shown in Table 8.4. No SAT score is statistically significant for blacks and only SATW matters for any other group. For whites, females, and males, an additional 100 SATW points corresponds to roughly 0.55–0.60 more first-year credit hours. High school GPA is a strong predictor of earned hours, and is strongest for blacks. One high school GPA point translates into an increase of 5.44 credit hours, or almost two full courses. The high school grades effect for the other groups is in the range of 3.3–3.7. Again, the model's fit is much better for blacks, whose regression R^2 is 0.57, compared with 0.39 for whites; where a student attended high school accounts for most of the difference. Dropping the high school controls yields R^2 values of 0.16 for blacks and 0.11 for whites. Finally, the coefficient estimate for AP credits remains insignificant at the usual levels but is more than five times larger than that of whites. For each three-credit AP course exemption, blacks are predicted to earn an average of about 0.5 additional credit hours.

To summarize, the data from UGA's 2006 freshman class suggest that SATV and SATM provide little independent explanatory power in predicting first-year GPA and earned hours, conditional on SATW, high school

TABLE 8.5 The Marginal Contribution of SAT Scores to Explaining the Variance in First-Year College GPA

	First-year GPA	Hours earned
White		
R^2 (without SAT scores)	0.488	0.386
R^2 (with SAT scores)	0.494	0.390
p-value of F-test for joint significance of SAT scores	0.000	0.003
Black		
R^2 (without SAT scores)	0.703	0.570
R^2 (with SAT scores)	0.708	0.570
p-value of F-test for joint significance of SAT scores	0.630	0.999
Female		
R^2 (without SAT scores)	0.560	0.460
R^2 (with SAT scores)	0.567	0.463
p-value of F-test for joint significance of SAT scores	0.000	0.011
Male		
R^2 (without SAT scores)	0.543	0.435
R^2 (with SAT scores)	0.547	0.438
p-value of F-test for joint significance of SAT scores	0.068	0.304

GPA, AP credits, some standard personal and background characteristics, and, importantly, high school attended. For blacks, none of the tests appear to matter very much. High school GPA, on the other hand, matters a great deal, and more so for blacks than for whites. While its effect is estimated less imprecisely for blacks, the same might be said for AP credits. Finally, controlling for where a student went to high school greatly improves prediction for all groups, but especially for blacks.

Testing the Joint Significance of the SAT Scores

The results in Tables 8.3 and 8.4 give the clear impression that SAT scores contribute little at the margin in predicting college success. The one exception is the new SATW score, which enters significantly for every group but blacks. However, it is possible that the three scores are sufficiently correlated with each other (or the other measures of high school achievement) that the regressions are unable to identify their independent contributions. In fact, the bivariate correlation between SATV and SATW is around 0.7, and between SATM and SATW, about 0.5.

Therefore, we directly tested the hypothesis that the three SAT scores are jointly insignificant in the college GPA and credit hours regressions, for each group. Table 8.5 reports the results of this exercise. For each case, the table presents the regression R^2 with and without the test scores included, as well as the p-value (actual significance level) of the F-statistic for the null hypothesis. Two things are immediately clear. First, including the test scores never produces more than a small marginal increase in fit. Second, the scores are jointly significant at the 5% level only for whites and females. There is weaker evidence that the test scores are jointly significant in the male first-year GPA regression.

Conclusions

The SAT and ACT are now fixtures in the college admissions landscape. They play a powerful role in quantifying academic merit. Complicating their use is the fact that scoring well on the SAT or ACT is strongly positively correlated with socioeconomic status. The growth in SAT and ACT prep courses both testify to the importance of the tests and reinforce the role of socioeconomic status in producing good scores. It was in this context that the College Board, in response to the University of California's criticisms, introduced the New SAT, adding a new Writing section and a host of changes to the traditional Math and Verbal sections.

The interesting empirical question for admissions offices is not so much what the SAT measures, but whether it aids in predicting college performance. Here we have reviewed the evidence on that question that we presented earlier (Cornwell et al., 2008) and extended our analysis to determine how the answers change by race and gender.

Perhaps surprisingly, we find that, at the margin, SATV and SATM add little to the prediction of first-year college GPA and earned hours. SATW scores contribute to the prediction of the performance of whites, but for blacks none of the tests are shown to matter. What does matter for everyone is high school GPA and, to a lesser degree, AP credits. Prediction is also significantly enhanced by controlling for where a student attended high school, especially for blacks. The importance of the high school attended is potentially troubling, because blacks in Georgia are overrepresented in districts with lower average school quality.

It is clear that the New SAT has contributed less than Georgia's HOPE Scholarship program, which is entirely based on high school grades, to the academic quality of undergraduates at the University of Georgia. Public universities may be better served by programs that partner them with high schools than by chasing after high test scores.

References

Cornwell, C. M., Mustard, D. B., & Van Parys, J. (2008, June 25). *How well does the New SAT predict academic achievement in college?* (Working paper). Athens: University of Georgia. Retrieved from http://www.terry.uga.edu/~mustard/New%20SAT.pdf

Zwick, R. (2007). College admission testing. *Report for National Association for College Admission Counseling,* pp. 1–44.

9

Predictors of Academic Success
at a Highly Selective
Private Research University

TERESA WONNELL, CHLOE MELISSA ROTHSTEIN,
and JOHN LATTING

There are two bodies of research on the impact of standardized tests on college admissions: one produced by those who work in the field of testing, often with direct ties to the organizations that sponsor the tests in question, such as the Educational Testing Service (ETS); and one that is drawn from independent studies done by individual colleges (Zwick, & Sklar, 2005). In the public discussion of the virtues or vices of high-stakes tests, the voices of professionals in the testing industry often crowd out the voices of individual college studies. This is an underappreciated yet critical problem, because the testing industry and individual colleges do not always agree on the importance of test scores in selecting academic talent (Bowen, Chingos, & McPherson, 2009; Cornwell, Mustard, & Van Parys, 2008; Geiser, 2002).

This topic was brought to national attention in 2008, when the National Association for College Admission Counseling (NACAC) issued a report calling on institutions of higher learning to "take back the conversation" about the use of standardized tests in admissions from "the media, commercial interests, and organizations outside of the college admission office" (2008). One of several recommendations laid forth in the report was that colleges and universities conduct their own validity studies evaluating the relative weight of standardized tests, high school grades, and other factors available in admissions files.

In response to NACAC's call, we, in the Office of Undergraduate Admissions at Johns Hopkins University, decided to do a validity study asking how significant standardized tests are in predicting which students will succeed at Hopkins. We were aware that we might offer a significant contribution. Our study is, to date, the only published empirical contribution evaluating the new post-2005 SAT to come from a top-tier private research university. Much of the public discussion of case studies on testing and admissions has been informed by research done at large public universities, such as the University of California and the University of Georgia, or at small liberal arts colleges, such as Bates College. We wanted to see, as some authors have suggested, if test scores were more important to highly selective private universities than to public universities or liberal arts colleges (Bowen et al., 2009).

To paint a quick picture of Johns Hopkins, we are located in Baltimore, Maryland, and are a private and highly selective research university with a current population of around 5000 undergraduate students. Johns Hopkins is known to draw students with a love of learning and an excitement about taking initiative in their studies and engaging in research. The academic quality of our students is high; for students matriculating in 2011, 87% were in the top 10% of their high school class. To use the metric of standardized tests, for the middle 50% of admitted students, their SAT Critical Reading scores fell between 630 and 740, their SAT Math scores between 660 and 770, and their SAT Writing scores between 640 and 740.

All applications receive a "holistic" review, taking into consideration both quantitative aspects (e.g., high school grades, the rigor of high school classes, and standardized tests) and more qualitative aspects (essays written by the student, recommendation letters written by teachers and counselors, and activities in which the student is involved). We make a point of not admitting or denying students purely based on quantitative aspects, such as grades and test scores.

One of our primary goals in the current study was to measure the relative contribution that high school grade-point average (HSGPA) and the SAT made to our ability to predict college grades. Previous studies agreed that HSGPA was a much stronger predictor of college GPA than the SAT. Nonetheless, there was the possibility that standardized tests were more predictive of performance at highly selective institutions than at less selective ones. In a national study of public universities, Bowen et al. (2009) found that, although HSGPA was more powerful than the SAT or ACT at every institution, the SAT/ACT had a relatively stronger predictive power at the most selective universities in their study group, in this case the University of California–Berkeley, University of California–Los Angeles (UCLA), University of Maryland–College Park, University of Michigan, University of North Carolina–Chapel Hill, and the University of Virginia. For a very selective private research university, such as Johns Hopkins, we wanted to see if standardized tests work better or less well than at less selective institutions.

Secondly, we wanted to see if the SAT works in a uniform way for all students or if there are differences by academic major in college. Most researchers have found variations between men and women, or blacks and whites, for example, in how well test scores predict college performance. We wanted to add to the literature on test-score differentials by looking at academic fields. For example, do students with hopes of majoring in engineering earn SAT Math scores that are more powerful predictors of their grades than Math scores for students who aspire to major in the humanities?

Lastly, some studies stress the advantage of "subject-based" tests, such as SAT Subject Tests or advanced placement (AP) exams, over "reasoning" tests, such as the SAT. California researchers (Geiser, 2002) found that combining the SAT II Writing test score with an SAT II score of the student's choice proved more predictive of success in college than the SAT or ACT. The Revised SAT, including a new "Writing section," materialized in 2005 largely in reaction to this research by the University of California, which showed that, among tests, the SAT II Writing test was one of the best predictors of academic performance in college. Those researchers also found that AP exam scores were very powerful indicators and the most significant predictor after high school GPA. However, they did not find that simply taking AP or other rigorous courses in high school predicted success in college (Geiser, 2009).

Method

Statistical linear regression was used to investigate the relative contributions of high school GPA as well as SAT and SAT Subject Test scores in predicting first-year college GPA. We began with a sample of 3316 students who fit these characteristics: (a) they were first-time, full-time degree-seeking freshmen; (b) they entered as a freshmen in 2006, 2007, or 2008; (c) they finished their first year of college; and (d) they had a complete set of control variables, SAT scores, and high school GPA. Students who submitted only ACT scores were not included. Our measure of student performance was spring-term college GPA. Fall GPA was not included because of a school policy that excludes freshman fall-term GPA from the cumulative GPA calculation.

Independent Variables

High school GPA, SAT scores, and SAT Subject Test scores were the independent academic variables considered in this study. As practiced by our admissions office, the HSGPA is recalculated for every applicant from a school that uses a 4.0 grading scale. This GPA, as a result, is unweighted, based on a 4.0 scale, and covers only academic courses taken in 10th and 11th grades. The SAT Critical Reading, Math, and Writing scores were used in all models that included SAT scores. The SAT Subject Test scores used were the Mathematics Level 2 score, which is strongly recommended for students applying to the engineering school, and the student's average of Biology, Chemistry, and/or Physics Subject Test scores, renamed the SAT Subject Test science score in our study. Many students interested in a major in the natural sciences take one or more of these subject tests, and using the average of the three maximized the number of observations included in analyses.

Control Variables

We controlled for demographic and high school characteristics, including gender, race/ethnicity, whether a student was recruited as an athlete, the number of AP or other rigorous courses taken in high school, the percentage of parents of students at each high school who have a bachelor's degree or higher, and whether a student was a first-generation college student. The latter two variables help control for socioeconomic status. We further controlled for socioeconomic factors by including whether the student received need-based grant aid. We also controlled for an "academic qualities" rating, which was assigned to each student by admissions counselors. This is a rating of a student's level of intellectual curiosity and engagement in learning, determined primarily from teacher and counselor recommendation letters and student essays. All of these variables are used by admissions staff to evaluate the candidate (in some cases indirectly, as with the high school's parent education level). Regression excludes cases with missing data, and thus students at high schools that do not issue grades or at foreign high schools were not included in the analyses, because we do not recalculate such grades into a 4.0 scale.

Table 9.1 shows the descriptive statistics for variables used in the analyses.

Results

Because admissions decisions are never made based on single variables, we focused on models with multiple variables. Table 9.2 shows the standardized regression coefficients and amount of variance in college GPA explained, for several models. All models contain the control variables and high school GPA, and they vary by whether SAT test scores are included, and what type (SAT and/or SAT Subject Test), in order to observe how much

TABLE 9.1   Summary Statistics

Variable	Mean	Std dev	Min	Max	N
Predictor variables					
High school GPA	3.70	0.28	2.30	4.00	3439
SAT Critical Reading	679	72	400	800	3350
SAT Mathematics	706	69	420	800	3350
SAT Writing	679	70	400	800	3304
SAT Subject Test Math Level 2	725	69	470	800	1982
SAT Subject Test science average	694	71	430	800	1987
Personal and high school characteristics					
Female	0.48	0.50	0	1	3533
White	0.48	0.50	0	1	3533
Black	0.07	0.25	0	1	3533
Hispanic	0.07	0.25	0	1	3533
Asian	0.23	0.42	0	1	3533
Other or unknown race	0.08	0.25	0	1	3533
Need-based grant	0.34	0.48	0	1	3533
AP courses index	0.70	0.46	0	1	3533
High school: % of parents with bachelor's degree	0.74	0.17	0	1	3346
First generation	0.09	0.29	0	1	3533
Academic quality rating	2.31	0.53	1	5	3533
Athlete	0.15	0.36	0	1	3533
Dependent variable					
First-year college GPA	3.20	0.58	0.125	4.00	3533

the inclusion of SAT scores added to the ability of the models to predict college GPA.

In all of the models shown in Table 9.2, high school GPA is the best predictor of college GPA, by a wide margin. As shown by the standardized regression coefficients for Model 2, a one standard deviation increase in high school GPA (0.26 grade points) is associated with an increase of 0.28 standard deviations in first-year college GPA, or 0.16 grade points. A one standard deviation increase in the SAT Critical Reading score is associated with an increase of 0.12 standard deviations in college GPA, or 0.07 grade points. The increases in college GPA associated with increases in the SAT Math and Writing scores (0.007 and 0.096 standard deviations) were smaller than for the SAT Critical Reading score. As seen by comparing Model 1 with Model 2, introducing SAT scores increased the explained variance by a little more than 2 percentage points, from around 18% to 20%, and reduced the regression coefficient of high school GPA by a very small amount. The Critical Reading and Writing scores were significant contributors to variance.

TABLE 9.2 Contribution of SAT Scores to Prediction of First Year College GPA

Model, all cohorts	N	% Explained variance	High school GPA	SAT Critical Reading	SAT Math	SAT Writing	SAT Subject Test Science	Gender	Race Black	Race Hispanic	Race Asian	JHU grant	High school rigor	Parent ed	First generation	Academic qualities rating	Athlete
Model 1	3316	17.6%	**0.291**	x	x	x	x	-0.028	**-0.148**	**-0.067**	**-0.039**	**-0.068**	**0.041**	**0.110**	**-0.034**	**0.050**	**-0.103**
Model 2	3097	19.8%	**0.280**	**0.118**	0.007	**0.096**	x	-0.014	**-0.087**	-0.031	**-0.043**	**-0.054**	0.008	**0.076**	-0.010	**0.037**	**-0.045**
Model 3[a]	1793	19.7%	**0.345**	**0.100**	0.037	**0.060**	x	0.006	**-0.066**	**-0.046**	-0.021	**-0.064**	0.009	**0.059**	0.025	**0.050**	-0.023
Model 4	1793	20.7%	**0.323**	**0.068**	-0.008	0.056	**0.135**	-0.021	**-0.066**	-0.044	-0.030	**-0.065**	-0.001	0.044	0.026	**0.045**	-0.016
Model 5	1833	19.4%	**0.323**	x	x	x	**0.166**	-0.039	**-0.075**	**-0.058**	-0.030	**-0.075**	0.009	**0.048**	0.016	**0.055**	-0.028

Notes: Standardized regression coefficients. Boldface indicates statistically significant at the 0.05 level or better. The reference group for gender is male and the reference group for race/ethnicity is white.

[a] Model 3 includes students with at least one science SAT Subject Test. However, the Subject Test science score is not incorporated as a variable.

Models 3 through 5 examine the contributions of the SAT Subject Test science average to the prediction of college GPA. Model 3 has the same variables as Model 2 (high school GPA, SAT scores, plus the control variables), but was run with just the observations that had at least one science Subject Test score in order to make better comparisons among models, because the number of observations is considerably lower. Including the Subject Test scores added surprisingly little to prediction—just 1 percentage point for the science test average (Model 3 vs. Model 4). It should be noted, however, that the Subject Tests had more predictive weight than any single SAT section, and that including the Subject Tests lowered the predictive weight of SAT scores.

Results by Academic Area of Interest

In reading applications, the primary major that an applicant indicates guides to some extent how much weight is given to various factors in his or her application. For instance, we would expect students interested in engineering or natural sciences to be stronger in mathematics and sciences, in terms of both grades and standardized testing, than students who intend to major in the humanities. Thus, we conducted separate sets of regressions for each of four broad academic areas: the natural sciences and mathematics, engineering, humanities, and social and behavioral sciences. We grouped students who had indicated that they wanted to enter the school of arts and sciences, but were undecided as to major, with the social and behavioral science students.

Natural Sciences and Mathematics

Table 9.3 shows the standardized regression coefficients and amount of variance in college GPA explained, for freshmen interested in majoring in the natural sciences or mathematics. Again, high school GPA was the single best predictor of college GPA. Including SAT scores increased the variance explained by 5.5 percentage points, from 22.9% to 28.4%, the largest increase associated with SAT scores for any of the four academic areas. The boost in variance explained due to SAT scores was large enough to capture our attention. Johns Hopkins tends to have a deep pool of qualified applicants in the natural sciences, rendering this finding potentially quite useful. The SAT Critical Reading and Math scores were both significant predictors.

When looking at the contribution of SAT Subject Tests, we again ran a regression (Model 3) with the same variables as Model 2 but only for observations that included an SAT Subject Test science average. Because subject tests are not required, many applicants do not submit scores. For this

TABLE 9.3 Contribution of SAT Scores to Prediction of First Year College GPA for Students with a Natural Science or Mathematics Interest at Time of Application

Model, all cohorts	N	% Explained variance	High school GPA	SAT Critical Reading	SAT Math	SAT Writing	SAT Subject Test Science	Gender	Race Black	Race Hispanic	Race Asian	JHU grant	High school rigor	Parent ed	First generation	Academic qualities rating	Athlete
Model 1	894	22.9%	**0.274**	x	x	x	x	0.040	**-0.238**	**-0.121**	-0.037	-0.010	0.050	**0.115**	-0.034	**0.061**	**-0.129**
Model 2	832	28.4%	**0.259**	**0.147**	**0.118**	**0.089**	x	0.047	**-0.116**	-0.058	-0.064	0.021	0.010	**0.074**	0.006	0.042	**-0.074**
Model 3[a]	512	22.4%	**0.320**	**0.152**	0.040	0.079	x	0.022	**-0.116**	**-0.096**	-0.042	0.060	-0.003	**0.089**	0.051	0.007	-0.034
Model 4	512	24.1%	**0.298**	0.106	0.001	0.064	**0.184**	-0.024	**-0.104**	-0.086	-0.043	0.056	-0.013	0.060	0.054	0.003	-0.022
Model 5	531	20.7%	**0.286**	x	x	x	**0.247**	-0.058	**-0.112**	**-0.106**	-0.035	0.023	-0.015	0.054	0.043	0.020	-0.024

Notes: Standardized regression coefficients. Boldface indicates statistically significant at the 0.05 level or better. The reference group for gender is male and the reference group for race/ethnicity is white.

[a] Model 3 includes students with at least one science SAT Subject Test. However, the Subject Test science score is not incorporated as a variable.

TABLE 9.4 Contribution of SAT Scores to Prediction of First Year College GPA for Students with an Interest in Engineering at Time of Application

Model, all cohorts	N	% Explained variance	High school GPA	SAT Critical Reading	SAT Math	SAT Writing	SAT Subject Test Math 2	Gender	Race Black	Race Hispanic	Race Asian	JHU grant	High school rigor	Parent ed	First generation	Academic qualities rating	Athlete
Model 1	1167	19.6%	**0.363**	x	x	x	x	0.038	**-0.090**	-0.042	0.042	**-0.103**	0.038	**0.092**	0.010	0.047	**-0.077**
Model 2	1125	21.5%	**0.348**	0.011	**0.166**	0.048	x	0.018	-0.043	-0.002	-0.003	**-0.097**	0.005	0.050	0.023	0.041	-0.049
Model 3	878	21.8%	**0.377**	0.009	**0.158**	0.031	x	0.028	-0.055	-0.032	-0.024	**-0.093**	0.028	0.037	0.036	0.034	-0.051
Model 4	878	23.1%	**0.367**	-0.003	0.070	0.017	**0.177**	0.008	-0.050	-0.028	-0.055	**-0.084**	0.009	0.023	0.038	0.027	-0.046
Model 5	894	22.9%	**0.367**	x	x	x	**0.218**	0.012	-0.058	-0.035	-0.051	**-0.085**	0.013	0.032	0.036	0.031	-0.053

Notes: Standardized regression coefficients. Boldface indicates statistically significant at the 0.05 level or better. The reference group for gender is male and the reference group for race/ethnicity is white.

[a] Model 3 was done with students with a Math 2 score.

smaller group, the variance explained by the model was 6 percentage points lower (Model 2 vs. Model 3) and the SAT Math score and Writing scores were no longer significant predictors. Including the SAT Subject Test science score (Model 4) increased the variance explained by 1.7 percentage points, from 22.4% to 24.1%. The Subject Test science average was a better predictor than the SAT Critical Reading score.

Engineering

Table 9.4 shows the standardized regression coefficients and amount of variance in college GPA explained, for freshmen interested in majoring in engineering. High school GPA was again the best predictor of first-year college GPA. Including SAT scores increased the explained variance in college GPA by about 2 percentage points, from 19.6% to 21.5% (Model 1 vs. Model 2). The SAT Math score was the only SAT section score that was a significant predictor.

When the SAT Mathematics Level 2 Subject Test score was introduced along with SAT scores, the explained variance increased just a little more than 1 percentage point, from 21.8% to 23.1% (Model 3 vs. Model 4). The standardized regression coefficient is similar in magnitude to that for the SAT Math score in Model 4. When the SAT Mathematics Level 2 Subject Test is considered in the model without SAT scores, as in Model 5, it does nearly as well as in Model 4, suggesting that SAT scores could be given less weight in making decisions for engineering applicants if the SAT Mathematics Level 2 Subject Test score is available.

Social and Behavioral Sciences

Table 9.5 shows the standardized regression coefficients and amount of variance in college GPA explained, for freshmen interested in majoring in the social or behavioral sciences. High school GPA was the best predictor of college GPA. Of the SAT scores, only the Critical Reading score was a significant predictor. SAT scores increased the variance by a little more than 1 percentage point, from around 26% to 27%.

Humanities

For freshmen interested in majoring in the humanities, conclusions about the relative contribution of SAT scores were more difficult to reach because of a cohort effect with the main model without SAT scores (Model 1). The variance explained by high school GPA and the control variables ranged from 10.6% for the 2006 cohort to 21.8% for the 2007 cohort, with 2008 in between. The cohort effect disappeared when SAT scores were introduced in

TABLE 9.5 Contribution of SAT Scores to Prediction of First-Year College GPA for Students with a Social and Behavioral Sciences Interest at Time of Application

Model, all cohorts	N	% Ex-plained variance	High school GPA	SAT Critical Reading	SAT Math	SAT Writing	Gender	Race Black	Race Hispanic	Race Asian	JHU grant	High school rigor	Parent ed	First gener-ation	Academic qualities rating	Athlete
Model 1	680	25.9%	**0.336**	x	x	x	−0.041	**−0.102**	−0.017	−0.005	−0.002	**0.075**	**0.184**	**−0.111**	0.060	**−0.136**
Model 2	633	27.2%	**0.316**	**0.180**	0.053	0.030	−0.054	−0.033	0.014	−0.014	0.015	0.001	**0.148**	**−0.094**	0.047	−0.043

Notes: Standardized regression coefficients. Boldface indicates statistical significance at the 0.05 level or better. The reference group for gender is male and the reference group for race/ethnicity is white. Also included in these regressions were students who were undecided arts and sciences applicants.

TABLE 9.6 Contribution of SAT Scores to Prediction of First-Year College GPA for Students with a Humanities Interest at Time of Application

Model and cohort	N	% Ex-plained variance	High school GPA	SAT Critical Reading	SAT Math	SAT Writing	Gender	Race Black	Race Hispanic	Race Asian	JHU grant	High school rigor	Parent ed	First gener-ation	Academic qualities rating	Athlete
Model 1 All cohorts	575	13.8%	**0.268**	x	x	x	−0.023	**−0.103**	−0.077	**−0.122**	−0.026	0.068	0.021	−0.069	0.039	**−0.118**
Model 1 2006	193	10.6%	**0.212**	x	x	x	0.017	−0.103	−0.063	−0.100	−0.001	0.049	0.136	**−0.188**	−0.028	−0.139
Model 1 2007	205	21.8%	**0.292**	x	x	x	−0.081	**−0.153**	**−0.147**	−0.129	−0.102	0.125	−0.061	−0.023	0.123	**−0.133**
Model 1 2008	177	11.9%	**0.304**	x	x	x	0.001	−0.038	−0.004	−0.146	0.064	−0.024	−0.048	0.020	0.022	−0.108
Model 2 All cohorts	507	19.3%	**0.278**	**0.281**	0.006	−0.031	−0.044	−0.039	−0.013	**−0.120**	−0.019	0.039	0.006	−0.058	0.027	−0.017

Notes: Standardized regression coefficients. Boldface indicates statistical significance at the 0.05 level or better. The reference group for gender is male and the reference group for race/ethnicity is white.

Model 2. For this group of students, a unique finding was that the SAT Critical Reading score was just as good a predictor of college GPA as high school GPA, perhaps the single piece of data in this study that most strongly supports the use of standardized tests. Another interesting result was that the SAT Writing test was not a significant predictor of college GPA.

Control Variables

We saw some interesting results regarding our control variables. Gender, for example, was not a significant predictor in any of the models. Race was significant in many models. For almost all academic areas, the introduction of SAT scores made the effects of race insignificant or considerably lessened. In other words, considering the SAT helped to mitigate the effect of race. However, for students interested specifically in the natural sciences, whether students were black or Hispanic was always a significant predictor of college GPA. Once SAT scores entered into the models, the regression coefficients for race became notably lower. For the group of engineering freshmen who took the Mathematics Level 2 Subject Test, race was never a factor, even in the model without SAT scores (Model 3).

Whether students received need-based aid was a significant predictor for the engineering models only, with students on aid having lower college GPAs than unaided students, on average. The high school level of parents' education, operationalized in this study as the percentage of parents at the student's high school with a bachelor's degree or higher, was a significant predictor in Model 1 for all academic areas except humanities. For natural science and engineering students, the effect of parent education went away with the introduction of SAT scores. For social and behavioral science students, parent education was a good predictor, as shown by the size of the regression coefficient. Parent education remained a significant factor when SAT scores were added to the equation and was even on par with the SAT Critical Reading score regarding its ability to predict college GPA. A second measure of parent education, whether a student was the first in his or her immediate family to attend college, was a significant predictor of college GPA only for the social and behavioral science students.

Conclusions

The data in this study show that the SAT adds little (2% overall) to our ability to predict the academic success of freshmen at Johns Hopkins. The data also indicate that HSGPA is in nearly all cases the single best predictor of first-year college GPA, a finding that can be applied to our admissions decision making.

However, there are a number of reasons to be cautious about appreciably changing the way in which we use SAT scores in our selection process. First, these results are based on one study with only one of several possible outcome variables. We would want to look at other measures of student success—such as upper-level GPA, grades in specific courses, or persistence to graduation—before considering more substantial changes.

Second, despite our inclusion of wide-ranging control variables, we are aware that no statistical model can capture all of the components of a student's academic potential. Some of these aspects are "softer" qualities, such as a student's academic engagement or personal hardships, which we consider while reading applications but are not necessarily quantifiable as variables. It is possible that test scores might be doing more than meets the eye when it comes to identifying academic potential.

Third, this study's sample was comprised only of enrolled students. However, it is the job of the Office of Undergraduate Admissions to assess thousands of applicants—more than 19,000 in the most recent cycle—some of whose profiles are quite different from those of our enrolled students. Although this study shows that standardized tests are not especially predictive of college GPA among students who have chosen to enroll at Hopkins, it is possible that test scores play a positive role as a discriminator among our entire applicant pool. In other words, restriction of range in our study sample may have lessened the ability of SAT scores to predict college GPA. However, we found that the percentage decrease in the standard deviation of HSGPA scores was greater than that of SAT scores when going from the applicant pool to our sample of enrolling students, suggesting that the restriction of range of HSGPA scores was greater than that of SAT scores. This, in turn, suggests that if restriction of range was not a factor, then HSGPA would be an even better predictor of college GPA than we found in this study, and it would still outperform SAT scores in prediction ability.

Fourth, we believe that it is reasonable to regard the SAT as a useful tool when it is employed flexibly to assess individual admissions applications. There are specific situations in which the SAT can prove valuable, and there are other cases in which test scores can be deemphasized. An example of a case in which one might deemphasize the SAT would be a student with relatively low SAT scores who nevertheless earned very high grades from a high school where grades are not given lightly and from which graduates have repeatedly proven themselves to be successful at Hopkins. In this case, it appears to be sensible to give less weight to testing when making an admissions decision.

In other cases, testing might reasonably occupy an important place in our decision making. For example, one can imagine a student who earns strong grades at a school that lacks a rigorous curriculum and has clear, documented grade inflation. When reading such a file, we would be cautious about deemphasizing SAT scores, especially if this hypothetical student wanted to major in the natural sciences, given that we now know that SAT scores explain the most variance in college GPA for freshman interested in the natural sciences. In cases where the transcript data leave the admissions committee with doubts regarding the quality or difficulty of coursework, the SAT can play a beneficial role. It seems to us to be sensible to proceed in this fashion, and to study at a later date whether test scores can help to fill a void that we sometimes see in documenting the academic preparation of applicants.

Regarding SAT Subject Tests, we were surprised they that did not add more to prediction in our sample given their significance in other studies. In future studies, we would like to examine the significance of another subject-based assessment, AP test scores. We found that merely taking rigorous classes, such as AP classes, is not a significant factor in predicting college GPA. However, it is possible that mastery of a subject, as evidenced through a high AP score, is valuable in predicting academic success in that or related subjects in college.

For example, we have internal data illustrating that AP calculus scores are powerfully correlated with grades received in Johns Hopkins introductory calculus courses. AP courses are prevalent among our applicants, admitted students, and enrolled students, and we certainly take note of high or low AP scores in the admissions process. Unfortunately, the data used in the current study did not include AP test scores, although the scores were available to admissions counselors at the time of admissions decisions. In future Hopkins research, we would like to examine AP test scores as predictor variables, because it is possible that we should emphasize these scores to a greater degree than we currently do in our selection process.

In addition to grades and testing, the admissions office will continue to consider many other factors as part of its holistic review process, never basing decisions solely on test scores or grades—or any other single measure, for that matter. That the admissions measures included in this study explain a relatively small amount of college GPA variance, in fact, is evidence that further research regarding how our office can predict academic success is necessary. Taking seriously factors such as extracurricular involvement, essays, and recommendations, which portray students in greater detail as people and students, is surely wise. And emphasis on this side of the application will remain as important as it has been.

Within the more quantitative portion of the admissions application—high school grades and standardized testing—this study suggests that it is sensible to revisit the weight we place on each of these components. But by no means does this investigation suggest that the debate about the role of standardized tests in our decision making is over. We will perennially investigate our admissions process—the aspects that we consider and the weight we place on each—and will continue to seek to uncover academic potential in all of its manifestations.

References

Bowen, W., Chingos, M., & McPherson, M. (2009). *Crossing the finish line: Completing college at America's public universities* (pp. 112–133). Princeton, NJ: Princeton University Press.

Cornwell, C., Mustard, D., & Van Parys, J. (2008). *How does the New SAT predict academic performance in college?* [working paper]. Athens: University of Georgia.

Geiser, S. (with Studley, R.). (2002). UC and the SAT: Predictive validity and differential impact of the SAT I and SAT II at the University of California. *Educational Assessment, 8*, 1–26.

Geiser, S. (2009). Back to the basics: In defense of achievement (and achievement tests) in college admissions. *Change, 41*(1), 16–23.

National Association for College Admission Counseling (NACAC). (2008). Report of the Commission on the Use of Standardized Tests in Undergraduate Admission. Arlington, VA: Author.

Zwick, R., & Sklar, J. (2005). Predicting college grades and degree completion. *American Educational Research Journal, 42*(3), 439–464.

PART III

Evaluations of Test-Optional Policies

10

Test Scores Do Not Equal Merit

Deemphasizing Standardized Tests in College Admissions

ROBERT SCHAEFFER

Approximately 850 accredited, bachelor's-degree-granting colleges and universities across the United States do not use the SAT or ACT to make admissions decisions about all or many of their incoming first-year students (FairTest, 2010). These test-optional institutions range in size and mission from multi-campus public systems, such as the University of Texas and California State University, to competitive liberal arts colleges such as Smith in Massachusetts, Muhlenberg in Pennsylvania, Lawrence in Wisconsin, and Pitzer in California. A growing number of top-ranked universities, including Wake Forest and Worcester Polytechnic Institute, have also eliminated SAT and ACT requirements.

Educators and policymakers are subjecting the SAT and ACT to unprecedented scrutiny. Increasingly, they identify standardized admissions tests as significant barriers to entry for thousands of academically qualified minority, first-generation, and low-income applicants. Often they have decided that the social and academic costs of continuing to rely heavily on these tests outweigh any possible benefits. By turning away from reliance on test scores, these institutions are promoting equity and excellence.

Many 4-year colleges and universities have long had broad concerns about the validity, equity, and educational impact of standardized admissions tests. Schools such as Bates and Bowdoin in Maine made the decision to go test-optional more than 25 years ago, recognizing that their entrance exam requirements were unnecessarily restricting their applicant pools. Other institutions, including many land grant colleges, did not require test scores from their inception, consistent with their missions. Many more analyzed their admissions numbers and found that standardized tests were simply not very good predictors of first-year college performance, which the tests purport to predict, let alone more important outcomes such as retention rates and graduation.

Schools that have dropped or sharply restricted the use of the SAT and ACT are widely pleased with the results. Regardless of size or selectivity, these institutions have seen substantial benefits, including increased diversity, more applicants, and better prepared students, as well as positive reactions from alumni, guidance counselors, and the public. Higher education institutions that reduce their emphasis on standardized admissions tests are sending a strong message that "test scores do not equal merit." For many years, one of the central arguments in favor of the SAT and ACT was that they serve as a "common yardstick." That, supposedly, enables admissions officials to compare students from different high schools and academic backgrounds. However, no one would seriously argue that a 1200 combined Critical Reading and Math score on the SAT at an affluent high school means the same thing as a similar score at a resource-starved school serving a low-income community. Even the Educational Testing Service, which produces the SAT, has criticized the "Myth of a Single Yardstick," arguing that there is "no single, primary ordering of people as 'best-qualified' or 'most meritorious' as simple notions of merit require" (Cole, 1997, p. A25). Test-optional schools have put into practice their skepticism about such false measures of merit as scores on a 3.5-hour, largely multiple-choice exam. In many cases, schools that join the ranks of test-optional colleges are merely making explicit and formal, long-standing admissions practices that depend very little on standardized admissions tests.

If, as the testmakers' publications acknowledge (Kobrin, Patterson, Shaw, Mattern, & Barbuti, 2008, p. 5) and many colleges practice, high school achievement is the strongest predictor of undergraduate academic performance, with test results providing no more than supplemental information, there are only two possible reasons for emphasizing such scores in the admissions process. Both involve changing the admit/deny decision that would be made in the absence of the test. If information from the SAT and ACT does not alter the fate of applicants, then these tests are clearly of no use to admissions officers.

The first possible justification for looking at test scores would be to identify students whose academic records indicate they are capable of performing successfully in their first year of college but who are not truly academically qualified because their high school grades and course-taking patterns overstate their preparedness. Such students—disproportionately minority and lower income—are at the heart of one debate over the reliance on test scores for admissions. Strict test score requirements will keep these students out of more competitive institutions, despite their records of achievement in classrooms, extracurricular activities, and community leadership.

By dropping or deemphasizing test scores for admissions, private colleges open up their campuses to these students and thereby promote both equity and excellence. Selective public institutions, often vital gateways to participation in a state's political, business, and community organizations, play down tests so as not to shut out talented and capable minority, low-income, rural, and first-generation college students.

The second justification for continuing use of test scores would be to flag applicants with greater promise than was revealed by their performance in high school. Although this may occur on occasion, it is unlikely that a significant body of students who had "underperformed" in high school would suddenly excel in college. A far larger number are likely to be "slackers" whose college grades would mirror their weak high school records. In any case, test-optional policies do not hurt these applicants because they can still submit SAT or ACT scores along with an explanation of their classroom performance. Thus, test-score-optional policies allow colleges to include many applicants with strong records of academic and other forms of achievement. At the same time, these policies do not exclude students who believe submission of test scores helps demonstrate their academic potential.

The Benefits of Making ACT and SAT Scores Optional

As the comprehensive statistical analyses in studies such as *The Case Against the SAT* (Crouse & Trusheim, 1988) and *Crossing the Finish Line* (Bowen, Chingos, & McPherson, 2009) demonstrate, deemphasizing the SAT in admissions would not harm colleges' abilities to accurately select their incoming classes. The former book concludes, "Our argument, in summary, is that from a practical viewpoint, most colleges could ignore their applicants' SAT score reports when they make selection decisions without appreciably altering the academic performance and graduation rates of the students they admit" (Crouse & Trusheim, 1988, p. 68). Similarly, the second book finds, "High school grades are a far better incremental predictor of graduation rates than are standard SAT/ACT test scores" and "The strong predictive power of high school GPA holds even when we know little or nothing about the quality of the high school attended" (Bowen et al., 2009, p. 226).

Tests Do Not Help Colleges

The practical experience of test-optional schools is fully consistent with the academic research. Having made submission of standardized exam scores optional back in 1969, Bowdoin College has a wealth of experience in admitting highly selective classes. Bowdoin's research shows that, since the test-optional policy was initiated, the academic performance of students who do not submit SAT or ACT results has been comparable to the performance of those students who do submit scores. In a multi-year study of its test-optional policy, Bates College found that the change "had no visible negative impact on the quality of enrollees, and seems in fact to have had a positive impact" (Hiss, 1990, p. 17). Other highly selective schools, such as Mount Holyoke and Muhlenberg, report similar findings. Peter Van Buskirk, the Dean of Admission at Franklin & Marshall College when his school began eliminating its admissions testing requirements, noted another advantage: "The decision was a point of liberation for my colleagues and me. Free from the tyranny of numbers, we could focus on the breadth of credentials in making decisions about young people whom we valued most" (Van Buskirk, 2010).

Of course, these highly selective schools, which receive multiple applications for each spot, must cull their applicant pools. However, most colleges and universities do not need to sort and rank their applicants. According to the National Association for College Admissions Counseling, more than half of all accredited, bachelor's-degree-granting institutions admit two-thirds or more of their applicants (Clinedinst & Hawkins, 2009, p. 15).

Deemphasizing Tests Helps Diversify Student Bodies

At Bates College, the test-optional policy resulted in a more diverse student body, with applications and enrollment by minority students more than doubling in the first 5 years (Clinedinst & Hawkins, 2009, p. 18). Members of minority groups make strong use of the policy, electing to withhold their ACT and SAT scores at a higher rate than the total applicant pool. Wheaton College in Massachusetts has attracted more minority students since its test-optional policy went into effect in 1992. When the Texas Higher Education Coordinating Board studied ways to promote diversity at the state's public universities, it concluded that "the use of standardized tests unduly limits admissions [and] . . . has had a chilling effect on the motivations and aspirations of underserved populations (Advisory Committee on Criteria for Diversity, 1997, p. 12). Research by the authors of *Crossing the Finish Line* reached a similar conclusion: "Overly heavy reliance on SAT/ACT scores in admitting students can have adverse effects on the diversity of the student bodies enrolled by universities" (Bowen et al., 2009, p. 226).

Going Test-Optional Helps Students

As more schools eliminate admissions testing requirements or deempha-size the role of the ACT and SAT, applicants will know that they will be evaluated more on the basis of their performance in the classroom. This should encourage greater attention to academics. Removing test scores from the equation will offer particular benefits to low-income, minority, first-generation, rural, female, and older students or, more generally, to stu-dents whose performance on tests does not provide a meaningful measure of their academic abilities. Reducing the role of one-shot tests will result in test coaching having less influence over the admissions process. Com-mercial test-prep courses cost $1000 or more and can increase students' composite SAT scores by more than 100 points combined for the Critical Reading and Math portions of the test (Stockwell, Schaeffer, & Lowenstein, 1991). Yet admissions officers have no way to determine which applicants have taken such courses. Thus, they cannot know whose scores were boosted by coaching and whose were not.

As more schools move away from the SAT and ACT, students will feel less pressure to take these expensive and time-consuming courses. William Hiss, the former Admissions Director at Bates College, who now serves as a Vice President, noted, "We think coaching distracts a student at precisely the critical moment when young people need to build up confidence and personal steam for critical thinking, effective writing, and developing strong analytical skills" (Hiss, 1990, p. 15). He added that Bates went test-optional in part as an "attempt to say to these young people, use your time and your energy to create real forward motion in your life" (p. 15). Stu-dents with lower test scores, even when they have otherwise strong aca-demic records, are often discouraged from applying to colleges with SAT/ACT requirements and higher average test scores for the student body. Many schools report that changing their test score requirements brought in new applicants, some with lower test scores, who did well after being admit-ted, but who would likely not have applied had test score requirements been in place.

Test-optional policies also give students greater say in the admissions process. After dropping its test submission requirement, Muhlenberg Col-lege included this statement in its "Questions and Answers About Muhlen-berg's Test-Optional Policy":

> We hope test-optional admissions policy will give some power back to students in the admissions process and give them a larger say in how to present their strongest portfolio of credentials. (quoted in *AGB Priorities*, 1998, p. 13)

Societal Benefits of Test-Optional Admissions Policies

A shift away from test-based admissions promotes more widespread access to selective colleges and universities. Students from families with greater household incomes typically post higher test scores than do those from families with lower incomes. There are still huge gaps in test results among whites, Asian Americans, and members of historically disenfranchised mi-

TABLE 10.1   Average SAT Scores of 2010 College-Bound Seniors, with Score Changes from 2006 (approximately 1.55 million test takers, of whom 53.4% were female)

	Critical Reading	Math	Writing	Total
All test takers	501 (–2)	516 (–2)	492 (–5)	1509 (–9)
Gender				
Female	498 (–4)	500 (–2)	498 (–4)	1496 (–10)
Male	503 (–2)	534 (–2)	486 (–5)	1523 (–9)
Ethnicity				
Asian, Asian American, or Pacific Islander	519 (+9)	591 (+13)	526 (+14)	1623 (+36)
White	528 (+1)	536 (0)	516 (–3)	1580 (–2)
African American or black	429 (–5)	428 (–1)	420 (–8)	1277 (–14)
American Indian or Alaskan Native	485 (–2)	492 (–2)	467 (–7)	1444 (–11)
Mexican or Mexican American	454 (0)	467 (+2)	448 (–4)	1369 (–2)
Puerto Rican	454 (–5)	452 (–4)	443 (–5)	1349 (–14)
Other Hispanic or Latino	454 (–4)	462 (–1)	447 (–3)	1363 (–8)
Other	494 (0)	514 (+1)	492 (–1)	1500 (0)
No response (4%)	487 (0)	514 (+8)	481 (–1)	1482 (+7)
Family income				
Less than $20,000/year	437	460	432	1329
$ 20,000–$40,000/year	465	479	455	1399
$ 40,000–$60,000/year	490	500	478	1468
$ 60,000–$80,000/year	504	514	492	1510
$ 80,000–$100,000/year	518	529	505	1552
$100,000–$120,000/year	528	541	518	1587
$120,000–$140,000/year	533	546	523	1602
$140,000–$160,000/year	540	554	531	1625
$160,000–$180,000	547	561	540	1648
More than $200,000/year	568	586	567	1721
No response (38%)	498	515	492	1505

Note: The No Child Left Behind requirement to test every child annually in grades 3–8 and at least once in high school went into effect in the 2005–2006 academic year. High school graduates in the class of 2006 were the first to take the SAT Writing test.

Source: Calculated by FairTest from: College Board, *College-Bound Seniors 2010: Total Group Profile Report* and *College-Bound Seniors 2006: Total Group Profile Report.*

TABLE 10.2 Average ACT Scores of 2010 College-Bound Seniors
(approximately 1.57 million test takers, of whom about 55% were female)

	Composite score
All test takers	21.0
Ethnicity	
Asian American or Pacific Islander	23.4
Caucasian American or white	22.3
African American or black	16.9
American Indian or Alaskan Native	19.0
Hispanic	18.6
Other/No response (9%)	20.6
Gender	
Female	20.9
Male	21.2

Source: ACT, *ACT High School Profile Report 2010.*

nority groups, particularly African Americans, Hispanics, and Native Americans (see Tables 10.1 and 10.2).

Heavy reliance on test scores in the admissions process assures that students who have had the greatest opportunities in life are further advantaged in terms of access to higher education. Moving away from policies that rely heavily on SAT or ACT scores opens the doors to academically qualified students whose test scores say more about their family backgrounds than about their capacity to perform well in college. At the same time, deemphasizing college entrance tests would benefit K–12 public education. Many admissions officers fear that a heavy focus on the ACT and SAT leads many students to invest a great deal of their time and energy on trying to raise their standardized exam scores rather than on their high school work. It also leads to high schools feeling pressure to devote precious resources to test preparation rather than more meaningful learning. Bill Mason, then Admissions Director at Bowdoin College, claimed, "[T]he natural outgrowth of a system . . . which relies solely on SAT scores" is high schools designing their courses "to accommodate multiple-choice exams." He added:

> The message we should be sending to high schools is that admissions offices at selective colleges are capable or making informed decisions without relying heavily or at all on the Educational Testing Service, not that we want them to design their courses to what can be tested by multiple-choice exams. By and large, that isn't the way we evaluate our students. Why should we require that high school students be evaluated in that fashion? (W. Mason, personal communication, August 5, 1987)

ACT and SAT scores are now used for everything from selecting scholarship winners to selling real estate. The quality of high schools, colleges, and even state education systems as a whole is often judged on the basis of test score averages. Yet experts—and the testmakers themselves—have long dismissed such comparisons as invalid because of the varying proportions of students taking the test and the differences within student populations. For instance, an increase in the number of students for whom English is a second language taking college entrance tests can alter a high school's average score without revealing anything about the quality of its education. By moving away from reliance on the ACT and SAT, colleges and universities would send a strong message that "test scores do not equal merit."

Why Some Colleges Still Use ACT and SAT Scores

Since "new" versions of the SAT and ACT were introduced in 2005, more than six dozen colleges and universities have eliminated their testing requirements. Still, the majority of undergraduate institutions do require most high school students to submit either ACT or SAT scores. Given all the problems with the exams and the many advantages of test-optional admissions policies, why do these schools still require applicants to submit test results? Admissions professionals offer three primary explanations.

Marketing and Rankings

Many colleges fear that dropping their ACT/SAT requirements might signal potential applicants and other important stakeholders that they are lowering academic standards. College rankings, particularly those from *U.S. News & World Report* magazine, which include average test scores in their calculations, help reinforce this concern. This belief is clearly mistaken. In fact, the *U.S. News* ranking formula only counts ACT or SAT averages as 7.5% of each school's total score (*U.S. News & World Report*, 2011, p. 87). Schools that have made submission of the tests optional have not suffered a drop in their rankings. If anything, the increases in both numbers of applicants and the quality of the high school records helps boost the ratings of institutions that eliminate test score requirements.

Currently about one-third of the top tier of national liberal arts colleges have test-optional policies (*U.S. News & World Report*, 2011, pp. 94–98). So do the top-ranked regional colleges in the South (such as Rollins), the second and third ranked colleges in the North (including Providence and Loyola Maryland), and highly regarded national universities such as Wake Forest and Worcester Polytechnic.

Political Pressure

At public institutions, in particular, administrators are subject to decisions made by state and local governments for political purposes. Raising average test scores is a cheap way of creating the impression that universities are raising academic standards and a convenient mechanism to cut the size of entering classes. In recent years, public universities in New York City, Massachusetts, and elsewhere have responded to political pressure to reduce enrollment or improve the appearance of academic quality by boosting ACT and SAT score requirements as a way to restrict access.

At the same time, however, other state university systems, including those in Texas and California, maintained diversity and academic excellence by creating admissions pathways that do not depend on test score. The Texas "Top 10%" rule, which has provided automatic entry for in-state students who graduate in the top 10% of their high school classes, having taken a college preparatory curriculum, is widely heralded for preserving diversity in the face of restrictions on affirmative action. To a lesser degree, the University of California's system of Eligibility in the Local Context, which has automatically qualified students in the top 4% of their high schools for state university seats, has had a similar effect. Because of its success, eligibility in California will be extended to the top 9% beginning with the class that graduates from high school in 2012 (Keller & Hoover, 2009).

Cost

Colleges pay nothing to receive applicants' test scores. Students and their parents bear the entire financial and psychological burden. Test scores are easy to process and require little time on the part of admissions offices. They also come with a vast body of demographic data that can be used for honing recruiting and "yield management" programs. Evaluating a more sophisticated, comprehensive set of admissions criteria does entail more staff time and somewhat higher costs.

The successful records of the nearly 850 test-optional colleges and universities undermine the purely economic argument. Yes, more time is needed to perform a "holistic" read of an applicant's file than to do a "triage" sort based on ACT/SAT scores. But the benefits from the additional investment are worth the extra effort to schools committed to maximizing equity and excellence. They recognize that trying to carry out admissions on the cheap has significant negative consequences in terms of diversity and academic quality.

Making the Change

Colleges and universities seeking to revamp their admissions processes by deemphasizing standardized tests can tap into a diverse set of experiences at public and private 4-year schools that have already taken these steps. Institutions that have gone test-optional have done so for a wide range of reasons and have chosen several different general approaches. No matter what the path, reducing the weight placed on ACT and SAT scores or dropping the testing requirement can and does work to promote the twin goals of equity and academic excellence.

Though each college or university must chart its own course when redesigning admissions requirements, there is a process, with roughly similar steps, necessary to develop, implement, and market a test-optional admissions policy.

Conduct a Standardized Test Audit

Before considering how to modify the use of standardized exams in its admissions process, a school must understand how it currently uses ACT and SAT results. There is often widespread misunderstanding about the role test scores play in the admissions process, even among faculty members, senior administrators, trustees, and other key stakeholders. Potential applicants, parents, guidance counselors, and others outside the school may also under- or overestimate how much decisions are driven by the ACT or SAT, often because written descriptions of requirements and policies are deliberately vague. Sometimes repeat calls to the same institution yield different answers about how the test is used in the admissions process. Websites may offer inconsistent information on different pages. At larger universities, individual programs may have different test score requirements, further complicating the picture.

For some schools, adoption of a test-optional admissions policy would have little impact on how selection decisions are actually made, although it might alter the applicant pool. At many others, however, such a shift would likely have an impact in areas ranging from the number and diversity of applicants, to the resources needed for the admissions office, to the school's reputation among high school counselors. A school that currently relies heavily on the ACT and SAT as an initial screen would have to turn to other methods. If a university uses a test score–based admissions index but wants to replace it with a more individualized approach to selection, changes in staffing likely would be necessary.

Some colleges, universities, and university systems continue to use eligibility or admissions formulas with fixed ACT or SAT requirements. Most schools do not publicize these formal "cutoffs" because they violate test-makers' guidelines for proper score use and the admissions profession's own standards of good practice. However, many appear to act as if they have required de facto score minimums that must be met before an application is thoroughly evaluated. On the other hand, many institutions waive test score submission requirements for applicants who have been out of school for several years, are transferring from other colleges, or have documented learning disabilities. Still others adjust scores for applicants from certain groups. Admissions officers at the Massachusetts Institute of Technology, for example, long used separate test score/grade-point average (GPA) indices to evaluate men and women (Johnson, 1993).

Admissions office practices vary significantly. In some cases, tests are used as an initial screening device but are not scrutinized thereafter. Alternatively, test scores sometimes serve as "tie-breakers," evaluated only when two or more candidates are closely matched in other ways. Test scores might be weighted so that they have more significance than grades and curriculum rigor, or are given less weight than high school performance.

Finally, some schools use standardized test scores to make decisions about "merit" scholarship awards and course placement. Any tuition award program that relies exclusively on ACT or SAT scores, with cutoffs, should be restructured because the tests are not meant for such precise use. Using absolute minimum score requirements also violates guidelines for proper test use.

Determine Whether Predicting First-Year GPA Is a Sufficient Criterion

The College Board and ACT have long justified their products on the basis of their capacity to predict first-year undergraduate grades, a task somewhat better performed by high school grades. With the increased focus on retention and graduation, schools should ask whether first-year grades are truly meaningful outcome criteria. William Sedlacek, a Professor of Education and Director of Testing at the University of Maryland, College Park, has identified some of the limitations of relying on first-year grades as the primary criterion for assessing the value of admissions test scores:

> Most scholars who research human abilities agree that the attributes first-year college students need to succeed differ from those they subsequently need. Typically, the first year of any curriculum is more didactic. Students learn facts and basic concepts in different disciplines. In later years, students are required to be more creative and to synthesize and reorganize their thoughts. Many students who do not do well in the first year often shine in the majors and in their later years of studies. (Sedlacek, 1998, p. 5)

Sedlacek adds that "standardized tests do not measure motivation, study habits, personal or professional goals, and other factors that can affect academic performance and persistence to graduation" (1998, p. 6). He has long been a leading advocate for incorporating noncognitive factors into the admissions process, noting that "student attitudes and expectations at matriculation are related to graduation five and six years later" (Sedlacek & Tracey, 1986, p. 12).

Recent research on predictors of graduation sponsored by the Mellon Foundation and published in *Crossing the Finish Line: Completing College at America's Public Universities* found that "High school grades are a far better predictor of both four-year and six-year graduation rates than are SAT/ACT test scores—a central finding that holds within each of the six sets of public universities that we study" (Bowen et al., 2009, p. 113). According to this analysis, the high school GPA of applicants is between 3 and 10 times more powerful as a predictor of college graduation than are their standardized test scores. The authors conclude, "In short, this analysis reinforces the point that high school grades measure a student's ability to 'get it done' in a more powerful way than do SAT scores—a conclusion that holds, we wish to emphasize, regardless of the high school attended" (Bowen et al., 2009, p. 123).

Look at Diversity and Outreach Issues

While it is important to gain a precise understanding of how a college is using standardized admissions tests, how well those exams predict performance at the institution, and whether there are alternatives that predict as well or better, it is also important to engage in a broader debate about a school's mission and its admissions goals, and how to achieve them. At some institutions that adopted test-optional admissions, the evaluation of ACT/SAT use was embedded in a broader debate about how to make the school more diverse while preserving rigorous academic standards. Elsewhere, as in the case of the University of Texas, the reworking of admissions requirements came in response to court-ordered bans on affirmative action and concerns about keeping campuses accessible to a range of applicants.

Even the best college GPA and graduation prediction equations cannot reveal whether otherwise qualified students were being deterred from applying by test score requirements. In Texas, higher education officials were deeply concerned with making sure that students from underrepresented groups still felt welcome at the state's public universities after the court ruling in the *Hopwood* reverse-discrimination case. Many liberal arts colleges wanted to develop more equitable ways of evaluating applicants and, at the same time, signal their openness to students with different learning styles and from a wide variety of backgrounds. To evaluate the potential impact of test score requirements on these outreach and recruitment issues, schools need to know who is applying, who from the pool of potential applicants is not applying and why, and whether the current mix is consistent with the institution's mission and goals. Schools should look at the mix of high schools, cities, regions, and states generating applicants. Are top students from low-income areas turned off from applying? Is a college developing new pools of applicants, especially from historically underrepresented groups?

Changing application and enrollment patterns requires modifications not just of outreach programs and admissions requirements but also of financial aid. Many institutions, including some that are test-optional for admissions, still have ACT or SAT score requirements for scholarships (Leider, 2007), a factor that also can deter some students from matriculating.

Develop Admissions Alternatives

Schools have deemphasized standardized tests in a variety of ways. The two most common approaches are making submission on ACT/SAT scores optional for all applicants and exempting students with proven high school records of achievement—usually measured by GPA or class rank—from submitting test score results. Each of these policies has numerous variants, which might include requiring applicants who choose the test-optional route to submit a graded research paper (e.g., Muhlenberg), project (e.g., Worcester Polytechnic Institute), or other evidence of academic accomplishment.

As the test-optional movement has grown and matured, additional alternatives have been developed and implemented. Sarah Lawrence College, for example, will not consider ACT and SAT results even if they are included in the application file, and American University will review students without regard to test scores if they apply before November 1.

As part of its review of admissions testing requirements, each institution needs to determine which particular policy would best fit its mission, goals, and staffing capability. At most selective liberal arts colleges, admissions officials already review individual applications and know far more about each student than just their test scores and grades. In such institutions, the transition to test-optional admissions is not particularly difficult, as dozens of schools have shown. For larger universities, which might receive 10,000 or more applications each year, the shift would be more complicated. Additional, trained file readers would be needed to ensure that each student's credentials are carefully reviewed. But, the extra investment will pay off in an undergraduate body that is more diverse in every possible way without any sacrifice in academic quality.

Build Support for New Policies

Mechanisms for making decisions about instituting broad admissions policy reforms vary substantially from college to college. In some cases, faculty members vote on whether to drop tests, whereas in others reforms may be initiated by the campus president (e.g., Drew University), admissions office staff, revisions in state law (e.g., University of Texas system), or policy changes at the trustee or regents level (e.g., University of California system). Whatever the process, broad dissemination of information about the current admissions policy and prospective changes will enhance the level of discussion. A report by the admissions office, a faculty task force, or a commission should provide an overview of the issues connected with standardized testing. It could make note of all current uses of test scores; the impact of such policies on admissions decisions; the effects of test requirements on different groups (by income, ethnicity, gender, and region); predictive data for grades, retention, and graduation by subgroup; and any available evidence about the role of test coaching.

Beyond the data, the report should also lay out the ethical issues connected with standardized admissions testing, including impact on high school curricula, psychological and financial costs to students, access to higher education, and societal notions about what constitutes "merit." In every case, efforts should be made to include all key stakeholder groups. These include faculty, administration, admissions staff, students, alumni, and donors, all of whom benefit from understanding how and why deemphasizing admissions test scores enhances equity and excellence.

Publicize Admissions Reforms

Once new admissions testing criteria have been put into place, it is very important to publicize the details to potential applicants, college counselors, parents, and the wide range of print and Internet guides that list college admissions requirements. For example, FairTest's online lists of test-optional colleges (www.fairtest.org/university/optional) host more than 200,000 unique visitors per year. Because of the many "flavors" of test-optional policies now in place, it is extremely important that the school's own website include highly visible links with clear language defining which students, if any, must submit test scores, and under which conditions. The same information needs to be incorporated into print materials distributed at college fairs, at school presentations, and to campus visitors.

Institutions, such as Bates (2004) and Mount Holyoke (2005), that have conducted and then broadly disseminated the results of internal studies about the impact of test-optional admissions provide an important service for the broader higher education community. By sharing their experiences, they help define a path that other institutions can follow.

Life After the SAT

The successful experience of test-optional schools demonstrates that there is life after the SAT (or ACT). At the majority of institutions that do not rely heavily on standardized tests to make admissions decisions, the transition to a test-optional policy could take place smoothly. For admissions offices that already read individual admissions files thoroughly, the SAT and ACT can easily be dropped or deemphasized. Data from the transcript and other items in the application will provide richer information than test scores would. The potential gains for individual schools from deemphasizing the ACT and SAT, in terms of the diversity and quality of applicants, is very clear from the track records of schools that have already adopted such policies. Broader gains, particularly for academically qualified students from underrepresented groups, also accompany moves toward test-optional admissions. The best admissions policies permit applicants to demonstrate their potential in a variety of ways. Eliminating test score requirements is a proven strategy for maximizing both excellence and equity.

Note

This chapter is adapted, revised, and updated from Charles Rooney with Bob Schaeffer, *Test Scores Do Not Equal Merit: Enhancing Equity & Excellence in College Admission by Deemphasizing SAT and ACT Results* (Cambridge, MA: National Center for Fair & Open Testing, 1998).

References

Advisory Committee on Criteria for Diversity. (1997). *Second status report*. Austin, TX: Texas Higher Education Coordinating Board.

AGB Priorities. (1998, Winter). Questions and answers about Muhlenberg's test-optional policy. *AGB Priorities, Newsletter of the Association of Governing Boards*, (10), 12–13.

Bates College. (2004). *SAT study: 20 years of optional testing*. Lewiston, ME: Author. Retrieved from http://www.bates.edu/ip-optional-testing-20years.xml

Bowen, W. G., Chingos, M. M., & McPherson, M. S. (2009). *Crossing the finish line*. Princeton, NJ: Princeton University Press.

Clinedinst, M., & Hawkins, D. (2009). *State of college admissions 2009*. Washington, DC: National Association for College Admissions Counseling.

Cole, N. (1997, September 19). Merit and opportunity: Testing and higher education at the vortex [Editorial]. *New York Times*, p. A25.

Crouse, J., & Trusheim, D. (1988). *The case against the SAT*. Chicago: University of Chicago Press.

FairTest. (2010). *Test score optional list: Schools that do not use SAT or ACT scores for admitting substantial numbers of students into bachelor degree programs*. Jamaica Plain, MA: FairTest National Center for Fair & Open Testing.

Hiss, W. (1990, September). Optional SATs: Six years later. *Bates: The Alumni Magazine*, pp. 15–19.

Johnson, E. S. (1993, Spring/Summer). College women's performance in a math-science curriculum: A case study. *College & University,* pp. 74–78.

Keller, J., & Hoover, E. (2009, February 5). U. of California to adopt sweeping changes in admissions policy. *Chronicle of Higher Education.* Retrieved from http://chronicle .com/article/U-of-California-to-Adopt/117340/

Kobrin, J. L., Patterson, B. F., Shaw, E. J., Mattern, K. D., & Barbuti, S. M. (2008). *Validity of the SAT for predicting first-year college grade point average.* (College Board Research Report No. 2008-5.) New York: College Board.

Leider, A. (2007). *The A's & B's of academic scholarships: 100,000 scholarships for top students.* Alexandria, VA: Octameron Associates.

Mount Holyoke College. (2005, March). *Early results from Mount Holyoke study reaffirm SAT-optional policy.* South Hadley, MA: Author. Retrieved from http://www.mtholyoke .edu/offices/comm/press/releases/satstudy.shtml

Sedlacek, W. (1998, Winter). Multiple choice for standardized tests. *AGB Priorities, Newsletter of the Association of Governing Boards,* (10), 5–6.

Sedlacek, W., & Tracey, T. (1986). *Prediction of college graduation using noncognitive variables by race.* (Research Report 2-86.) College Park: Counseling Center, Office of Vice Chancellor for Student Affairs, University of Maryland.

Stockwell, S., Schaeffer, R., & Lowenstein, J. (1991). *The SAT coaching cover-up.* Cambridge, MA: National Center for Fair & Open Testing.

U.S. News & World Report. (2011). How we calculate the rankings. In *2011 Best colleges guide.* New York: Author.

Van Buskirk, P. (2010, September 8). *Testing and college: Keep your options open.* The Admission Game College Planning Blog. Retrieved from http://www.theadmission game.com/blog/archives/279.

11

Going Test-Optional

A First Year of
Challenges, Surprises, and Rewards

MARTHA ALLMAN

When it comes to standardized testing, we have all seen the data: regression analyses, correlations, predictive comparisons. We understand the debates: ethical, cultural, and philosophical. The test-optional argument is certainly based on numbers and theory, but there is also a very real and human aspect to this issue. In 2008, in the Wake Forest University Admissions Office, the abstract became real. We were no longer "rethinking admissions"; we were literally re*doing* admissions. And so it began.

In May 2008, Wake Forest made the announcement that after much discussion and careful investigation, we had decided to dramatically revamp our admissions process in three important ways: (a) we would no longer require standardized tests for admission, (b) the written response portion of our application would be expanded to include a series of provocative short-answer questions such as "What outrages you?" "Define cool." "Argue a position that you don't support." "Tell us about your intellectual epiphany." and so forth, and (c) an interview with an admissions officer would become a strongly encouraged component of each application.

The media went nuts. TV cameras swarmed the office. Phone lines blinked incessantly with calls from national and local newspaper reporters. Friends called and said, "I was stuck in traffic and heard you on the radio." We became the darlings of the media. I received love mail from alums and faculty. I received hate mail from alums and faculty. My mother was beside herself with excitement.

We were surprised by the magnitude of the storm initiated by our test-optional announcement. Some alumni wrote to us that it was their proudest moment, while others insisted that we had utterly destroyed the academic reputation of their alma mater. Some Wake Forest students applauded bringing more diversity to campus, while others feared that their diplomas would be devalued. Parents of current Wake Forest students expressed concern that test-optional would cause our *U.S. News and World Report* rankings to fall (in fact they rose), while others championed our decision. Some faculty worried about academic concessions, while others anticipated students who would bring lively discussion to their classrooms. Strong opinions abounded.

So how did we as admissions officers feel? Like Little Red Riding Hood in *Into the Woods,* "excited and scared." Many times I thought and said, "I wish I had a crystal ball. If only I knew what it was actually going to be like." Other test-optional institutions gave us some hints: "Your applications are going to go up." But I wondered—by how much? "Your minority apps are really going to go up." But I wondered—by how much? And the interviews—could we physically do it? And the application—would applicants balk at the increased writing requirements and just choose not to apply? Could the air conditioning and plumbing systems in our beloved old Starling Hall stand up to the crowds of campus visitors coming here to interview?

Our first challenge was find a way to make sure that our prospect pool knew that we had changed our policy concerning the submission of standardized tests and were placing a new emphasis on the personal interview. We contacted everyone in our database electronically and by mail, we scheduled a series of high school counselor breakfasts to discuss our changes, and we amped up our admissions website to reflect the new policy.

In staff meetings in May, my young and idealistic staff members looked at each other and said, "We are *so* doing the right thing. We are sending a powerful message about what's important, about what a 'student' should be. We know we have sometimes used the SAT as a crutch or a tie-breaker, and now we are going to have to prove our mettle as admissions officers. Our process has always been holistic, but now we are going to examine high schools and curricula even more closely. We are going to read applications even more carefully, and we will listen intently and discerningly when we interview. We are going to look for talent, for creativity, for curiosity, for 'fire in the belly.' We are going to expand the definition of merit to a whole new level as we assess each student's fitness for our Wake Forest community. We are going to seek individuals who will enrich this place, each in his or her own way." We were energized like never before. Little did we know what grueling admissions labor lay ahead.

The Challenges of Redoing Admissions

From June 1 through December 15, we conducted 4000 personal interviews in the Admissions Office with a professional staff of 12. The bulk of the interviews were done during the steaming southern summer months. Sometimes we would each do as many as 10 interviews a day. We were exhausted, and the Admissions Office felt like Grand Central Station. Hot and crowded. Traffic jams in the parking lot. Managing the visitors became a real challenge. We petitioned our Provost for a mobile addition to the office, and we cheered and celebrated when our "trailer" arrived. We added two professional staff members. We called in help from emeriti faculty who had served with us on scholarship committees. They loved interviewing, prospective students loved the conversations, and we loved having them as part of the process. The conversations were rich.

Some interviews we did on the road. One Saturday morning in the fall, I sat in the back room of the only coffee shop in a small town in the North Carolina mountains interviewing applicants. One, who is now pursuing a successful Wake Forest undergraduate career, brought with her a notebook detailing her summer research with the U.S. Forest Service. When I asked her, "Why Wake Forest?" she responded with my favorite answer, "Because I just want to make something of myself."

We worried that there were those for whom a visit to Winston-Salem was financially or logistically impossible. In our desire to expand our pool to include those who perhaps had not before considered Wake Forest an option, we certainly did not want to place new impediments in their way. We turned to the Wake Forest Information Systems Department, which assigned a team of programmers and systems specialists to help us, and they began working on virtual interview options.

In September, we began offering webcam interviews via SKYPE and Adobe Connect; by December 1, we had conducted 200 of these interviews. Occasionally connectivity issues or time zone confusion arose, but for the most part, the virtual interviews were quite productive. High school counselors called us to make sure they had properly set up computers in their media centers so that students who did not have computers at home could still interview with us. And when time ran out and we had to turn our attention to application reading, our Information Systems project team again came to the rescue and developed for us a written online virtual interview. Applicants could log in only once, and they had 30 minutes to answer randomly generated questions such as "If you had a 'do over' button for your high school career, what would you do over?" or "Who has had more impact on your life, William Shakespeare or Ryan

Seacrest?" It was our hope that this format would simulate a face-to-face interview, giving us a sense of how students thought on their feet. When all was said and done, 80% of our applicant pool completed one of the three interview options.

In the midst of all this interviewing, we found something surprising. Time and again we asked students to tell us how they became interested in Wake Forest. Many times the response was "because of the test-optional policy." We expected that from those who had done poorly on the test, but what surprised us was the frequency of those with SAT scores of 1500+ who said, "I'm just with you philosophically. You are really trying to understand who I am. I want to attend a school that sees me for who I am, not just a big score."

We also found that the interviews truly helped us differentiate among applicants. We talked with those who were really curious and excited about the life of the mind, genuinely eager for the challenge of college; those who were well informed about current events, and who really did read *The Economist* (and those who said they did but didn't). There were those whose primary goal in college was to get away from their family, join a fraternity, and have as much fun as possible. We found those whose minds were closed so tightly a crowbar couldn't open them and those whose compassion for their fellow man was dictated only by their high school's community service requirement. We learned that interviews cannot be one-size-fits-all. Some students came prepped and ready for the challenge, while others were nervous and unpolished. It was our responsibility to tailor our questions and our approach to each candidate. It was challenging, but the more interviews we conducted, the more we wondered how we ever chose a class without them.

While the face-to-face and SKYPE interviews were extremely helpful in the admissions selection process, the online timed written interview proved problematic. Students found the process technically challenging, and some sought to beat the system by logging in multiple times, thus defeating the purpose of a simulated interview and instead giving us simply another set of essay responses. Interestingly, however, sometimes the responses on the timed interview differed markedly from the responses to the short-answer questions and the essay on the admissions application. Was the application perhaps a product of coaching and editing, while the real student—with bad grammar and inappropriate subject matter—shone through on the timed interview?

The Surprises of Test-Optional Applications

With fall came early decisions. The economy was starting to tank and we feared our early-decision applications would too, but actually the numbers went up slightly. We ended up admitting the same number of early-decision students as the previous year and enrolled roughly 25% of our class early. But this time, early-decision enrollment included 15% students of color (up from 9% the previous year) and 31% without standardized test scores. All were interviewed face to face, so the process was very different. We felt that we knew them and were hand-picking our class with more confidence than ever. To spread out the workload, we instituted a non-binding Early Action for North Carolina applicants for the first time. Among these applicants, 29% were non-score-submitters, but only 14% were admitted with no scores. One out of four students admitted through Early Action was a member of an ethnic minority.

Then came the long-awaited January 15 regular decision deadline. With it came an overall 16% increase in applications. Applications from students of color increased 46%, with applications by African Americans up 70%. North Carolina applications increased 52%, and for the first time in Admissions Office recorded history, we received applications from all 100 North Carolina counties—from the Appalachian Mountains to the Outer Banks. International applications increased 36%. Not only were the numbers impressive, the applications themselves were simply remarkable to read. Our admissions committee meetings were more difficult and more lively than ever, and late-night e-mails among readers shared incredible stories from student essays. There were stories of abuse, of poverty, and there was a recurring theme of students saying over and over, "I just want to make something of myself."

Take, for example, an applicant who was an Afghan immigrant. At age 6, he was working with tiny bleeding fingers making rugs in a sweatshop in Kabul. He immigrated to the United States at age 12, compiled an exemplary high school record, and became proficient in four languages. He submitted no test scores. Or consider the valedictorian from a small rural high school, with one parent unemployed and one suffering from misdiagnosed lymphoma, whose application burned with a passion to explore politics and theology. Or take the young artist who escaped his world of poverty—"smoke, screaming children and loud rap music"—by designing and sewing incredible prom dresses for his friends who otherwise could not afford them.

We reviewed a virtually flawless application from a student who attended a laboratory school associated with a large research university. We agreed her myriad talents and lively mind would make her a wonderful fit for Wake Forest, and then we "accidentally" saw her nonreported SAT scores tucked away on the back page of a transcript. We took a deep breath and admitted her. Again, we found ourselves feeling both excited and scared.

We received applications from students with poor grades and no scores who misunderstood our test-optional decision. There were those with compelling stories whose academic backgrounds were just too weak. We saw valedictorians from failing schools with no scores and whose curriculum, writing, and interviews demonstrated that Wake Forest was just not the right fit. Making these decisions was both sad and difficult. We were earning our keep as admissions officers.

We spent great amounts of time on the telephone with guidance counselors trying to determine how particular applicants measured up against their peers. We asked for class rank. We asked specific questions about strength of curriculum. We worked hard to learn about schools we didn't know much about. We publicly stated that 4 years of high school should be more important that a 4-hour test and so, true to our word, we painstakingly evaluated transcripts and profiles and shared with each other our knowledge of high schools. We all became better admissions officers.

The Rewards of Looking Beyond the Numbers

To our relief but not really our surprise, our typical applicant—the International Baccalaureate (IB) diploma candidate or the AP scholar with excellent SAT scores—didn't go away just because we became test-optional. We still attracted students from the flagship public schools and the strong private schools, many of whom continued the praise for our test-optional decision. This comment came from an applicant with a perfect SAT score:

> [At Wake Forest] you look past the arbitrary veneer of test scores so that an absent dowry or peerage doesn't disqualify a worthy suitor. Even with the technological resources of a much larger, impersonal and cumbersome institution, you maintain high standards of individual, face-to face instruction. You have realized that intellectual development is useless without a corresponding ethical maturation. You want me to fully develop my talents for humanity and I'd like you to be there with me when I finally do.

And another:

> The thing that intrigues me most about Wake Forest is how progressive it is. Wake Forest ranks second in the nation in the undergraduate study

abroad programs. It is the only school I know of that conducts virtual admissions interviews and it became the first top 30 national university to drop the SAT requirement for undergraduate admissions. These three signs of progress show me that Wake Forest is leading the way into the future and I definitely want to attend a school that is leading the way, not just following.

The decision to become test-optional was resonating with students. It seemed right and fair to them and a reflection of the soul of Wake Forest. We were attracting exactly the kind of students that we wanted to attract— intellectuals who were compassionate, creative, independent, and self-motivated. They were more than numbers, and they appreciated the fact that we recognized that.

But let's get back to the admissions cycle. After hours upon hours of reading and discussing, with many tears and occasional raised voices and an unusually large number of late nights, we settled on the class and mailed our regular decision letters. We had admitted the most accomplished and the most geographically, ethnically, and socioeconomically diverse class in Wake Forest history. We had painstakingly handcrafted this class, going beyond the numbers in the most labor-intensive endeavor we had ever undertaken. We had rethought and redone admissions. Now the question was, would they enroll?

The world did not stand still while we made our great change, however. As a matter of fact, the economic downturn threw colleges into a maelstrom of waiting lists and scholarship bidding wars. But in the midst of it all, despite the uncertainties, we brought in a class like Wake Forest has never seen before. The number of students who had graduated in the top 10% of their classes rose substantially. We doubled the number of international students, and 23% of our enrolling freshmen were students of color, up from 18% the previous year. More than 10% of the entering class was first-generation college students. Twenty percent submitted no test scores. We have made a dramatic statement about fairness, inclusion, and giving a chance to students, regardless of their backgrounds, who are hungry for the life of the mind and the rigor of academe—those who truly "want to make something" of themselves.

In retrospect, we could not have anticipated the dramatic increase in workload, the labor-intensiveness of the process, the challenge of attempting to interview the entire applicant pool, the technical challenges of written online interview options, nor the volume of comment from our constituencies. However, perhaps the most important lesson we learned was that, indeed, just as we had expected, test scores really *don't* matter that much. In tracking our first class of test-optional students, no difference emerged in our enrolled submitters and nonsubmitters—either in freshman GPA or in attrition rates. Just as we had hypothesized, a detailed, writing-heavy admissions application, a high school transcript, and reference letters from counselors and teachers could lead us to a valid admissions decision, with or without test scores.

Students are more than numbers, and they are so much more than standardized test scores. As an outstanding applicant wrote in one my favorite application essays:

> I am the only child of two only children. I am the babysitter down the street, the girl at the coat check on Thursday nights. Sometimes I am a number. For the degree of scoliosis curve that restricts me now from playing the sports I used to love, I am a 34. Sometimes I am a 0 for the number of those in my family who graduated from college, a statistic that will happily see its demise in 2013. I am also a 1, a tiny minute out of the thousands of applicants you will consider, but hopefully one that will stand out in your mind. I am thankful that these digits do not identify me, like those branded onto my grandmother's arm at Mauthausen, because I really do believe that I have more to offer the world than can be accounted for numerically.

For many years, we have decried the state of college admissions and the inequities of the selection process. Now we have taken a step from statement to action. Change is always unsettling, and we in the Wake Forest Admissions Office are still a little scared. But now, with a cycle behind us, most of all we are excited—profoundly and splendidly excited.

12

Diversity Outcomes of Test-Optional Policies

THOMAS J. ESPENSHADE and CHANG YOUNG CHUNG

Over the years, a disproportionate reliance on SAT scores in college admissions has generated a growing number and volume of complaints (Syverson, 2007). Some applicants, especially members of underrepresented minority groups, believe that the test is culturally biased. Other critics argue that high school grade-point average (GPA) and results on SAT Subject Tests are better than scores on the SAT Reasoning Test at predicting college success, as measured by grades in college and college graduation. Finally, there is mounting evidence that SAT scores are correlated not only with race but also with parental income and education, which produces an upward social-class bias in the profile of admitted students (Atkinson & Geiser, 2009; Gerald & Haycock, 2006; Soares, 2007).

Owing partly to these concerns, growing numbers of four-year colleges are moving away from the SAT test, giving students the option of submitting SAT scores or eliminating them altogether from consideration in the admission decision (Jaschik, 2006).[1] At the beginning of 2010, the website of the National Center for Fair and Open Testing (FairTest, 2009) listed the names of more than 830 four-year colleges that do not use the SAT I or the ACT test to admit substantial numbers of freshmen. Many of these schools are nonselective institutions that have never required standardized tests, but momentum for test-optional admissions is picking up, especially among smaller liberal arts colleges. At the same time, the percentage of colleges indicating that they attach "considerable importance" to admissions test scores has risen from 46% in 1993 to 60% in 2006 (National Association for College Admission Counseling [NACAC], 2008).[2] Public institutions (68%) and those that enroll more than 10,000 students (81%) are most likely to fall into this category. Meanwhile, the percentage of schools that attribute "considerable importance" to grades in college preparatory courses and the strength of the high school curriculum has fallen slightly, from 82% in 1993 to 74% in 2005.

Left in the middle are those colleges and universities that still require standardized test results for admission but attach little importance to them. A survey of 461 senior-level admissions deans and enrollment managers at four-year colleges conducted by the *Chronicle of Higher Education* in early 2008 found that 88% of respondents said their institutions required the submission of standardized test scores (Hoover, 2008). But fully one-half of these administrators indicated these test scores had "little" or "no" influence on admission outcomes, and only one-sixth said they had "great" influence. It is presumably these schools that the National Association for College Admission Counseling's Commission on the Use of Standardized Tests in Undergraduate Admission had in mind when they encouraged institutions to

> consider dropping the admission test requirements *if it is determined that the predictive utility of the test or the admission policies of the institution . . . support that decision and if the institution believes that standardized test results would not be necessary for other reasons such as course placement, advising, or research.* (NACAC, 2008, p. 7, emphasis in the original)

There has been research discrediting the belief that SAT or ACT tests are biased against members of minority groups. The Commission on the Use of Standardized Tests in Admission concluded, "A substantial body of literature indicates that test bias has been largely mitigated in today's admissions tests due to extensive research and development of question items on both the SAT and ACT" (NACAC, 2008, p. 10). Consequently, this chapter focuses on the remaining two criticisms leveled at standardized tests. We begin by presenting new evidence on how well SAT I scores predict college academic outcomes for students at academically selective colleges and universities. But we reserve most of our attention for an examination of how adopting test-optional policies in admissions or disregarding standardized test scores altogether would affect the racial, socioeconomic, and academic profiles of admitted students.

Factors That Predict College Success

Evaluation studies that predict success in college are concerned with factors that are most highly correlated with college GPA or class rank at the end of the first year, with the likelihood of graduating, and with cumulative GPA or class rank at graduation. Steven Syverson, Dean of Admissions and Financial Aid at Lawrence University, has argued that both the SAT and the ACT are useful in predicting how well students will perform in their early years of college (Syverson, 2007, p. 57).[3]

Much debate, however, has centered on which measures of a student's high school academic performance are the *best* predictors of college success. Arguments typically emphasize two different sets of factors: scores on standardized aptitude tests versus indicators that students have mastered curriculum content. In a recent evaluation based on 150,000 students from 110 four-year colleges and universities, the New SAT introduced in the spring of 2005, which has a required writing section, does almost as well as high school GPA at predicting first-year college GPA. The two used in combination do best (Kobrin, Patterson, Shaw, Mattern, & Barbuti, 2008). At private and academically selective schools, the edge goes to the New SAT. Moreover, white males are the only demographic group for which high school GPA is a better predictor of first-year college GPA than the New SAT (Mattern, Patterson, Shaw, Kobrin, & Barbuti, 2008).

The National Study of College Experience (NSCE) includes data to inform this debate. Initiated at Princeton University, the NSCE collected data on all applicants for admission in the early 1980s, 1993, and 1997 to a subset of the selective colleges and universities contained in the College and Beyond database analyzed by Bowen and Bok (1998). NSCE data include information on whether applicants were admitted, whether they subsequently enrolled, and their later college academic experiences as measured by first-year GPA, cumulative GPA at graduation, and whether students graduated within 6 years. A rich variety of student demographic and high school academic performance measures are also included in the NSCE data.

The data in Table 12.1 demonstrate how well standardized admissions test scores, achievement test scores, high school classroom performance, and high school curriculum predict college success at the eight selective NSCE institutions for which relevant data are available. The top section of the table shows the effects of SAT I scores. This variable includes a conversion from ACT to SAT I scores if students submitted only ACT scores as part of their college application. It is clear that standardized admissions test scores are statistically significant and substantively important predictors of college grades. This conclusion stands whether academic performance is measured at the end of the first year of college or cumulatively at graduation. Other things held constant, a swing in SAT I scores from the bottom category of less than 1000 (on the old system of a maximum of 1600 points) to the top range of 1400 or above is associated with a gain of roughly 30 percentile points in class rank. Admissions test scores are not associated with the likelihood of graduating.

Other measures of academic potential are also associated with college academic performance. As one would expect, students who have demonstrated a mastery of curriculum content by scoring well on the SAT II Subject

TABLE 12.1   Academic Predictors of College Success

Predictor variables	First-year class rank[a]	Graduated in 6 years[b]	Class rank at graduation[c]
SAT I score[d]			
1400–1600	10.7**	1.00	8.7**
1300–1399	3.1	1.17	3.3
(1200–1299)	—	—	—
1100–1199	−6.2†	0.95	−7.3**
1000–1099	−8.7*	0.87	−15.3***
<1000	−20.8***	1.21	−22.0***
Average SAT II score			
750 and above	16.3***	1.45	19.8***
650–749	8.7**	0.91	5.5**
(<650)	—	—	—
High school GPA			
A+	15.1***	2.67*	16.3***
A	6.5†	1.93†	9.9**
A−	4.9	1.17	2.8
(B+ or lower)	—	—	—
High school class rank			
Top 10%	5.2	0.88	2.4
Next 10%	0.1	1.04	−2.4
(Bottom 80%)	—	—	—
Elite high school			
Yes	2.3	4.67***	3.4
(No)	—	—	—
Number of observations	2224	4390	3788

Notes: All models use weighted observations. Reference categories are shown in parentheses. Other variables incorporated in these models include race, social class, sex, immigrant generation, first-generation college student, home ownership, help with homework, legacy student, received financial aid, held campus job, recruited athlete, satisfaction with college social life, academic selectivity of college, number of AP and SAT II exams taken, merit scholar, and high school type. The model for class rank at graduation also includes college major as a predictor variable.

[a] Class rank expressed as a percentile. Coefficients are estimated from a linear regression. Data are based on first-year students who enrolled at one of eight NSCE colleges or universities in the fall of 1997. $R^2 = 0.311$.

[b] Coefficients are odds ratios estimated from a logistic regression. Dependent variable = 1 if student graduated within 6 years; 0 otherwise. Data are based on students who enrolled at one of eight NSCE colleges or universities in the fall of 1993 or 1997. $F(63, 4248) = 5.39$. Prob > F = 0.0000.

[c] Class rank expressed as a percentile. Coefficients are estimated from a linear regression. Data are based on students who enrolled at one of eight NSCE colleges or universities in the fall of 1993 or 1997 and graduated within 6 years. $R^2 = 0.314$.

[d] Includes ACT scores converted to SAT I scores for students who reported only an ACT score.

† $p < 0.10$; * $p < 0.05$; ** $p < 0.01$; *** $p < 0.001$.

Source: Authors' calculations from the National Study of College Experience (NSCE); Espenshade and Radford (2009).

Tests and by having a high school GPA in the A or A+ range are predicted to do well in college. SAT II test scores are not associated with graduation rates, but having a high GPA in high school does matter. Students with a reported high school GPA of A+ are 167% more likely to graduate within 6 years than students with a high school GPA in the range of B+ or lower. Classroom performance in high school, when measured by high school class rank at graduation, does not appear to be associated with any of the NSCE measures of college success. Finally, high school curriculum—approximated here by whether a student graduated from one of 72 elite secondary schools, as identified by two senior admissions officers at Princeton University—is strongly associated with graduation rates but not with other college academic outcomes. Students who graduated from an elite high school are nearly five times as likely to graduate within 6 years as other students.[4]

We conclude from this brief review of the NSCE data that standardized admissions test scores are significant predictors of later college classroom performance—but not of 6-year graduation rates—at the selective schools considered in the National Study of College Experience. High school GPA matters, too, as do scores on SAT II achievement tests. Because each of these indicators contributes something important to an evaluation of an applicant's readiness to handle the academic demands at selective colleges and universities, admissions officers at elite colleges typically evaluate candidates by using a combination of academic indicators and do not rely on a single measure.

Diversity Outcomes of Test-Optional Policies

In this section we lay the groundwork for a systematic empirical examination of how test-optional admissions policies are likely to affect the racial and socioeconomic composition of admitted students at selective colleges and universities. We begin by presenting information on the relation between race and social class on the one hand and measures of academic achievement and performance in high school on the other. Then we describe the nature of test-optional policies and their anticipated effects not only on admission decisions but also on the composition of applicant pools. The following section describes the results of our simulation analyses.

Admissions Test Scores and Inequality

Those who worry about racial and socioeconomic diversity in higher education and about access on the part of underrepresented minority and lower-income students to the nation's top schools are concerned that an overemphasis on standardized test scores in the admissions process produces an entering freshman class that is disproportionately white or Asian and from upper social-class backgrounds (Shanley, 2007; Zwick, 2007). Because graduating from a selective college imparts later economic rewards, these observers argue that the current system of selective college application, admissions, and enrollment reinforces an existing pattern of inequality from one generation to the next.

The heart of the matter is a strong correlation between standardized admissions test scores, parental income and education, and race. An admissions process that rewards applicants with high test scores tilts the outcome in favor of students who come from more socioeconomically privileged backgrounds. At the same time, a perception on the part of potential applicants and their parents that SAT scores loom large in the selection process may discourage students with more modest test scores from applying in the first place. As a consequence, a disproportionate reliance on SAT or ACT test outcomes in college admissions—whether in fact or in perception—tends to exclude students from more marginal groups in society and to create an entering freshman class that is largely white and affluent (Bowen, Kurzweil, & Tobin, 2005; Gerald & Haycock, 2006; Soares, 2007; Zwick, 2007).[5]

Table 12.2 contains new information on patterns in the NSCE data between students' race, social-class background, and four academic outcomes. These data are based on students in the combined applicant pool of one or more of seven selective NSCE institutions in the fall of 1997. Respondents who reported in the NSCE student survey that they came from an upper-middle-class or upper-class family are grouped into the "high" social class. Students from lower- or working-class backgrounds are combined into the "low" category. Data in the first two columns show clear positive associations between social-class background and performance on the SAT I exam and SAT II achievement tests. The correlations appear to be somewhat stronger for SAT I. Among students from the high social-class group, 29% received a score of 1400 or better on the combined SAT I Math and Verbal examinations. This percentage falls steadily with social class to 14%—just half as much—among students from low social-class backgrounds. The same association can be seen with average SAT II scores, ranging from 54% who are high scorers among the high social-class group to 32% among students in the bottom social-class category.

Column 3 in Table 12.2 suggests an inverse association between social class and high school classroom performance. Slightly fewer than one-quarter (24%) of students from a high social class report having a high school GPA of A+. This proportion increases as one moves down the social-class scale to a figure topping one-third (35%) among low social-class groups. This negative association is not what one would expect within a

TABLE 12.2   Academic Outcomes in High School Among Applicants to Selective
Colleges, by Social Class and Race[a]

Item	Percent with			
	SAT I score 1400+	Average SAT II score 650+	High school GPA of A+	Top 10% of graduating class
Total	25.4	48.5	26.6	61.8
Social class[b]				
High	28.7	53.8	23.9	61.4
Middle	24.0	46.2	27.7	63.4
Low	13.9	31.8	35.2	58.0
Race				
White	24.9	50.9	27.3	61.7
Black	7.2	18.3	11.4	34.2
Hispanic	14.6	38.5	25.5	59.9
Asian	36.0	52.8	29.6	70.8

[a] Data are based on applicants to seven NSCE colleges or universities for the 1997 entering class.

[b] "High" includes upper-middle and upper classes; "Low" includes lower and working classes.

Source: Authors' calculations from the National Study of College Experience (NSCE); Espenshade and Radford (2009).

particular high school, but NSCE applicants are drawn from many different high schools across the United States. The final column of the table exhibits relatively little correlation between social class and graduating in the top 10% of one's high school class.

The bottom half of the table suggests how students' reported race and measures of high school academic performance are associated. These data conform to widely observed patterns. Regardless of which academic outcome is considered, underrepresented minority students are least likely to be high scorers, whereas white and especially Asian students perform at the top. To use SAT I scores as an example, one-quarter of white students who took the SAT exam, and more than one-third of Asian students, received a score of 1400 or better. These figures stand in sharp contrast to that for Hispanic students, just 15% of whom achieved a score as high. Only 7% of black students taking the SAT achieved a score of at least 1400. Racial disparities are somewhat less pronounced for the remaining academic indicators, but they consistently favor white and Asian students over blacks and Hispanics.

Data from other sources confirm these findings. Geiser and Santelices (2007) examined the pattern of correlations between test scores and high school GPA on the one hand and parental income and education on the other among first-time freshmen entering the University of California system between the fall of 1996 and the fall of 1999. All associations they found are positive, but the strongest ones are between SAT I Math and Verbal scores and parental socioeconomic status (ranging between 0.24 and 0.39). Weak positive correlations were measured between high school GPA and family income (0.04) and between GPA and parents' education (0.06).

SAT and ACT score reports for all test takers in 2007 show the same regularities. The SAT range that separates students from lower-income families (less than $10,000) and those from upper-income families (more than $100,000) exceeds 100 points on each of the three components of the New SAT test (Critical Reading, Mathematics, and Writing). For example, the average score on the Critical Reading component varies from 427 for students in the lowest income category to 544 among students in the highest income group (NACAC, 2008). A range of more than 100 points is also evident when students are arrayed by highest level of parental education (from no high school diploma to graduate degree). Black and Hispanic students receive the lowest average ACT scores (17.0 and 18.7, respectively), versus 22.1 for white test takers and 22.6 for Asian American and Pacific Islander test takers (NACAC, 2008).

SAT-Optional Policies

To increase diversity and help counteract these associations between standardized admissions test scores and parental socioeconomic status (SES), a growing number of colleges and universities are leaving it up to students to decide whether to submit SAT and ACT scores with their application packets. The nature of SAT-optional or test-optional admissions policies at selective institutions varies widely, depending on the type of institution and available alternatives (Hoover & Supiano, 2008). For example, at Wake Forest University, the first university ranked in the top 30 by *U.S. News & World Report* to adopt an SAT-optional policy, prospective students are told that submitting SAT I or ACT scores is up to applicants.[6] Candidates may submit these test results if they feel the scores appropriately reflect their academic abilities and accomplishments. But a failure to submit standardized admissions test scores will not be held against students in the admissions decision. In describing the new admissions process, the Wake Forest University (2008) website advises applicants, "If test scores are not submitted, there will be no negative effect on the admissions decision. An admissions decision will be based on what applicants do submit, not [on] what they do not."

A mental experiment is enough to anticipate the effect that adopting a test-optional admissions policy may have on the composition of admitted students. First, if the new policy is widely advertised, the number of applications is likely to increase. Students who previously believed they stood no chance of being admitted because of modest standardized test scores might now be encouraged to apply. Moreover, the composition of the applicant pool is likely to swing toward lower-income and underrepresented minority groups, because students in these groups typically receive lower scores on admissions tests (Bates College, 2004). Another reason the number of applications is likely to increase is that students from more affluent backgrounds who appreciate the educational benefits of diversity may be more likely to apply to an institution whose student body becomes more racially and socioeconomically diverse.

These expectations are supported by experiences of schools that have adopted test-optional policies.[7] In the year immediately following the implementation of new policies, total applications were up by 18% at Knox College, 12% at Lawrence University, and 18% at Drew University (Jaschik, 2006). Holy Cross reported a 41% increase in applications in one year, a gain that was accompanied by more geographic and ethnic diversity (McDermott, 2008). The proportion of admitted students from outside New England rose from 46% to 50%, and nonwhite admittees increased their share from 17% to 21%.

Not only is the applicant pool resized and reshaped by moving to a test-optional admissions policy, but the likelihood that a student with low admissions test scores will be admitted is higher, other things remaining the same. None of the schools in the NSCE sample has adopted a test-optional policy, and at these institutions there is a large admissions payoff to having high SAT or ACT scores. For instance, a student with an SAT score in the 1500–1600 range has a likelihood of being admitted to a selective private NSCE institution that is more than 10 times the likelihood of someone with a score in the 1100–1199 range, other things being equal. If a student with a top score (between 1500 and 1600) is compared with a student in the bottom category (an SAT score lower than 1000), the differential admissions advantage increases to a factor of 550 to 1 (Espenshade & Radford, 2009). The evidence suggests that there are similarly steep gradients associated with ACT and SAT scores at public NSCE schools. With so much weight placed on how one performs on standardized tests, the chances of being admitted to a top school would surely rise if the stigma attached to low scores could be erased from the minds of admissions deans.

The New Look of the Student Body

As the number of schools that have adopted test-optional admissions policies increases, there is mounting anecdotal evidence on the diversity implications of these changes. But there is little or no systematic research on

FIGURE 12.1   Hypothetical Relationships Between an Applicant's SAT Score and the Likelihood of Being Admitted to a Selective College, Other Things Being Equal

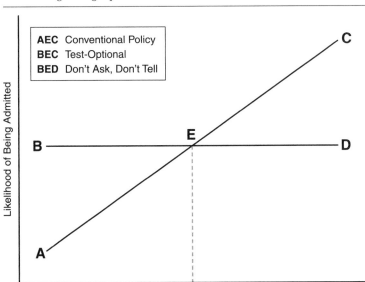

how a change from a more conventional admissions policy that emphasizes standardized test scores, along with other indicators of academic potential, to one that downplays the importance of such scores would alter demographic and academic profiles of admitted students (Syverson, 2007).

We begin by examining two alternative admissions policies. Figure 12.1 illustrates different hypothetical relationships between an applicant's "SAT score" and the chances of being admitted to a selective college or university, all other things being equal. In this illustration "SAT score" stands not just for scores on the SAT I Reasoning test but for outcomes on other standardized admissions tests as well, including the ACT test. The standard relationship between such scores and the probability of being offered a seat in the first-year class is shown by the line AEC. In this relationship, there is a strong positive and monotonic association between test results and admission probabilities. Students with higher scores always have a better chance of admission than students with lower scores, other things held constant.

Adopting an SAT-optional policy is equivalent to telling applicants, "We won't hold a low test score against you." This conclusion follows partly from the fact that students who do not submit standardized test scores typically have below-average test results. For example, based on their 20-year experience with optional SATs for admissions, Bates College found that nonsubmitters score about 90 points lower than submitters on the Verbal SAT and 70 points lower than submitters on the Math SAT, for a total SAT gap of about 160 points (Hiss, 2004). In addition, admissions deans are saying to students that failure to submit standardized test scores will not harm a candidate's chances of success (Wake Forest University, 2008). This kind of test-optional policy is captured in Figure 12.1 by the line BEC. Now, instead of suffering an admissions disadvantage, students with below-average SAT scores have the same chance of being accepted as students with average scores. At the same time, however, students with above-average scores stand an above-average chance of being admitted.

An alternative admissions strategy can also be modeled by using Figure 12.1. Sarah Lawrence College has adopted an expanded version of SAT-optional admissions. They disregard students' SAT and ACT standardized test scores. According to their website for undergraduate admissions, "Our recent decision to remove all standardized testing from the admission process reflects the College's emphasis on writing rather than testing. That's right; we no longer look at standardized test scores" (Sarah Lawrence College, 2009). Under this policy, the College does not ask for admissions test scores, and if students submit them, they are ignored. This is a policy that we might characterize as "Don't Ask, Don't Tell." Because SAT and ACT scores are removed altogether from the admissions equation, they have no bearing on admissions outcomes. Other things being equal, students who have lower scores stand the same chance of being admitted as students with very high scores. In terms of Figure 12.1, a Don't Ask, Don't Tell admissions policy is reflected by the horizontal line BED.

Our analysis of the effects of alternative admissions policies takes as a starting point equations that predict the odds of being admitted to selective private and public colleges, respectively (Espenshade & Radford, 2009). These prediction equations include a large number of explanatory variables, including an applicant's race, social-class background, sex, citizenship, athlete and legacy status, academic characteristics (SAT and ACT test scores, as well as other academic indicators), high school type, participation in extracurricular activities, and character.[8] To model the effects of a change to an SAT-optional admissions policy, SAT I scores below 1200 are assigned the *same* weight as scores between 1200 and 1299. The weights on higher SAT scores are left unchanged. In addition, ACT scores below 25 are given the same weight as scores in the 25–29 range. Weights on ACT scores of 30 or higher are not altered. When Wake Forest University (2008) described its new policy, it announced, too, that "the high school curriculum and classroom performance combined with the student's writing ability and evidence of character and talent are the most important criteria." To capture these additional features, our analysis gives 25% more weight than the standard prediction equations to high school GPA, high school class rank, average score on SAT II examinations, whether a student graduated from one of the 72 "elite" secondary schools in the United States, extracurricular participation, and evidence of character.

Under the Don't Ask, Don't Tell admissions alternative, the importance of standardized admissions test scores is eliminated altogether by assigning zero weight to all categories of SAT I and ACT test scores. However, the additional weight given to other predictors of admissions outcomes under the SAT-optional approach is retained.

The earlier discussion highlighted the experience institutions have had with expanded applicant pools after they adopt a test-optional policy. We incorporate this experience into our analysis in two ways. Under the first alternative, we assume that students who are black or Hispanic or who come from lower- or working-class family backgrounds will apply to SAT-optional institutions in larger numbers than before. After Worcester Polytechnic Institute dropped its SAT requirement, minority applications rose by 30% (Jaschik, 2008).[9] We use this percentage increase and apply it to applicants who are black, Hispanic, or from lower- or working-class families.[10] Under a second approach, we identify candidates who have below-average standardized test scores and assume that students in these categories will be 30% more likely to apply for admission. NSCE students who apply to selective colleges are already highly accomplished academically. As a result, "below-average" SAT I scores are defined as those less than 1200, and below-average ACT scores are those less than 25.

Changes to Applicant Pools

At the private NSCE institutions in our study, the total size of the applicant pool increases by 6.6% when students who typically have below-average admissions test scores are assigned more weight in the applicant pool. Of course, the number of applicants who are black, Hispanic, or from lower- or working-class backgrounds grows by 30%. But other categories of applicants are also somewhat affected. The number of white applicants increases by 2.7%, while the increase for Asians is 3.6%. The growth in applicants from middle-, upper-middle-, or upper-class backgrounds ranges between 2.7% and 4.2%. Alternatively, when 30% more weight is applied directly to applicants with low SAT or ACT scores, the applicant pool increases by 4.7%. Growth is greatest for black (10.7%) and Hispanic (12.1%) applicants and less for whites (3.6%) and Asians (4.0%). Applicants from lower-class backgrounds experience the largest increase (9.6%), followed by those from the working class (8.8%). For students from higher social-class categories, the increase ranges between 3.2% and 5.4%.

The increase in the total applicant pool is 4.2% at public NSCE institutions when 30% more weight is given to black, Hispanic, and lower- or working-class students. This growth is less than the 6.6% gain registered at private colleges because groups whose weight is increased are relatively less numerous at public than at private NSCE schools. For instance, blacks and Hispanics account for 13.3% of all applicants to private NSCE institutions (before receiving more weight), compared with 9.5% at public NSCE schools. And NSCE students from lower- and working-class family backgrounds make up 12.3% of all applicants at private colleges, compared with 7.0% at public universities.

However, the size of the total applicant pool at public NSCE universities jumps by 15.0% when more weight is applied to applicants with low test scores. The increase is greatest for black (24.5%) and Hispanic (16.0%) students, but white (14.2%) and Asian (14.1%) students also gain. Growth is large among applicants from lower-class (25.5%) backgrounds, but increases in other social-class categories are also substantial and range from 13.8% to 16.6%. The reason that overall growth in applicant numbers is larger at public than at private NSCE institutions when more weight is applied directly to students with low scores is that the relative number of low scorers is so much greater at public institutions. Our definition of what constitutes a low SAT I score (less than 1200) or a low ACT score (less than 25) is based on the total NSCE student sample and does not distinguish between applicants to private and public institutions. Applicants to public institutions have much lower SAT scores than do applicants to private schools (1189 vs. 1340), making relatively more applicants to public institutions eligible for the boost given to candidates with low test scores.

Results

Our examination of the diversity implications of test-optional admissions policies is based on a new series of simulation analyses conducted separately for private and public NSCE institutions. Each student observation in the relevant applicant pool is passed through an admissions prediction equation, and a probability of admission is estimated by using that student's characteristics. The admission probability is multiplied by the sampling weight assigned to that case to estimate the expected number of students admitted with those characteristics. The constant term on the prediction equation is controlled so that the total number of students who are admitted equals the number who were actually admitted in the fall of 1997. In other words, an increase in the size of the applicant pool has the effect of making these schools more selective (the percentage of students admitted declines) and not the effect of growing the number of students admitted.

Our results for private colleges are displayed for five different scenarios in Table 12.3. The first column, labeled "Observed baseline admitted," shows the actual profile of students admitted to private NSCE schools for the fall semester of 1997. The remaining four columns show results from the simulations. Each simulation uses one of the two test-optional admissions policies—either the one we have called SAT-optional or the one described as Don't Ask, Don't Tell. In addition, each simulation incorporates one of two approaches for expanding the size of the applicant pool—either the one where more weight is targeted on specific demographic groups (labeled "More apps: I") or the one in which students with low test scores receive more weight (called "More apps: II").

The results show unambiguously that increased racial and socioeconomic diversity can be achieved by switching to test-optional admissions policies. Under the baseline condition in which low SAT scores diminish one's chances of being admitted, 8.3% of admitted candidates are black and 7.9% are Hispanic, for a total minority share of 16.2%. Figures in the remaining four columns show changes in the percentages compared with the baseline condition. For example, under an SAT-optional policy applied to an applicant pool enlarged by giving more weight to black, Hispanic, and low-SES candidates, the percentage of admitted students who are black would increase by 3.0 percentage points to 11.3%, and the Hispanic share would rise to 10.6%. The biggest impact on racial diversity is created by combining a Don't Ask, Don't Tell admissions policy with increased applications from black, Hispanic, and low-SES candidates. Here the share of black and Hispanic students among those admitted rises to slightly more than one-quarter (25.8%).

If we consider as our measure of socioeconomic diversity the share of admitted students who are lower- or working-class, then this type of diversity also increases under all four scenarios. In the baseline, 9.9% of admitted students fall into the low-SES category. This proportion reaches a maximum of 16.0% in the fourth column under a Don't Ask, Don't Tell policy.

One might reasonably ask whether the academic profiles of admitted students would be somewhat weaker as the share of minority and low-SES students increases. We can test this possibility by examining several indicators of academic potential. Average SAT I scores in Table 12.3 are lower in each hypothetical scenario than in the baseline, with declines ranging from about 20–25 SAT points under an SAT-optional policy to about 60 points with a Don't Ask, Don't Tell policy. At the same time, an SAT-optional policy produces slightly higher proportions of admitted students in the top categories of SAT II scores, high school GPA, and high school class rank. If one believes that performance in the high school classroom and mastery of curriculum content are the surest indicators of later college success, then both diversity and college preparedness are increased when

TABLE 12.3 Implications of Alternative Admission Policies and Changing Applicant Pools for the Profile of Admitted Students at Selective Private Institutions

| | | Difference from observed baseline admitted | | | |
| | | SAT-optional[a] | | Don't Ask, Don't Tell[b] | |
Item	Observed baseline admitted	More apps: I[c]	More apps: II[d]	More apps: I[c]	More apps: II[d]
Total	12,233	0	0	0	0
Race (%)					
White	59.9	−5.1	−2.6	−6.1	−3.2
Black	8.3	3.0	1.6	5.5	3.8
Hispanic	7.9	2.7	1.3	4.1	2.6
Asian	23.9	−0.6	−0.3	−3.5	−3.2
Social class (%)					
Upper	7.2	−0.7	−0.4	0	0.4
Upper-middle	49.6	−4.0	−2.9	−6.6	−5.4
Middle	33.4	1.3	1.5	0.4	0.6
Working	8.3	2.5	1.2	5.1	3.5
Lower	1.6	0.8	0.5	1.0	0.7
Mean SAT I score	1405	−21	−23	−59	−63
SAT II score (%)[e]					
750 and above	15.1	0.5	0.6	−3.1	−3.0
650–749	56.8	−1.6	−2.1	−6.1	−6.8
Below 650	28.0	1.2	1.6	9.3	9.8
High school GPA (%)[e]					
A+	42.1	1.5	1.2	−2.3	−2.6
A	37.9	−0.3	−0.3	−0.6	−0.6
A−	14.3	−0.9	−0.6	2.0	2.4
B+ or lower	5.8	−0.4	−0.5	0.8	0.7
High school class rank (%)[e]					
Top 10%	81.1	0.6	0.2	−4.0	−4.4
Next 10%	14.8	0	0.4	2.9	3.4
Bottom 80%	4.1	−0.6	−0.6	1.1	1.0

[a] Applicants with SAT I scores below 1200 or ACT scores below 25 are assumed to have the same chances of being admitted, other things being equal, as applicants with SAT I scores between 1200 and 1299 or ACT scores between 25 and 29, respectively. Twenty-five percent more weight is given to high school GPA, high school curriculum, class rank at high school graduation, scores on SAT II or Subject Tests, having won a large number of awards or held leadership positions in academic extracurricular activities, and character (as measured by participation in a large number of community-service activities).

[b] Applicants' SAT I and ACT scores are given no weight in the admission process. The Don't Ask, Don't Tell policy gives the same amount of additional weight as the SAT-optional policy to performance in high school courses, participation in academic extracurricular activities, and character. See note a.

[c] This alternative assumes that the number of applicants who are black, or Hispanic, or from lower- or working-class backgrounds will increase by 30 percent.

[d] This alternative assumes that the number of applicants with SAT I scores below 1200 or ACT scores below 25 will grow by 30%.

[e] Percentage distribution is calculated on the basis of known outcomes.

Source: Authors' calculations.

colleges shift from more conventional to SAT-optional policies. A different picture emerges, however, when standardized admissions test results are disregarded altogether, as they are under Don't Ask, Don't Tell. In this case, not only do average SAT scores for admitted students decline, so do average scores on SAT II Subject Tests, high school GPA, and high school class rank. Because a Don't Ask, Don't Tell policy results in a greater increase in racial and socioeconomic diversity than does an SAT-optional policy, our results suggest that at some point a tradeoff emerges between diversity and college preparedness.[11]

Results for public universities are shown in Table 12.4. The picture regarding diversity outcomes is qualitatively much the same as it is for private institutions, but the quantitative effects are smaller for public NSCE schools. More racial and socioeconomic diversity is produced by admissions policies that downplay the importance of SAT and ACT scores. The largest increases in diversity come through Don't Ask, Don't Tell policies. For example, when these policies are combined with higher application rates from black, Hispanic, and low-SES students, the share of admitted students who are black or Hispanic rises by 4.2 percentage points (from 9.3% in the baseline to 13.5%). This scenario also produces the largest gain in socioeconomic diversity, from 6.6% of admitted students who are low-SES in the baseline to 10.4% in the simulation.

The story regarding academic preparedness is more varied, just as it was at private institutions. Average SAT I scores are lower in each of the four scenarios, but not by much. The decline is contained within a range of 8–16 SAT points. The proportion of students in the lowest SAT II category (an average score below 650) rises as one moves away from the baseline, and the increases are steepest under Don't Ask, Don't Tell. But in no instance are the changes particularly large. On the other hand, the proportion of students in the admitted student population who have excelled in their coursework in high school—as indicated either by high school GPA or high school class rank—is uniformly larger in each of the four scenarios than in the baseline. It is worth noting that the largest increases in proportions of students with high school GPAs in the A+ range and with high school class ranks in either the top decile or the top two deciles occur with the admissions policy that also produces the most substantial gains in racial and socioeconomic diversity—Don't Ask, Don't Tell.

At both private and public NSCE schools, a relaxed emphasis on SAT and ACT test scores in admissions decisions is accompanied by more racial and social-class diversity. However, each time a different hypothetical scenario is compared with the baseline, two things are changing—institutional admissions policies and the size of the applicant pool. How much of the greater diversity achieved through test-optional policies can be attributed to different admissions policies *per se* and how much to the changing size

TABLE 12.4   Implications of Alternative Admission Policies and Changing Applicant Pools for the Profile of Admitted Students at Selective Public Institutions

| | | Difference from observed baseline admitted | | | |
| | | SAT-optional[a] | | Don't Ask, Don't Tell[b] | |
Item	Observed baseline admitted	More apps: I[c]	More apps: II[d]	More apps: I[c]	More apps: II[d]
Total	14,185	0	0	0	0
Race (%)					
White	87.3	−2.3	−0.6	−4.2	−2.6
Black	7.8	2.1	1.0	3.5	2.3
Hispanic	1.5	0.4	0	0.7	0.3
Asian	3.4	−0.2	−0.4	0	0
Social class (%)					
Upper	2.8	0	−0.1	−0.2	−0.1
Upper-middle	52.5	0.3	1.7	−1.4	0.1
Middle	38.1	−1.9	−2.4	−2.2	−2.2
Working	6.1	1.4	0.7	3.6	2.1
Lower	0.5	0.1	0.1	0.2	0.1
Mean SAT I score	1206	−11	−16	−8	−14
SAT II score (%)[e]					
750 and above	0	0	0	0	0
650–749	35.6	−0.4	−1.5	−2.7	−4.6
Below 650	64.4	0.4	1.5	2.7	4.6
High school GPA (%)[e]					
A+	26.1	1.4	1.5	1.9	1.8
A	37.7	−0.5	0.9	0.8	2.4
A−	15.3	−0.1	−0.2	0.7	0.5
B+ or lower	20.9	−0.7	−2.1	−3.4	−4.7
High school class rank (%)[e]					
Top 10%	52.2	0.6	0.3	3.7	4.0
Next 10%	30.3	0.5	2.3	−0.6	0.5
Bottom 80%	17.5	−1.0	−2.6	−3.1	−4.5

[a] Applicants with SAT I scores below 1200 or ACT scores below 25 are assumed to have the same chances of being admitted, other things being equal, as applicants with SAT I scores between 1200 and 1299 or ACT scores between 25 and 29, respectively. Twenty-five percent more weight is given to high school GPA, high school curriculum, class rank at high school graduation, and scores on SAT II or Subject Tests.

[b] Applicants' SAT I and ACT scores are given no weight in the admission process. The Don't Ask, Don't Tell policy gives the same amount of additional weight as the SAT-optional policy to performance in high school courses. See note a.

[c] This alternative assumes that the number of applicants who are black, or Hispanic, or from lower- or working-class backgrounds will increase by 30%.

[d] This alternative assumes that the number of applicants with SAT I scores below 1200 or ACT scores below 25 will grow by 30%.

[e] Percentage distribution is calculated on the basis of known outcomes.

Source: Authors' calculations.

TABLE 12.5 Relative Contribution of Alternative Admission Policies to Greater Racial and Socioeconomic Diversity on Campus

	Percentage of total change			
	SAT-optional[a]		Don't Ask, Don't Tell[a]	
Item	More apps: I[a]	More apps: II[a]	More apps: I[a]	More apps: II[a]
Selective private institutions				
Larger share black and Hispanic[b]	32	69	57	84
Larger share lower and working class[b]	30	62	60	85
Selective public institutions				
Larger share black and Hispanic[b]	6	25	40	67
Larger share lower and working class[b]	0[c]	6	55	80

[a] See notes to Tables 12.3 and 12.4 for definitions.

[b] Among admitted students.

[c] Calculated value is –3 before rounding to zero.

Source: Authors' calculations; Tables 12.3 and 12.4.

and composition of applicant pools that typically accompany new admissions practices?

Answers to this question are contained in Table 12.5. Numbers in the table represent the percentage of the total change in racial or socioeconomic diversity that can be assigned to new admissions policies at private and public NSCE institutions.[12] Clearly the proportions vary substantially, from zero in one instance to 85% in another. Some generalizations can be drawn nevertheless. First, the proportions of total change in diversity assigned to admissions practices are uniformly larger at private colleges than at public ones. Second, altered admissions policies account for surprisingly similar relative amounts of change in racial and socioeconomic diversity. This is especially the case at private institutions. Third, new admissions practices exert their smallest influence on enhanced racial and socioeconomic diversity in the first column of Table 12.5, where SAT-optional admissions are combined with higher application rates from black, Hispanic, and low-SES students. On the other hand, at both private and public institutions, a switch to a test-optional policy accounts for the largest share of overall change in diversity outcomes when a Don't Ask, Don't Tell policy is invoked and accompanied by more applications from students with below-average admissions test scores regardless of the applicants' race or socioeconomic status.

The Varied Implications of Going Test Optional

In an open letter to faculty colleagues extolling his university's decision to adopt an SAT-optional admissions policy, Wake Forest professor Joseph Soares (2008) wrote:

> Making the SAT optional is a win-win situation for us. It allows us to tell the truth about the SAT: that it is not the gold standard for predicting college performance—insofar as any academic measure does that, it is HSGPA. And SAT "not required" admissions will give us greater social diversity and academically stronger students.

This claim is only partially supported when data from some of the most academically selective colleges and universities in the nation are examined.

We concur that a move away from conventional admissions practices that give substantial weight to standardized admissions test results and toward test-optional admissions policies is likely to produce more diversity on campus—both racial and socioeconomic. The proportion of admitted students who are black or Hispanic or who come from the bottom two social classes is greater in each of the four simulations than in the baseline case at both private and public NSCE institutions. In all instances, the greatest amount of additional diversity relative to the baseline is found when a Don't Ask, Don't Tell admissions policy is paired with an applicant pool enlarged because there are more applications from black, Hispanic, and low-SES students. This outcome might be anticipated because a Don't Ask, Don't Tell policy pays no attention to applicants' SAT or ACT test scores.

But it is not at all clear that a more diverse student body is also an academically stronger one. The outcome depends on which measure one uses to gauge academic strength, what kind of test-optional policy is implemented, and whether the evaluation takes place among selective private or public schools. Average SAT I scores among admitted students are uniformly lower under all of the test-optional simulations. In general, at private colleges, other measures of academic merit (including average scores on SAT II Subject Tests, high school GPA, and high school class rank) are somewhat higher with an SAT-optional policy compared with the baseline, but markedly lower against the baseline with a Don't Ask, Don't Tell policy. When the analysis is directed to public institutions, either kind of test-optional policy produces lower average SAT II scores compared with the baseline. But the same policies appear to produce academically stronger students when measured by high school GPA and high school class rank. This is especially true when admissions deans are free to disregard altogether an applicant's scores on standardized admissions tests.

Finally, among the schools we studied, it is not true that SAT I scores lack power to predict college performance. Enrolled students' expected class ranks, measured either at the end of the freshman year or at graduation, can fluctuate by as much as 30 percentile points depending on whether a student's SAT I score is less than 1000 or greater than 1400. Other measures of academic potential, including SAT II scores, high school GPA and class rank, and high school curriculum, are also predictive of college academic outcomes. Selective college admissions deans typically rely on a combination of these academic indicators rather than on a single factor.

Our take-away message is this: given the great variety of postsecondary institutions in the United States—variety in terms of size, endowment, mission, geography, degree of selectivity, and whether private or public, among others—it is difficult to generalize to all campuses about the likely consequences of a move to a test-optional admissions policy. Such a change could have substantial benefits for some schools but not necessarily for all. One is reminded of a conclusion reached by the Commission on the Use of Standardized Tests in Undergraduate Admission: "a 'one-size-fits-all' approach for the use of standardized tests in undergraduate admission does not reflect the realities facing our nation's many and varied colleges and universities" (NACAC, 2008, p. 7).[13]

We close with two final comments. First, our simulations have emphasized the diversity implications of test-optional admissions policies for the profile of admitted students. But what admissions deans and enrollment managers care about ultimately is the impact on the entering first-year class. To carry our analysis one step further would require additional assumptions about what the yield from admitted students is likely to be. Yield rates can be highly variable, especially in times of economic uncertainty (Supiano, 2009; Zernike, 2009). Worcester Polytechnic Institute experienced a substantial jump in yield rates once it abandoned its SAT requirement. Yield rates increased most for women, underrepresented minority students, and students outside New England. Aiming for a first-year class of 810 students, it received deposits from 959 would-be freshmen (Jaschik, 2008). Our simulations hold constant the number of admitted students, but they could lead to freshman classes that are too big or too small. We prefer to cast our lot with admissions deans and confess to a large dose of uncertainty. Rather than trying to model yield rates explicitly, it seems preferable simply to acknowledge this limitation and move on.

Second, it is unclear how the current economic downturn will affect application rates to schools that have recently adopted test-optional admissions policies. The diversity-inducing effects of these newly instituted policies could be blunted if lower-income students are discouraged from applying. Admissions policies, too, might need to be adjusted to reflect the new economic realities. Constraints on financial aid budgets could mean that schools can no longer afford to admit as many students from lower social-class categories, even if these students make it into the applicant pool. In short, today's economic climate could produce greater racial diversity at colleges with test-optional admissions policies but little more (or even less) socioeconomic diversity.

Notes

This chapter is adapted from a presentation delivered by Thomas Espenshade at the "Rethinking Admissions" conference held April 15–16, 2009, at Wake Forest University. Partial support for this research came from the Eunice Kennedy Shriver National Institute of Child Health and Human Development (grant #5R24HD047879).

1. Bryn Mawr College (2009), Loyola College (2009), and New York University (2009) are some of the most recent examples of four-year institutions that have announced a form of test-optional or test-flexible admissions policies.

2. Supporting empirical evidence on the behaviors of selective postsecondary institutions is provided by Alon and Tienda (2007) and Horn and Yun (2008).

3. Zwick (2002, 2007) provides additional empirical evidence that total (Math plus Verbal) SAT scores and ACT composite scores are useful in predicting first-year college grade point averages and college graduation rates.

4. Other research has shown that the predictive capacity of SAT I scores is overstated if parental socioeconomic status is not controlled (Geiser & Studley, 2001; Rothstein, 2004). Each of the regressions in Table 12.1 includes measures of parents' social class and other dimensions of socioeconomic status. We find that neither the number of advanced placement (AP) exams nor the number of SAT II achievement tests taken is related to any measure of college success. Significant predictors of college graduation rates are more likely to include institutional selectivity, parental socioeconomic status, a student's race, whether a student is foreign born or has a foreign-born parent, and how satisfied students are with the social aspects of college life.

5. West-Faulcon (2009) has argued that state bans on affirmative action coupled with substantial reliance on SAT scores in admissions to selective public universities have the effect of discriminating against racial minorities, in violation of Title VI of the 1964 Civil Rights Act, thereby setting the stage for race-based affirmative action as a remedial measure.

6. Scores on SAT II Subject Tests are already optional at Wake Forest University (2008).

7. Syverson (2007, p. 64) says that, "Virtually every college that has been test-optional for an extended period of time reported substantial growth in applications and matriculation among underrepresented students in the years since the introduction of their test-optional policy."

8. The remaining academic indicators include number of AP tests taken, number of SAT II or Subject Tests taken, average score on SAT II exams, high school GPA, high school class rank, and whether an applicant is a National Merit Scholar or a National Achievement Scholar. High school type is measured in two ways: (a) by whether the school is a public/nonmagnet, public/magnet, parochial/religious, or private school; and (b) by whether it is one of the 72 "most outstanding" high schools in the United

States as identified by two former Princeton University admissions officers. Participation in extracurricular activities is identified by having won "a large number of academic awards or leadership positions" in high school—the only extracurricular activity related to admissions outcomes at private colleges. "Character" in our models is measured by having participated in "a large number of community service activities." Variables for extracurricular participation and character are not included in the prediction equations for public universities because the regression coefficients are too unstable.

9. In the first year after Providence College introduced its test-optional admissions policy, applications from nonwhite students and from first-generation college students both increased by 21%. The enrolled first-year class included 31% more nonwhite students than in the previous year and 19% more students who were the first in their family to attend college. The percentage of the class that was eligible for Pell Grants increased from 7.3% to 11.8% (Shanley, 2007).

10. In practice, we increased the sampling weights for applicants in these categories by 30%.

11. Zwick's (2007) analysis also draws attention to the tension between promoting access and maintaining college selectivity.

12. To estimate these proportions, simulations at private and public institutions were redone by changing one input at a time. For example, the baseline case was compared with a simulation in which an SAT-optional policy was adopted but the applicant pool did not change. In this way, the amount of change in racial and economic diversity produced by each of the two admissions policies and each of the two ways of expanding applicant pools can be estimated. Numbers reported in Table 12.5 are the average of two figures—the percentage amount of change in diversity produced by a different admissions policy and 100 minus the percentage amount of change in diversity produced by an enlarged applicant pool.

13. In a similar vein, the President of Providence College, reflecting on his institution's decision to stop requiring SAT or ACT test scores for admission, concluded that, "Other institutions considering this initiative should do so in the context of their missions rather than simply joining the current trend" (Shanley, 2007, p. 435).

References

Alon, S., & Tienda, M. (2007). Diversity, opportunity, and the shifting meritocracy in higher education. *American Sociological Review, 72*(4), 487–511.

Atkinson, R. C., & Geiser, S. (2009). Reflections on a century of college admission tests. *Educational Researcher, 38*(9), 665–676.

Bates College. (2004). *SAT study: 20 years of optional testing.* Retrieved February 7, 2009, from http://www.bates.edu/ip-optional-testing-20years.xml

Bowen, W. G., & Bok, D. (1998). *The shape of the river: Long-term consequences of considering race in college and university admissions.* Princeton, NJ: Princeton University Press.

Bowen, W. G., Kurzweil, M. A., & Tobin, E. M. (2005). *Equity and excellence in American higher education.* Charlottesville: University of Virginia Press.

Bryn Mawr College. (2009). *Bryn Mawr adopts new testing policy promoting greater flexibility and emphasis on subject mastery.* Retrieved June 23, 2009, from http://news.bryn mawr.edu/?p=2793

Espenshade, T. J., & Radford, A. W. (2009). *No longer separate, not yet equal: Race and class in elite college admission and campus life.* Princeton, NJ: Princeton University Press.

FairTest. (2009). [Website of The National Center for Fair and Open Testing.] http://fairtest.org; last accessed December 28, 2009.

Geiser, S., & Santelices, M. V. (2007). Validity of high-school grades in predicting student success beyond the freshman year: High-school record vs. standardized tests as indicators of four-year college outcomes. *Research and Occasional Papers Series: CSHE.9.07.* Berkeley: Center for Studies in Higher Education, University of California. Retrieved October 2, 2007, from http://cshe.berkeley.edu/publications/publications.php?id=265

Geiser, S., & Studley, R. (2001, October 29). *UC and the SAT: Predictive validity and differential impact of the SAT I and SAT II at the University of California.* Oakland: Office of the President, University of California.

Gerald, D., & Haycock, K. (2006). *Engines of inequality: Diminishing equity in the nation's premier public universities.* Washington, DC: Education Trust.

Hiss, W. C. (2004, October 1). *Optional SAT, VP Bill Hiss '66 speaker notes.* Paper presented at the 60th Annual Meeting of the National Association for College Admission Counseling, Milwaukee, Wisconsin. Retrieved February 7, 2009, from http://www.bates.edu/x61659.xml

Hoover, E. (2008). What admissions officials think. *Chronicle of Higher Education, 54*(34), B3.

Hoover, E., & Supiano, B. (2008). Wake Forest U. joins ranks of test-optional colleges. *Chronicle of Higher Education, 54*(39), A21.

Horn, C. L., & Yun, J. T. (2008). Is 1500 the new 1280? The SAT and admissions since *Bakke.* In P. Marin & C. L. Horn (Eds.), *Realizing Bakke's legacy: Affirmative action, equal opportunity, and access to higher education* (pp. 145–169). Sterling, VA: Stylus.

Jaschik, S. (2006, May 26). Momentum for going SAT-optional. *Inside Higher Ed.* Retrieved February 2, 2009, from http://insidehighered.com/news/2006/05/26/sat

Jaschik, S. (2008, May 27). Another first for SAT-optional movement. *Inside Higher Ed.* Retrieved May 29, 2008, http://www.insidehighered.com/news/2008/05/27/wake

Kobrin, J. L., Patterson, B. F., Shaw, E. J., Mattern, K. D., & Barbuti, S. M. (2008). *Validity of the SAT for predicting first-year college grade point average.* (College Board Research Report No. 2008-5.) New York: College Board. Retrieved July 4, 2008, from http://professionals.collegeboard.com/profdownload/Validity_of_the_SAT_for_Predicting_First_Year_College_Grade_Point_Average.pdf

Loyola College. (2009). Loyola announces launch of test-optional policy. Retrieved June 5, 2009, from http://admissions.loyola.edu/admissions/admissions/freshman-admission/testoptional.asp

Mattern, K. D., Patterson, B. F., Shaw, E. J., Kobrin, J. L., & Barbuti, S. M. (2008). *Differential validity and prediction of the SAT.* (College Board Research Report No. 2008-4.) New York: College Board. Retrieved July 4, 2008, from http://professionals.collegeboard.com/profdownload/Differential_Validity_and_Prediction_of_the_SAT.pdf

McDermott, A. B. (2008). Surviving without the SAT [Commentary]. *Chronicle of Higher Education, 55*(7), A41.

National Association for College Admission Counseling (NACAC). (2008). *Report of the Commission on the Use of Standardized Tests in Undergraduate Admission.* Arlington, VA: Author.

New York University. (2009). *New standardized testing policy.* Retrieved April 20, 2009, from http://admissions.nyu.edu/

Rothstein, J. M. (2004). College performance predictions and the SAT. *Journal of Econometrics, 121,* 297–317.

Sarah Lawrence College. (2009). *Frequently asked questions.* Retrieved February 10, 2009, from http://www.slc.edu/admission/Frequently_Asked_Questions.php

Shanley, B. J. (2007). Test-optional admission at a liberal arts college: A founding mission affirmed. *Harvard Educational Review, 77*(4), 429–435.

Soares, J. A. (2007). *The power of privilege: Yale and America's elite colleges.* Stanford, CA: Stanford University Press.

Soares, J. A. (2008, September 24). *University makes SAT, ACT optional: Open letter to faculty on Wake Forest's new admissions policy.* Retrieved February 7, 2009, from http://www.wfu.edu/wowf/2008/sat-act/soares/

Supiano, B. (2009). For admissions offices, a spring of uncertainty. *Chronicle of Higher Education, 55*(22), A22.

Syverson, S. (2007, Summer). The role of standardized tests in college admissions: Test-optional admissions. *New Directions for Student Services, 118,* 55–70. Retrieved from www.interscience.wiley.com (DOI: 10.1002/ss.241).

Wake Forest University. (2008). *Questions and answers on Wake Forest's new SAT/ACT policy.* Retrieved May 29, 2008, from http://www.wfu.edu/admissions/sat-act/

West-Faulcon, K. (2009). The river runs dry: When Title VI trumps state anti-affirmative action laws. *University of Pennsylvania Law Review, 157*(4), 1075–1160.

Zernike, K. (2009, March 8). In a shifting era of admissions, colleges are sweating. *New York Times.*

Zwick, R. (2002). *Fair game? The use of standardized admissions tests in higher education.* New York: RoutledgeFalmer.

Zwick, R. (2007). College admissions in twenty-first-century America: The role of grades, tests, and games of chance. *Harvard Educational Review, 77*(4), 419–429.

Conclusion

JOSEPH A. SOARES

Some of our nation's top researchers and innovators in the field of college admissions have contributed to this volume. The discussion began with an overview of admissions and testing, and continued with specific critiques of the SAT and ACT. Case studies of the variables that best predict college performance—within different types of institutional settings—were presented, as were accounts of implementation of test-optional policies. In these concluding remarks, I review the high points of the discussion and look ahead to how institutions can strengthen their admissions processes. In addition, I provide the update on the social composition and academic performance of Wake Forest's first test-optional cohorts that I promised in the Introduction.

To begin, Pulitzer Prize winner Daniel Golden provided us with shocking examples of how elite colleges, even today, make admissions decisions that privilege the rich. The President Emeritus of the University of California, Richard Atkinson, and his research associate, Saul Geiser, reviewed a century of standardized testing and made the case for secondary school curriculum-based achievement tests over the SAT/ACT. John Aubrey Douglass gave us a historical account of the vicissitudes of testing politics at the University of California, reminding us that research rarely drives policy and institutional memories are short. California began using the SAT in 1968, and retained it in 2009, against the advice of key researchers. The politics of boards of governors and the visions of administrators play more important roles in admissions policies than faculty senates or scholarly statistics. Beginning in 2012, the University of California system will admit anyone within the top 9% of each high school graduating class, but the situation still is not optimal, as SAT/ACT test scores continue to be required of everyone. Robert Sternberg (now Provost at Oklahoma State) offers us one possible solution: tests of creativity, practical ability, and wisdom such as those he designed and piloted while he was at Tufts University. Sternberg's new tests outperform the SAT in predicting grades, and they do so without the SAT's racial or gender disparities. Jay Rosner, Executive Director of the Princeton Review Foundation, found serious racial and gender biases in the question selection process for the SAT, and it remains to be seen whether or not the Educational Testing Service (ETS) will open its records to independent scholars to evaluate that damning charge.

The track record of the ETS with respect to sharing data on its technical internal procedures is not encouraging. It took pressure from the University of California, and 2 years of in-house dithering, for the ETS to release data relevant to a previous charge of racial bias. Roy Freedle, a retired researcher with 30 years of employment at the ETS to draw on, found racial and social-class biases in the ETS's scoring of vocabulary questions. The ETS reluctantly provided data to the University of California to test Freedle's case, and the work was done by two independent scholars, Maria Veronica Santelices, Catholic University of Chile, and Mark Wilson, Professor in the Graduate School of Education, UC Berkeley. They substantiated Freedle's conclusion that the test has a racial bias, reporting that Freedle's findings "hold for current test forms. . . . The confirmation of unfair test results throws into question the validity of the test and, consequently, all decisions based on its results. . . . [It is] biased against the African American[s] . . . and could be exposed to legal challenge" (Santelices & Wilson, 2010, p. 126). Naturally, the ETS rejects these findings and continues to resist independent evaluation of its data. Nonetheless, Freedle's case was partially made, and that lends support to the notion that Rosner's charges of bias are also true.

The three institutional case studies presented in this book focus on the variables that best predict college performance, and they all tell the same story. Whether the findings are from a highly selective private university, a highly selective private liberal arts college, or a selective public university, the numbers are similar and perfectly clear. High school GPA is the best academic predictor of college grades, and the SAT/ACT adds only very modestly to the power of statistical models. If for students going into particular fields, such as engineering, test scores contribute more to the prediction of college grades than the 2% they do in most fields, then a university may feel the need to request test scores from prospective students in those areas. But the question of what good is served by requiring test scores of all remains unanswered.

Three discussions of implementation of test-optional policies made up the final section of the book. Robert Schaeffer treated us to an overview of the experiences of the early pioneers for this policy, liberal arts colleges. He also provided a step-by-step procedural list for institutions thinking about going test-optional. Martha Allman, Wake Forest's admissions director, contributed a narrative on that institution's transition year to test-optional admissions policies. Princeton's Thomas Espenshade and Chang Young Chung provided statistical simulations, using national data from selective private and public universities. Their models suggest that test-optional works best at private colleges, and a policy of "Don't Ask, Don't Tell" on testing (i.e., test scores are not requested, and any scores submitted are ignored) works best at public universities. Regardless of whether a selective institution is private or public, its undergraduate school would become more diverse and academically stronger with adoption of some alternative to mandatory testing.

One proven option for public universities that has not been explored in depth in this book is the local high school rank exemption strategy. As noted earlier, the University of California is introducing such a policy in 2012; the University of Texas has had a similar system in place since 1997. Texas law guarantees admission at a public university in the state to students who graduate in the top 10% of their local high school class—without any regard to standardized test scores.

Since its enactment in 1997, the Texas top-10% rule has been the subject of controversy. Misunderstandings about the rule even extend into our legal system. The U.S. Court of Appeals for the Fifth Circuit in January 2011 issued a mistaken opinion on the impact of the Texas top-10% program on academic selectivity. The ruling claims that "the Top Ten Percent Law eliminated the consideration of test scores, and correspondingly reduced academic selectivity" (Jaschik, 2011a), and that is wrong. Not only does the court equate one measure (an SAT/ACT score) with academic selectivity while denigrating another measure (high school GPA ranking) as somehow not being a metric of academic selectivity, but it also ignores the research done at the University of Texas that shows the value and virtue of high school ranking as a predictor of college grades and graduation. As Vice Provost and Director of Admissions at UT Austin, Bruce Walker released multiple reports on the 10% solution, showing how high school ranking is an excellent and reliable predictor of college GPA and graduation.

Being admitted to the university from the top 10% of any high school graduating class allows a youth to overcome the disadvantages of coming from a low-income family, of having parents without high school degrees, and of attending a low-performing high school. Walker (2009) found that top-10% youths from families with the lowest incomes (below $20,000 per year) and from the least desirable high schools (those officially ranked "low performing") do better academically at the University of Texas than youths from below the top 10% even when those individuals attended "exemplary" high schools, come from high-income families, and have college-educated parents. The special qualities that it takes for a youth to be in the top 10% of his or her high school graduating class lift that youth

academically above youths from the "best" schools and wealthiest families, when they are not also in the top 10%. Schools have different resources
and draw from communities with different racial and socioeconomic
makeups, but being in the "talented tenth," to borrow a phrase from
W.E.B. Du Bois (1903), signals one's academic promise far better than any
standardized test. High school records remain, as they always have been,
the best measure of "academic selectivity" and the best predictor of grades
and graduation rates. It is time for the courts and the public to learn the
relative merits of school grades versus test scores.

The issue of variations between schools, or grade inflation within them,
as a justification for keeping the SAT/ACT has been addressed by the Texas
experience, but a definitive refutation of the notion that high school grades
are unreliable was offered in a book published in 2009. That book is titled
Crossing the Finish Line, and it was written by William Bowen, Emeritus
President of both Princeton University and the Mellon Foundation; Michael
McPherson, President of the Spencer Foundation and Emeritus President of
Macalester College; and Matthew Chingos, research associate at the Mellon
Foundation and graduate student at Harvard. These authors debunk the
idea that differences among high schools matter to the predictive power of
the high school GPA. In a thorough examination, using a national data set
for public universities at three different levels of selectivity, Bowen and his
collaborators found "the main story line is straightforward. High school
grades are a far better predictor of both four-year and six-year graduation
rates than are SAT/ACT test scores . . . even when we cannot (or do not)
take account of the characteristics of the high schools that the student
attended" (Bowen, Chingos, & McPherson, 2009, pp. 113, 123).

It is a myth that SAT/ACT scores perform better as predictors than high
school grades because those tests are "nationally normed," whereas high
school grades are not. No matter how counterintuitive it may sound, in
study after study, including those done by the College Board, high school
GPA works better than the SAT despite the latter being nationally normed.
"Nationally normed" simply means that test scores are translated into a
percentile ranking distributed on a curve that looks like the Liberty Bell.
The bell curve never changes, regardless of whether students are more or
less accomplished than those of previous generations. On a scoring curve
shaped like a bell, there will always be 7% at the undesirable left-hand side
of the curve, 24% next to them, 38% in the middle, 24% to the right of the
middle, and 7% at the desirable far right. The College Board has managed
to norm scores in that fashion from 1926 to the present. But how do they
know that intelligence is distributed in our population in the shape of a
bell curve? What law of nature or god determines that human intelligence
is always parceled out in such a stingy fashion? For decades, critics have

objected that the bell curve is not empirically valid (see Gould, 1981). The SAT bell curve remains stagnant despite strong evidence that intelligence test scores should be rising. James R. Flynn discovered the famous "Flynn effect," a rising tide of intellectual performance. As he explains it, the "'Flynn effect' . . . [shows that] each generation outscores the previous generation on IQ tests often by huge margins" (Flynn, 2000, p. 35). The College Board's belief in the immutable validity of the bell curve is insufficient to refute empirical evidence and does *not* lift SAT scores above high school grades as effective predictors of first-year college grades, cumulative college GPA, or even whether a youth will graduate from college within 6 years.

Few names today are more associated with the bell curve than Charles Murray's, and yet he also has come out against the SAT/ACT. He still accepts the psychometric soundness of the test but argues that its positive usefulness to identity underprivileged talent is long gone. If it was ever a democratizing stairway for promising nonaffluent youths, that passageway has become blocked by the inheritors of the privilege of upper socioeconomic status. Murray is also against test-optional admissions; his contribution to this volume suggests that even administering the test sends out the wrong signal about merit and inheritance.

The authors represented in this volume may not all agree on whether subject tests are superior to aptitude tests; on whether racial or ethnic biases are built into the SAT; or on whether the SAT should be downplayed, made optional, or rejected. But there are broad areas of agreement, particularly on two fundamentals: (a) high school grades are the best single academic predictor of college grades and graduation rates, and (b) institutions of higher education should all reexamine the effectiveness and fairness of their admissions standards. We must, as the NACAC commissioners urge, "take back the conversation" on admissions (NACAC, 2008, p. 21).

I hope that as part of this conversation each college would find ways to move beyond the SAT/ACT. When we in higher education require SAT/ACT test scores, we undercut the economic, racial, and creative diversity of our applicant pool. When scores are used to select between two comparable candidates, we surrender our judgment to statistical tea leaves. And when we reference scores to describe our students or our institution, we display the nose hairs of social class snobbery.

What grounds are there for optimism that colleges will move toward test-optional policies and embrace, in addition to the academic evaluations contained in the high school record, new tools to assess creativity, practical ability, and wisdom? Which trends or actors are going to move us forward? If the future of higher education were left entirely up to faculty senates, we would be in for a snail-slow slog toward change. As winners in the high-stakes standardized-test-selection machine, many professors are disinclined to notice its faults. Most campuses that have gone test-optional have done so because administrators and admissions staff have pushed for the change. It was a milestone when Richard Atkinson, as President of the University of California, put the controversy over the SAT/ACT on the table. And another milestone was reached when the professional association for admissions workers, NACAC, in September 2008 put its authority into encouraging each college to do its own internal study. In addition to NACAC's moral push, there is an incentive provided by the job market for admissions staff and top administrators. As more and more colleges go test-optional, there is an incentive for mobile and progressive administrators to be the ones to lead their colleges into the 21st century on admissions. But there is an even stronger push under way from the K–12 side of education that works against the SAT/ACT. As standards in schools become more uniform, and as assessment tools become more sophisticated, the space in which the SAT/ACT can operate shrinks. It would be a poetic historic reversal if new and effective assessment tests in K–12 drove out the bad old admissions tests for college.

The movement for common curriculum standards and assessment tests is being led by associations of states. The Common Core State Standards Initiative movement so far has 36 states participating. The National Governors Association has gotten 48 states to work together to find common standards in math and reading, and the White House supports that effort. The U.S. Department of Education has put $330 million into the coordinated efforts of 44 states to devise new computer-based performance-assessment tests for math and reading. In the words of an education professor at UC Berkeley, Bruce Fuller, quoted in the *New York Times* regarding this move, "If these plans work out, it'll turn the current testing system upside down" (Dillon, 2010). The testing requirements for college admissions will look antiquated alongside the new performance-assessment tests scheduled for use in high schools by 2014. Once schools are using new types of tests, the case for colleges going test-optional and embracing Robert J. Sternberg's alternatives for capturing information on creativity and wisdom will be even more attractive. There is an important opening here for the ETS in a post-SAT 21st century, which it has already seized, helping the U.S. Department of Education and America's state governments devise and implement common core-curriculum performance-assessment tests.

In the meantime, we will continue to evaluate the evidence, which returns us to the question raised in the Introduction: how well did Wake Forest's (WFU) test-optional cohorts do academically? Before answering the question about academic performance, we should review the basic facts on how

TABLE 13.1   Wake Forest University's Test-Optional Application Pool and Yield, 2009 and 2010

- WFU applications went up by 16%
- Non-test-submitters were 32–36% of applicant pool
- African American applications went up by 70%
- Our 2009 "yield" was 1201 matriculating students: 23% black or Hispanic, 7% Asian, 10% first generation, 8% Pell Grant recipients, 75% from outside North Carolina, and 26% non-test-submitters.
- For the fall 2010 "yield," there were 22% black or Hispanic, 9% Asian, 11% first generation, 11% Pell Grant recipients, 78% from outside North Carolina, and 28% non-test-submitters.
- Percentage of students from top 10% of their high school class went up from 65% in 2008 to 75% in 2009, and up again in 2010 to 81%.

WFU, like all of the other institutions that have gone test-optional, increased its applicant pool and its social and racial diversity through the new policy. After the test-optional policy was announced, our applicant pool, even in the worst economic year in recent history, went up by 16%; our minority applicants increased by 70%. As reported in *The Journal of Blacks in Higher Education,* 6% of Wake Forest's senior cohort were minorities of color before the policy change; in the two cohorts admitted thus far as test-optional, the percentage of black and Hispanic students has gone up to 23%. Asian student numbers have increased to 11%. First-generation youths, where neither parent went to college, jumped to 11%; Pell Grant youths, whose families earn near the poverty line, nearly doubled to 11%. In 2009, 78% of WFU undergraduates came from outside North Carolina. (See Table 13.1.)

We looked at the logistic odds of one of our matriculating students being among the 26% who came in without reporting a test score. First-generation students were 1.89 times more likely than their counterparts to be nonsubmitters; females were 1.64 times more likely than males to be nonsubmitters; minority youths of color were 1.54 times more likely than whites to be nonsubmitters; North Carolina youths were 1.44 times more likely than those from outside the state to be nonsubmitters; high-financial-aid-need students were 1.23 times more likely than full-pays to be nonsubmitters. Test-optional was opening up space for talented first-generation, female, and minority youths; for North Carolinians; and for high-financial-aid-need youths to apply and be selected.

What about academic records? Were we getting stronger students, as Espenshade and Chung's simulations predicted? Yes, we were. In the last class to matriculate at WFU before test-optional, the class entering in 2008, 65% were from the top 10% of their high school graduating class. In our first year of test-optional, the class entering in 2009, the percentage from

TABLE 13.2 Wake Forest's First Test-Optional Cohort in 2009, Divided by Financial Status and Whether or Not a Test Score Was Submitted, with Details on First-Generation, Minority, or Asian Composition

Non-submitters: 26%	Test score submitters: 74%
Of those without financial need: 4% first generation 14% minority 5% Asian	Of those without financial need: 2% first generation 15% minority 5% Asian
Of those with low-financial need: 7% first generation 14% minority 3% Asian	Of those with low-financial need: 7% first generation 17% minority 8% Asian
Of those with high-financial need: 36% first generation 56% minority 12% Asian	Of those with high-financial need: 21% first generation 34% minority 9% Asian

the top 10% went up to 75%; in Year 2 of test-optional, 2010, our youths from the top 10% of their local high schools went up to 81%. To judge from high school ranking, our students were getting stronger every year under test-optional admissions.

What about the academic record of these students in college? On the criterion of retention, the percentage of students who returned after a freshman year for a sophomore year at WFU remained exactly as high as before test-optional, at 94%. There were no differences between nonsubmitters and submitters on continuing their educations at WFU.

What about grades? We looked at first-year grade-point averages (FYGPA) as carefully as possible. We wanted to compare "apples with apples," so we statistically controlled for gender, race, first generation, financial-aid status, athletic status, high school grades, rigor of high school curriculum, and region of the country. Then we compared nonsubmitters with submitters to see if there were any statistical differences between them on FYGPA. Table 13.2 shows how some of these variables broke down.

In multivariate regression models, we found that for full-pay students there was no statistical difference in FYGPA between test-score submitters and nonsubmitters. For high-need students (family contribution below $25,000) there was no difference for FYGPA. For low-need students (family contribution between $25,000 and $50,000) from North Carolina, no difference was found. For low-need students from anywhere in United States but one region (which will remain anonymous), there was no difference. For low-need students from the anonymous region, there was a difference.

This group was made up of 20 students, among whom test submitters (12) had an average GPA of 3.2 and nonsubmitters (8) had an average GPA of 2.8. At WFU, a B+ grade starts at GPA 3.33 and B– starts at 2.67; thus, all of the difference for those 20 students falls within the B grade range. Between nonsubmitters and submitters, we did not find differences—the one anonymous region's few low-need students notwithstanding—that would lead us to reconsider our test-optional policy. We will monitor everything possible about our students, but so far, so very good.

First-year grades and retention rates are important, but they represent just one dimension of success in college. We looked at other indicators of the contribution to our campus being made by the test-optional cohorts. We heard plenty of anecdotes from faculty about more lively class discussions and about students looking more diverse, not just racially but also in terms of attire and comportment. Student organizations told us that more students, first-years in particular, were volunteering than previously. The one place where we could get solid statistics on the difference the new cohorts made was in library usage. Librarians are marvelous for keeping track of their domain, and from them we learned that library usage went up dramatically: 63% increase in personal research sessions, 55% increase in instructional library sessions, 26% increase in credited library instructional classes, 10% increase in daily average visits, and 62% increase in daily unique library website visits.

Whether in terms of social diversity, top-10% ranked high school graduates, FYGPA, retention, campus life, classroom excitement, or library usage, test-optional is clearly working for Wake Forest in the 21st century.

I am confident that we would as a nation benefit immensely from dropping the SAT/ACT and focusing our attention, and our prospective students' minds, on their high school classwork. Cognitive analytical abilities, "book smarts," are best judged by a youth's performance over the years in the classroom. It is also time to emphasize that other attributes and skills, in addition to analytic cognitive ones—including diversity, creativity, athletic abilities, problem solving, leadership, and ethical maturity—are all highly valuable to a collegiate community. All students, regardless of race, ethnicity, or gender, learn best in a community with a diversity of talents and demographics.

Colleges do not function in separate tiers, and youths are not reducible to test scores. Our world is *not* best served by a test-score social Darwinism in support of a collegiate caste system. Going to college should be for both the youth and the institution a process of finding the right fit and the right mix of those who will make the best of their opportunities and contribute the most to our world.

Moving beyond high-stakes standardized tests is a beginning, not a panacea. There are many issues, in addition to testing, that must be addressed if we are to respond to the challenges of our time. The age of transparency and accountability is upon higher education, and that is a good thing. It is hypocritical for colleges to sit in judgment of the measure of a youth, while refusing to allow that youth to know the measure of the education being offered.

At present, sadly, youths rely too much on the ratings industry to learn about the "value added" by any particular college. Ratings are dominated by commercial magazines that care more about sales than about getting the information right. College officials do not help when they lament the inadequacy of the magazine's methodology and yet brag about any upward movement of their college's score.

There are a few leading the way on fixing the ratings game, Lloyd Thacker and the Education Conservancy among them, as well as Yale's admissions dean, Jeffrey Brenzel. We in higher education have, as Brenzel told *Inside Higher Ed,* "a moral obligation" (Jaschik, 2008) to provide an alternative to the commercial magazine ratings game.

Higher education must take back the conversation on ratings in the same way it must do so on testing. The ways we evaluate colleges must undergo a complete transformation. Education is not a zero-sum game for youths, and it should not be one for colleges. A college should not be rated "excellent" because in the popularity contest it has many times more qualified applicants than it can accommodate, and thus it beats rivals by rejecting a higher percentage of its applicant pool. A college should be rated more by what it does within its walls than by how many it excludes at the door.

Fortunately, higher education is in the contentious yet healthy process of reevaluating its metric for success. As Syracuse University's Vice President for Enrollment Management, Donald A. Saleh, put it, "there is this tension in higher education between the old ways in which colleges described the quality of their class—test scores and G.P.A. . . . and the new metric, . . . socioeconomic diversity, the percentage of students who are first-generation in college" (Jaschik, 2011b). Saleh and Syracuse, where Pell Grant students jumped from 14% to 26% and minorities from 16% to 30%, have it right (Jaschik, 2011b). Access and diversity should matter more than "selectivity" based on rejections.

Getting diverse youths in the door must be matched by an effective learning community and by high completion rates. What happens to one's students inside college and afterward should matter to our metric of success. Assessing how well our students are learning should be as important as testing what they know. Colleges should be able to say, and youths should understand, the value that is added by their education. If colleges are not measurably enhancing the critical thinking and communication skills of our youths, if our youths are not developing a broader and deeper knowledge of the world, and if our youths are not graduating equipped to move on, then we have failed them in the test of life.

References

Bowen, W., Chingos, M., & McPherson, M. (2009). *Crossing the finish line: Completing college at America's public universities.* Princeton, NJ: Princeton University Press.

Dillon, S. (2010, September 2). U.S. asks educators to reinvent tests, and how they are given. *New York Times.*

Du Bois, W.E.B. (1903). The talented tenth. In *The negro problem* (pp. 31–75). New York: James Pott.

Flynn, J. R. (2000). IQ trends over time: Intelligence, race, and meritocracy. In K. Arrow, S. Bowles, & S. Durlauf (Eds.), *Meritocracy and economic inequality* (pp. 35–60). Princeton, NJ: Princeton University Press.

Gould, S. J. (1981). *The mismeasure of man.* New York: W. W. Norton.

Jaschik, S. (2008, September 26). Creating the anti-rankings. *Inside Higher Ed.*

Jaschik, S. (2011a, January 19). Key win for affirmative action. *Inside Higher Ed.*

Jaschik, S. (2011b, March 2). Is there a price for inclusiveness? *Inside Higher Ed.*

Santelices, M. V., & Wilson, M. (2010). Unfair treatment? The case of Freedle, the SAT, and the standardization approach to differential item functioning. *Harvard Educational Review, 80*(1), 106–133.

Walker, B. (2009). *Overcoming the effects of social structure on college-going behavior and academic performance: Texas and the top 10% solution.* Austin: University of Texas.

About the Contributors

Martha Allman is Dean of Admissions at Wake Forest University.

Richard C. Atkinson is President Emeritus of the University of California and Professor Emeritus of Cognitive Science and Psychology at the University of California, San Diego.

Chang Young Chung is Statistical Programmer and Data Archivist of the Office of Population Research, Princeton University. He has published several articles on elite college admissions with Thomas J. Espenshade.

Christopher Cornwell is a Professor of Economics in the Terry College of Business at the University of Georgia, an Adjunct Professor of Public Administration and Policy in the School of Public and International Affairs, and a Senior Fellow in the University's Institute for Higher Education.

John Aubrey Douglass is a Senior Research Fellow in the Center for Studies in Higher Education, University of California, Berkeley. He is the author of *The Conditions for Admission: Access, Equity, and the Social Contract of Public Universities* (2007).

Thomas J. Espenshade is a Professor of Sociology and a Faculty Associate of the Office of Population Research, Princeton University. He is a co-author (with Alexandria Walton Radford) of *No Longer Separate, Not Yet Equal: Race and Class in Elite College Admission and Campus Life* (2009).

Saul Geiser is a Research Associate in the Center for Studies in Higher Education, University of California, Berkeley. He is former Director of Research for Admissions and Outreach for the University of California system.

Daniel Golden, Pulitzer Prize Winner, is Editor-at-Large at Bloomberg News, former Senior Editor at Conde Nast *Portfolio,* and former Deputy Bureau Chief in the Boston Bureau of the *Wall Street Journal.* He is the author of *The Price of Admission: How America's Ruling Class Buys Its Way into Elite Colleges—and Who Gets Left Outside the Gates* (2006).

David Hawkins is National Research and Public Policy Director of the National Association for College Admission Counseling (NACAC), Washington, DC.

John Latting is Dean of Undergraduate Admissions at Johns Hopkins University. He worked previously in the offices of Undergraduate Admissions at the California Institute of Technology and at Stanford University.

Charles Murray is the W. H. Brady Scholar at the American Enterprise Institute for Public Policy Research, Washington, DC. He is a co-author (with Richard J. Herrnstein) of *The Bell Curve: Intelligence and Class Structure in American Life* (1994).

David B. Mustard is an Associate Professor of Economics in the Terry College of Business at the University of Georgia, an Adjunct Professor of Public Administration and Policy in the School of Public and International Affairs, and a Senior Fellow in the University's Institute of Higher Education. He is also a Research Fellow at the Institute for the Study of Labor in Bonn, Germany.

Kevin Rask is a University Research Professor of Economics at Colorado College and a former Professor of Economics at Wake Forest University. He has published numerous articles related to admissions and student choice in higher education.

Jay Rosner is Executive Director of the Princeton Review Foundation. He testified as an expert witness before the U.S. Supreme Court in the landmark *Grutter v. Bollinger* case, which upheld the affirmative action admissions policy of the University of Michigan Law School.

Chloe Melissa Rothstein is Assistant Director of Undergraduate Admissions at Johns Hopkins University.

Robert Schaeffer is Public Education Director, National Center for Fair & Open Testing (FairTest), Cambridge, MA. He is a co-author (with John Weiss and Barbara Beckwith) of *Standing Up to the SAT* (1989) and of many FairTest publications, including *The SAT Coaching Cover-Up* (1991) and *Test Scores Do Not Equal Merit* (1998).

Joseph A. Soares is a Professor of Sociology at Wake Forest University. His book *The Power of Privilege: Yale and America's Elite Colleges* (2007) was instrumental in Wake Forest's decision to go test-optional in admissions. An earlier book on universities in the United Kingdom, *The Decline of Privilege: The Modernization of Oxford University* (1999), won a national award from the American Sociological Association. For most of 2008, he was a member of the National Education Policy Group for Barack Obama's campaign for U.S. President. Dr. Soares organized the national "Rethinking Admissions" conference held at Wake Forest University in April 2009.

Robert J. Sternberg is Provost, Senior Vice President, and Professor of Psychology at Oklahoma State University. Previously, he was Dean of the School of Arts and Sciences at Tufts University (where the Kaleidoscope Project was conducted) and, before that, IBM Professor of Psychology and Education at Yale University (where the Rainbow Project was conducted). He is the author of *Admissions for the 21st Century* (2010). Dr. Sternberg was the 2003 President of the American Psychological Association and is President-Elect of the International Association for Cognitive Education and Psychology.

Jill Tiefenthaler is President and Professor of Economics at Colorado College and former Provost and Professor of Economics at Wake Forest University.

Jessica Van Parys is a Ph.D. student in the Department of Economics, Columbia University.

Teresa Wonnell is Coordinator of Enrollment Research for the School of Arts and Sciences and the School of Engineering at Johns Hopkins University. Her presentation of material from her contribution to this volume won the Best Paper Award from the Maryland Association for Institutional Research in 2010.

Index

Abolition of SAT, proposal for, 5, 69–80
Achievement tests, 30–43, 79
  ACT as, 30–32. *See also* ACT
  Advanced Placement exams as, 32–36.
    See also Advanced Placement exams
  criterion-referenced, 41, 42
  K–12 standards-based assessments as, 29,
    36–40
  predictive value of, 33–34, 40–41, 70–71
    of ACT, 178–181
    of Advanced Placement exams, 27, 33–
      34, 40
    in combination with SAT and high
      school grades, 70–71, 73
    and proposal for SAT abolition, 69–80
    of SAT Subject Tests, 27, 33, 35–36, 44–
      45nn5–6, 139, 149
  SAT compared to, 70, 73
  SAT Subject Tests as, 32–36. *See also* SAT
    Subject Tests
  shift from prediction focus to, 40–43, 79,
    80
  and socioeconomic status, 35, 46n14,
    135
  in University of California admissions,
    28, 30, 33, 35, 37–38, 45–46nn12–13,
    51, 52, 57–58, 59, 61, 70–71
ACT, 2–3, 30–32
  annual number of tests taken, 2, 23
  areas measured by, 85
  audit on current use of, 162–163
  augmentation with supplemental mea-
    sures, 90
  below-average scores on, 188, 189
  bias in, 178
  cutoff scores in, 162–163
  as false measure of merit, 154
  in Johns Hopkins University, 139
  justifications for, 154–155, 160–162, 204
  misuses and misunderstandings of, 2, 160
  National Study of College Experience on,
    179
  predictive value of, 178–181
  as SAT rival, 53, 127

  and socioeconomic status, 135
  in University of California, 30, 51, 52, 59,
    61
ACT-optional admissions policies. *See* Test-
  optional admissions policies
Administrators of college, admissions preference for children of, 18
Advanced placement classes, 35, 45n11,
  149
  in University of Georgia study, 128–135
Advanced Placement exams, 23, 32–36, 70
  ACT compared to, 31
  in Johns Hopkins University, 139, 149
  predictive value of, 27, 33–34, 40, 139,
    197n4
Affirmative action programs, 14, 27, 63, 64,
  116, 164, 197n5
African American students, 97
  ACT scores of, 159, 184
  in Kaleidoscope Project, 97
  in Rainbow Project, 93
  SAT scores of, 74, 104, 158, 183
    in Johns Hopkins University, 139–142,
      144, 146, 147
    question selection and test bias affect-
      ing, 113–114, 202
  in test-optional admission policies, 2–3,
    159, 173, 188–194, 195, 207
  in University of California, 27
AGB Priorities, 157
Agronow, S., 44n3
A-Levels, 87, 90
Allman, Martha, 8, 202
Alon, S., 197n2
Alumni, legacy preference for children of,
  15–16, 20–21, 22
American Association of Universities (AAU),
  38
American Council on Education, 51
American Educational Research Association,
  32
American Psychological Association, 32
American University, 165
Analogy questions, 28, 31, 64, 104, 127